CompTIA®
Data+

Study Guide
Exam DA0-001

Mike Chapple
Sharif Nijim

SYBEX®
A Wiley Brand

To my aspiring engineer, Chris. Your mother and I are so proud of you and can't wait to see all of the incredible things that you accomplish!
—Mike

To my parents, Basheer and Germana. Thank you for your constant love and support, and for showing me how to live.
—Sharif

Acknowledgments

Books like this involve work from many people, and as authors, we truly appreciate the hard work and dedication that the team at Wiley shows. We would especially like to thank senior acquisitions editor Kenyon Brown. We have worked with Ken on multiple projects and consistently enjoy our work with him.

We also greatly appreciated the editing and production team for the book. First and foremost, we'd like to thank our friend and colleague, Dr. Jen Waddell. Jen provided us with invaluable insight as we worked our way through the many challenges inherent in putting out a book covering a brand-new certification. Jen's a whiz at statistics and analytics, and we couldn't have completed this book without her support. We also benefited greatly from the work of two of our students at Notre Dame. Ricky Chapple did a final read-through of this book to ensure that it was ready to go, and Matthew Howard helped create the instructor materials that accompany this book.

We'd also like to thank the many people who helped us make this project successful, including Adaobi Obi Tulton, our project editor, who brought years of experience and great talent to the project, and Barath Kumar Rajasekaran, our content refinement specialist, who guided us through layouts, formatting, and final cleanup to produce a great book. We would also like to thank the many behind-the-scenes contributors, including the graphics, production, and technical teams who make the book and companion materials into a finished product.

Our agent, Carole Jelen of Waterside Productions, continues to provide us with wonderful opportunities, advice, and assistance throughout our writing careers.

Finally, we would like to thank our families who support us through the late evenings, busy weekends, and long hours that a book like this requires to write, edit, and get to press.

About the Authors

Mike Chapple, Ph.D., CySA+, is author of the best-selling *CISSP (ISC)² Certified Information Systems Security Professional Official Study Guide* (Sybex, 2021) and the *CISSP (ISC)² Official Practice Tests* (Sybex, 2021). He is an information technology professional with two decades of experience in higher education, the private sector, and government.

Mike currently serves as a teaching professor in the IT, Analytics, and Operations department at the University of Notre Dame's Mendoza College of Business, where he teaches undergraduate and graduate courses on cybersecurity, data management, and business analytics.

Before returning to Notre Dame, Mike served as executive vice president and chief information officer of the Brand Institute, a Miami-based marketing consultancy. Mike also spent four years in the information security research group at the National Security Agency and served as an active duty intelligence officer in the U.S. Air Force.

Mike has written more than 30 books. He earned both his B.S. and Ph.D. degrees from Notre Dame in computer science and engineering. Mike also holds an M.S. in computer science from the University of Idaho and an MBA from Auburn University.

Learn more about Mike and his other certification materials at `CertMike.com`.

Sharif Nijim is an assistant teaching professor in the IT, Analytics, and Operations department at the Mendoza College of Business at the University of Notre Dame, where he teaches undergraduate and graduate courses in business analytics and information technology.

Prior to Notre Dame, Sharif co-founded and served on the board of a customer data integration company serving the airline industry. Sharif also spent more than a decade building and optimizing enterprise-class transactional and decision support systems for clients in the energy, healthcare, hospitality, insurance, logistics, manufacturing, real estate, telecommunications, and travel and transportation sectors.

Sharif earned both his B.B.A. and M.S. from the University of Notre Dame.

About the Technical Editor

Jennifer Waddell is a teaching professor, assistant department chair, and the director of undergraduate studies in the IT, Analytics, and Operations department at the University of Notre Dame, specializing in the areas of statistical methodology and analytics. Over the last 20 years, she has educated students at the undergraduate, graduate, and executive levels in these disciplines, focusing on their theoretical understanding as well as technical skill implementation. In addition to her time in the classroom, she has worked as a statistical consultant on research projects in healthcare systems and educational services.

Contents at a Glance

Contents

Introduction

If you're preparing to take the Data+ exam, you'll undoubtedly want to find as much information as you can about data and analytics. The more information you have at your disposal and the more hands-on experience you gain, the better off you'll be when attempting the exam. This study guide was written with that in mind. The goal was to provide enough information to prepare you for the test, but not so much that you'll be overloaded with information that's outside the scope of the exam.

We've included review questions at the end of each chapter to give you a taste of what it's like to take the exam. If you're already working in the data field, we recommend that you check out these questions first to gauge your level of expertise. You can then use the book mainly to fill in the gaps in your current knowledge. This study guide will help you round out your knowledge base before tackling the exam.

If you can answer 90 percent or more of the review questions correctly for a given chapter, you can feel safe moving on to the next chapter. If you're unable to answer that many correctly, reread the chapter and try the questions again. Your score should improve.

Don't just study the questions and answers! The questions on the actual exam will be different from the practice questions included in this book. The exam is designed to test your knowledge of a concept or objective, so use this book to learn the objectives behind the questions.

The Data+ Exam

The Data+ exam is designed to be a vendor-neutral certification for data professionals and those seeking to enter the field. CompTIA recommends this certification for those currently working, or aspiring to work, in data analyst and business intelligence reporting roles.

The exam covers five major domains:

1. Data Concepts and Environments
2. Data Mining
3. Data Analysis
4. Visualization
5. Data Governance, Quality, and Controls

These five areas include a range of topics, from data types to statistical analysis and from data visualization to tools and techniques, while focusing heavily on scenario-based learning. That's why CompTIA recommends that those attempting the exam have 18–24 months of hands-on work experience, although many individuals pass the exam before moving into their first data analysis role.

The Data+ exam is conducted in a format that CompTIA calls "performance-based assessment." This means that the exam combines standard multiple-choice questions with other, interactive question formats. Your exam may include several types of questions such as multiple-choice, fill-in-the-blank, multiple-response, drag-and-drop, and image-based problems. More details about the Data+ exam and how to take it can be found here:

http://www.comptia.org/certifications/data

You'll have 90 minutes to take the exam and will be asked to answer 90 questions during that time period. Your exam will be scored on a scale ranging from 100 to 900, with a passing score of 675.

You should also know that CompTIA is notorious for including vague questions on all of its exams. You might see a question for which two of the possible four answers are correct—but you can choose only one. Use your knowledge, logic, and intuition to choose the best answer and then move on. Sometimes, the questions are worded in ways that would make English majors cringe—a typo here, an incorrect verb there. Don't let this frustrate you; answer the question and move on to the next one.

CompTIA frequently does what is called *item seeding*, which is the practice of including unscored questions on exams. It does so to gather psychometric data, which is then used when developing new versions of the exam. Before you take the exam, you will be told that your exam may include these unscored questions. So, if you come across a question that does not appear to map to any of the exam objectives—or for that matter, does not appear to belong in the exam—it is likely a seeded question. You never really know whether or not a question is seeded, however, so always make your best effort to answer every question.

Taking the Exam

Once you are fully prepared to take the exam, you can visit the CompTIA website to purchase your exam voucher:

https://store.comptia.org/Certification-Vouchers/c/11293

Currently, CompTIA offers two options for taking the exam: an in-person exam at a testing center and an at-home exam that you take on your own computer.

This book includes a coupon that you may use to save 10 percent on your CompTIA exam registration.

In-Person Exams

CompTIA partners with Pearson VUE's testing centers, so your next step will be to locate a testing center near you. In the United States, you can do this based on your address or your ZIP code, while non-U.S. test takers may find it easier to enter their city and country. You can search for a test center near you at the Pearson Vue website, where you will need to navigate to "Find a test center."

```
http://www.pearsonvue.com/comptia
```

Now that you know where you'd like to take the exam, simply set up a Pearson VUE testing account and schedule an exam on their site.

On the day of the test, take two forms of identification, and make sure to show up with plenty of time before the exam starts. Remember that you will not be able to take your notes, electronic devices (including smartphones and watches), or other materials in with you.

At-Home Exams

CompTIA began offering online exam proctoring in response to the coronavirus pandemic. As of the time this book went to press, the at-home testing option was still available and appears likely to continue. Candidates using this approach will take the exam at their home or office and be proctored over a webcam by a remote proctor.

Due to the rapidly changing nature of the at-home testing experience, candidates wishing to pursue this option should check the CompTIA website for the latest details.

After the Data+ Exam

Once you have taken the exam, you will be notified of your score immediately, so you'll know if you passed the test right away. You should keep track of your score report with your exam registration records and the email address you used to register for the exam.

What Does This Book Cover?

This book covers everything you need to know to pass the Data+ exam.

Chapter 1: Today's Data Analyst

Chapter 2: Understanding Data

Chapter 3: Databases and Data Acquisition

Chapter 4: Data Quality

Chapter 5: Data Analysis and Statistics

Study Guide Elements

This study guide uses a number of common elements to help you prepare. These include the following:

Summaries   The summary section of each chapter briefly explains the chapter, allowing you to easily understand what it covers.

Exam Essentials   The exam essentials focus on major exam topics and critical knowledge that you should take into the test. The exam essentials focus on the exam objectives provided by CompTIA.

Chapter Review Questions   A set of questions at the end of each chapter will help you assess your knowledge and whether you are ready to take the exam based on your knowledge of that chapter's topics.

Interactive Online Learning Environment and Test Bank

This book comes with a number of additional study tools to help you prepare for the exam. They include the following.

Go to https://www.wiley.com/go/sybextestprep to register and gain access to this interactive online learning environment and test bank with study tools.

Sybex Test Preparation Software

Sybex's test preparation software lets you prepare with electronic test versions of the review questions from each chapter, the practice exam, and the bonus exam that are included in this book. You can build and take tests on specific domains, by chapter, or cover the entire set of Data+ exam objectives using randomized tests.

Electronic Flashcards

Our electronic flashcards are designed to help you prepare for the exam. Over 100 flashcards will ensure that you know critical terms and concepts.

Glossary of Terms

Sybex provides a full glossary of terms in PDF format, allowing quick searches and easy reference to materials in this book.

Bonus Practice Exams

In addition to the practice questions for each chapter, this book includes two full 90-question practice exams. We recommend that you use them both to test your preparedness for the certification exam.

 Like all exams, the Data+ certification from CompTIA is updated periodically and may eventually be retired or replaced. At some point after CompTIA is no longer offering this exam, the old editions of our books and online tools will be retired. If you have purchased this book after the exam was retired or are attempting to register in the Sybex online learning environment after the exam was retired, please know that we make no guarantees that this exam's online Sybex tools will be available once the exam is no longer available.

Exam DA0-001 Exam Objectives

CompTIA goes to great lengths to ensure that its certification programs accurately reflect the IT industry's best practices. It does this by establishing committees for each of its exam programs. Each committee consists of a small group of IT professionals, training providers, and publishers who are responsible for establishing the exam's baseline competency level and who determine the appropriate target-audience level.

Once these factors are determined, CompTIA shares this information with a group of hand-selected subject matter experts (SMEs). These folks are the true brainpower behind the certification program. The SMEs review the committee's findings, refine them, and shape them into the objectives that follow this section. CompTIA calls this process a job-task analysis (JTA).

Finally, CompTIA conducts a survey to ensure that the objectives and weightings truly reflect job requirements. Only then can the SMEs go to work writing the hundreds of questions needed for the exam. Even so, they have to go back to the drawing board for further refinements in many cases before the exam is ready to go live in its final state. Rest assured that the content you're about to learn will serve you long after you take the exam.

CompTIA also publishes relative weightings for each of the exam's objectives. The following table lists the five Data+ objective domains and the extent to which they are represented on the exam.

Domain	% of Exam
1.0 Data Concepts and Environments	15%
2.0 Data Mining	25%
3.0 Data Analysis	23%
4.0 Visualization	23%
5.0 Data Governance, Quality, and Controls	14%

DA0-001 Certification Exam Objective Map

Objective	Chapter
1.0 Data Concepts and Environments	
1.1 Identify basic concepts of data schemas and dimensions	Chapter 3
1.2 Compare and contrast different data types	Chapter 2
1.3 Compare and contrast common data structures and file formats	Chapter 2
2.0 Data Mining	
2.1 Explain data acquisition concepts	Chapter 3
2.2 Identify common reasons for cleansing and profiling datasets	Chapter 4
2.3 Given a scenario, execute data manipulation techniques	Chapter 4
2.4 Explain common techniques for data manipulation and query optimization	Chapter 3
3.0 Data Analysis	
3.1 Given a scenario, apply the appropriate descriptive statistical methods	Chapter 5
3.2 Explain the purpose of inferential statistical methods	Chapter 5
3.3 Summarize types of analysis and key analysis techniques	Chapter 5
3.4 Identify common data analytics tools	Chapter 6

Exam objectives are subject to change at any time without prior notice and at CompTIA's discretion. Please visit CompTIA's website (www .comptia.org) for the most current listing of exam objectives.

Assessment Test

1. Lila is aggregating data from a CRM system with data from an employee system. While performing an initial quality check, she realizes that her employee ID is not associated with her identifier in the CRM system. What kind of issue is Lila facing? Choose the best answer.

    A. ETL process

    B. Record linkage

    C. ELT process

    D. System integration

2. Rob is a pricing analyst for a retailer. Using a hypothesis test, he wants to assess whether people who receive electronic coupons spend more on average. What should Rob's null hypothesis be?

    A. People who receive electronic coupons spend more on average.

    B. People who receive electronic coupons spend less on average.

    C. People who receive electronic coupons do not spend more on average.

    D. People do not receive electronic coupons spend more on average.

3. Tonya needs to create a dashboard that will draw information from many other data sources and present it to business leaders. Which one of the following tools is least likely to meet her needs?

    A. QuickSight

    B. Tableau

    C. Power BI

    D. SPSS Modeler

4. Ryan is using the Structured Query Language to work with data stored in a relational database. He would like to add several new rows to a database table. What command should he use?

    A. SELECT

    B. ALTER

    C. INSERT

    D. UPDATE

5. Daniel is working on an ELT process that sources data from six different source systems. Looking at the source data, he finds that data about the sample people exists in two of the six systems. What does he have to make sure he checks for in his ELT process? Choose the best answer.

    A. Duplicate data

    B. Redundant data

    C. Invalid data

    D. Missing data

6. Samantha needs to share a list of her organization's top 50 customers with the VP of Sales. She would like to include the name of the customer, the business they represent, their contact information, and their total sales over the past year. The VP does not have any specialized analytics skills or software but would like to make some personal notes on the dataset. What would be the best tool for Samantha to use to share this information?

    A. Power BI

    B. Microsoft Excel

    C. Minitab

    D. SAS

7. Alexander wants to use data from his corporate sales, CRM, and shipping systems to try and predict future sales. Which of the following systems is most appropriate? Choose the best answer.

    A. Data mart

    B. OLAP

    C. Data warehouse

    D. OLTP

8. Jackie is working in a data warehouse and finds a finance fact table links to an organization dimension, which in turn links to a currency dimension that is not linked to the fact table. What type of design pattern is the data warehouse using?

    A. Star

    B. Sun

    C. Snowflake

    D. Comet

9. Encryption is a mechanism for protecting data. When should encryption be applied to data? Choose the best answer.

    A. When data is at rest

    B. When data is at rest or in transit

    C. When data is in transit

    D. When data is at rest, unless you are using local storage

10. What subset of the Structured Query Language (SQL) is used to add, remove, modify, or retrieve the information stored within a relational database?

    A. DDL

    B. DSL

    C. DQL

    D. DML

11. Which of the following roles is responsible for ensuring an organization's data quality, security, privacy, and regulatory compliance?

   A. Data owner

   B. Data steward

   C. Data custodian

   D. Data processor

12. Jen wants to study the academic performance of undergraduate sophomores and wants to determine the average grade point average at different points during an academic year. What best describes the data set she needs?

   A. Sample

   B. Observation

   C. Variable

   D. Population

13. Mauro works with a group of R programmers tasked with copying data from an accounting system into a data warehouse. In what phase are the group's R skills most relevant?

   A. Extract

   B. Load

   C. Transform

   D. Purge

14. Which one of the following tools would not be considered a fully featured analytics suite?

   A. Minitab

   B. MicroStrategy

   C. Domo

   D. Power BI

15. Omar is conducting a study and wants to capture eye color. What kind of data is eye color? Choose the best response.

   A. Discrete

   B. Categorical

   C. Continuous

   D. Alphanumeric

16. Lars is looking at home sales prices in a single zip code and notices that one home sold for $938,294 when the average selling price of similar homes is $209,383. What type of data does the $938,294 sales price represent? Choose the best answer.

   A. Duplicate data

   B. Data outlier

   C. Redundant data

   D. Invalid data

17. Trianna wants to explore central tendency in her dataset. Which statistic best matches her need?

   A. Interquartile range

   B. Range

   C. Median

   D. Standard deviation

18. Shakira has 15 people on her data analytics team. Her team's charter requires that all team members have read access to the finance, human resources, sales, and customer service areas of the corporate data warehouse. What is the best way to provision access to her team? Choose the best answer.

   A. Since there are 15 people on her team, create a role for each person to improve security.

   B. Since there are four discrete data subjects, create one role for each subject area.

   C. Enable multifactor authentication (MFA) to protect the data.

   D. Create a single role that includes finance, human resources, sales, and customer service data.

19. What is the median of the following numbers?

   13, 2, 65, 3, 5, 4, 7, 3, 4, 7, 8, 2, 4, 4, 60, 23, 43, 2

   A. 4

   B. 4.5

   C. 63

   D. 18

20. Lewis is designing an ETL process to copy sales data into a data warehouse on an hourly basis. What approach should Lewis choose that would be most efficient and minimize the chance of losing historical data?

   A. Bulk load

   B. Purge and load

   C. Use ELT instead of ETL

   D. Delta load

21. Carlos wants to analyze profit based on sales of five different product categories. His source data set consists of 5.8 million rows with columns including region, product category, product name, and sales price. How should he manipulate the data to facilitate his analysis? Choose the best answer.

   A. Transpose by region and summarize.

   B. Transpose by product category and summarize.

   C. Transpose by product name and summarize.

   D. Transpose by sales price and summarize.

22. According to the empirical rule, what percent of the values in a sample fall within three standard deviations of the mean in a normal distribution?

    A. 99.70%

    B. 95%

    C. 90%

    D. 68%

23. Martin is building a database to store prices for a items on a restaurant menu. What data type is most appropriate for this field?

    A. Numeric

    B. Date

    C. Text

    D. Alphanumeric

24. Harrison is conducting a survey. He intends to distribute the survey via email and wants to optionally follow up with respondents based on their answers. What quality dimension is most vital to the success of Harrison's survey? Choose the best answer.

    A. Completeness

    B. Accuracy

    C. Consistency

    D. Validity

25. Mary is developing a script that will perform some common analytics tasks. In order to improve the efficiency of her workflow, she is using a package called the tidyverse. What programming language is she using?

    A. Python

    B. R

    C. Ruby

    D. C++

Answers to Assessment Test

1. B. While this scenario describes a system integration challenge that can be solved with either ETL or ELT, Lila is facing a record linkage issue. See Chapter 8 for more information on this topic.

2. C. The null hypothesis presumes the status quo. Rob is testing whether or not people who receive an electronic coupon spend more on average, so the null hypothesis states that people who receive the coupon do spend more on average. See Chapter 5 for more information on this topic.

3. D. QuickSight, Tableau, and Power BI are all powerful analytics and reporting tools that can pull data from a variety of sources. SPSS Modeler is a machine learning package that would not be used to create a dashboard. See Chapter 6 for more information on this topic.

4. C. The INSERT command is used to add new records to a database table. The SELECT command is used to retrieve information from a database. It's the most commonly used command in SQL because it is used to pose queries to the database and retrieve the data that you're interested in working with. The UPDATE command is used to modify rows in the database. The CREATE command is used to create a new table within your database or a new database on your server. See Chapter 6 for more information on this topic.

5. A. While invalid, redundant, or missing data are all valid concerns, data about people exists in two of the six systems. As such, Daniel needs to account for duplicate data issues. See Chapter 4 for more information on this topic.

6. B. This scenario presents a very simple use case where the business leader needs a dataset in an easy-to-access form and will not be performing any detailed analysis. A simple spreadsheet, such as Microsoft Excel, would be the best tool for this job. There is no need to use a statistical analysis package, such as SAS or Minitab, as this would likely confuse the VP without adding any value. The same is true of an integrated analytics suite, such as Power BI. See Chapter 6 for more information on this topic.

7. C. Data warehouses bring together data from multiple systems used by an organization. A data mart is too narrow, as Alexander needs data from across multiple divisions. OLAP is a broad term for analytical processing, and OLTP systems are transactional and not ideal for this task. See Chapter 3 for more information on this topic.

8. C. Since the dimension links to a dimension that isn't connected to the fact table, it must be a snowflake. With a star, all dimensions link directly to the fact table. Sun and Comet are not data warehouse design patterns. See Chapter 3 for more information on this topic.

9. B. To provide maximum protection, encrypt data both in transit and at rest. See Chapter 8 for more information on this topic.

10. D. The Data Manipulation Language (DML) is used to work with the data stored in a database. DML includes the SELECT, INSERT, UPDATE, and DELETE commands. The Data Definition Language (DDL) contains the commands used to create and structure a relational database. It includes the CREATE, ALTER, and DROP commands. DDL and DML are the only two sublanguages of SQL. See Chapter 6 for more information on this topic.

11. B. A data steward is responsible for leading an organization's data governance activities, which include data quality, security, privacy, and regulatory compliance. See Chapter 8 for more information on this topic.

12. A. Jen does not have data for the entire population of all undergraduate sophomores. While a specific grade point average is an observation of a variable, Jen needs sample data. See Chapter 5 for more information on this topic.

13. C. The R programming language is used to manipulate and model data. In the ETL process, this activity normally takes place during the Transform phase. The extract and load phases typically use database-centric tools. Purging data from a database is typically done using SQL. See Chapter 3 for more information on this topic.

14. A. Power BI, Domo, and MicroStrategy are all analytics suites offering features that fill many different needs within the analytics process. Minitab is a statistical analysis package that lacks many of these capabilities. See Chapter 6 for more information on this topic.

15. B. Eye color can only fall into a certain range of values; as such, it is categorical. See Chapter 2 for more information on this topic.

16. B. Since the value is more than four times the average, the $938,294 value is an outlier. See Chapter 4 for more information on this topic.

17. C. The median is the middle observation of a variable and is, therefore, a measure of central tendency. Interquartile range is a measure of position. Range and standard deviation are both measures of dispersion. See Chapter 5 for more information on this topic.

18. D. While MFA is a good security practice, it doesn't govern access to data. Creating a single role for her team and assigning that role to the individuals on the team is the best approach. See Chapter 8 for more information on this topic.

19. B. To find the median, sort the numbers in your dataset and find the one located in the middle. In this case, there are an even number of observations, so we take the two middle numbers (4 and 5) and use their average as the median, making the median value 4.5. The mode is 4, the range is 63, and the number of observations is 18. See Chapter 5 for more information on this topic.

20. D. Since Lewis needs to migrate changes every hour, a delta load is the best approach. See Chapter 3 for more information on this topic.

21. B. We can transpose this data by product category to perform this analysis broken out by product category. Transposing by sales price, region, or product name will not further his state analytical goal. See Chapter 4 for more information on this topic.

22. A. According to the empirical rule, 68% of values are within one standard deviation, 95% are within two standard deviations, and 99.7% are within three standard deviations. See Chapter 5 for more information on this topic.

23. A. Prices are numbers stored in dollars and cents; as such, the data type needs to be capable of storing numbers. See Chapter 2 for more information on this topic.

24. A. Accuracy is for measuring how well an attribute matches its intended use. Consistency measures an attribute's value across systems. Validity ensures an attribute's value falls within an expected range. While all of these dimensions are important, completeness is foundational to Harrison's purpose. See Chapter 4 for more information on this topic.

25. B. The tidyverse is a collection of packages for the R programming language designed to facilitate the analytics workflow. The tidyverse is not available for Python, Ruby, or C++, all of which are general-purpose programming languages. See Chapter 6 for more information on this topic.

Chapter 1

Today's Data Analyst

Analytics is at the heart of modern business. Virtually every organization collects large quantities of data about its customers, products, employees, and service offerings. Managers naturally seek to analyze that data and harness the information it contains to improve the efficiency, effectiveness, and profitability of their work.

Data analysts are the professionals who possess the skills and knowledge required to perform this vital work. They understand how the organization can acquire, clean, and transform data to meet the organization's needs. They are able to take that collected information and analyze it using the techniques of statistics and machine learning. They may then create powerful visualizations that display this data to business leaders, managers, and other stakeholders.

Welcome to the World of Analytics

We are fortunate to live in the Golden Age of Analytics. Businesses around the world recognize the vital nature of data to their work and are investing heavily in analytics programs designed to give them a competitive advantage. Organizations have been collecting this data for years, and many of the statistical tools and techniques used in analytics work date back decades. But if that's the case, why are we just now in the early years of this Golden Age? Figure 1.1 shows the three major pillars that have come together at this moment to allow analytics programs to thrive: data, storage, and computing power.

Data

The amount of data the modern world generates on a daily basis is staggering. From the organized tables of spreadsheets to the storage of photos, video, and audio recordings, modern businesses create an almost overwhelming avalanche of data that is ripe for use in analytics programs.

Let's try to quantify the amount of data that exists in the world. We'll begin with an estimate made by Google's then-CEO Eric Schmidt in 2010. At a technology conference, Schmidt estimated that the sum total of all of the stored knowledge created by the world at that point in time was approximately 5 exabytes. To give that a little perspective, the file containing the text of this chapter is around 100 kilobytes. So, Schmidt's estimate is that the world in 2010 had total knowledge that is about the size of 50,000,000,000,000 (that's 50 trillion!) copies of this book chapter. That's a staggering number, but it's only the beginning of our journey.

FIGURE 1.1   Analytics is made possible by modern data, storage, and computing capabilities.

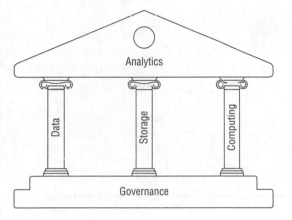

Now fast-forward just two years to 2012. In that year, researchers estimated that the total amount of stored data in the world had grown to 1,000 exabytes (or one zettabyte). Remember, Schmidt's estimate of 5 exabytes was made only two years earlier. In just two years, the total amount of stored data in the world grew by a factor of 200! But we're still not finished!

In the year 2020, IDC estimates that the world created 59 zettabytes (or 59,000 exabytes) of new information. Compare that to Schmidt's estimate of the world having a total of 5 exabytes of stored information in 2010. If you do the math, you'll discover that this means that on any given day in the modern era, the world generates an amount of brand-new data that is approximately 32 times the sum total of all information created from the dawn of civilization until 2010! Now, *that* is a staggering amount of data!

From an analytics perspective, this trove of data is a gold mine of untapped potential.

Storage

The second key trend driving the growth of analytics programs is the increased availability of storage at rapidly decreasing costs. Table 1.1 shows the cost of storing a gigabyte of data in different years using magnetic hard drives.

TABLE 1.1   Gigabyte storage costs over time

Year	Cost per GB
1985	$169,900
1990	$53,940
1995	$799
2000	$17.50
2005	$0.62
2010	$0.19
2015	$0.03
2020	$0.01

Figure 1.2 shows the same data plotted as a line graph on a logarithmic scale. This visualization clearly demonstrates the fact that storage costs have plummeted to the point where storage is almost free and businesses can afford to retain data for analysis in ways that they never have before.

Computing Power

In 1975, Gordon Moore, one of the co-founders of Intel Corporation, made a prediction that computing technology would continue to advance so quickly that manufacturers would be able to double the number of components placed on an integrated circuit every two years. Remarkably, that prediction has stood the test of time and remains accurate today.

Commonly referred to as *Moore's Law*, this prediction is often loosely interpreted to mean that we will double the amount of computing power on a single device every two years. That trend has benefited many different technology-enabled fields, among them the world of analytics.

In the early days of analytics, computing power was costly and difficult to come by. Organizations with advanced analytics needs purchased massive supercomputers to analyze their data, but those supercomputers were scarce resources. Analysts fortunate enough to work in an organization that possessed a supercomputer had to justify their requests for small slices of time when they could use the powerful machines.

Today, the effects of Moore's Law have democratized computing. Most employees in an organization now have enough computing power sitting on their desks to perform a wide variety of analytic tasks. If they require more powerful computing resources, cloud services allow them to rent massive banks of computers at very low cost. Even better, those resources are charged at hourly rates, and analysts pay only for the computing time that they actually use.

FIGURE 1.2   Storage costs have decreased over time.

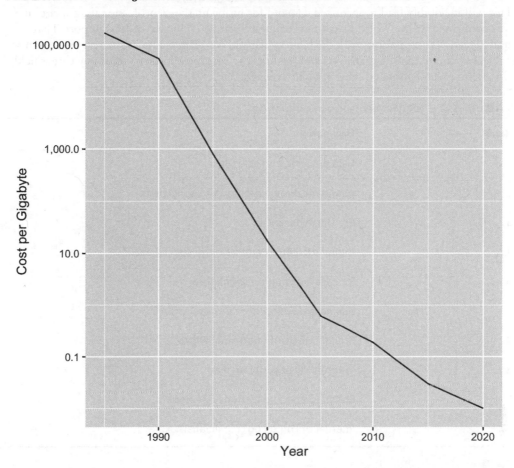

These three trends—the massive volume of data generated by our businesses on a daily basis, the availability of inexpensive storage to retain that data, and the cloud's promise of virtually infinite computing power—come together to create fertile ground for data analytics.

Careers in Analytics

As businesses try to keep up with these trends, hiring managers find themselves struggling to identify, recruit, and retain talented analytics professionals. This presents a supply-and-demand situation that is problematic for businesses but excellent news for job candidates seeking to break into the field.

In their 2020 Global State of Enterprise Analytics survey, the firm MicroStrategy found that 94 percent of firms believe that analytics is crucial to the growth of their businesses and that 65 percent of firms planned to increase their analytics investment in the coming year. This will inevitably lead to increased demand for hiring analytics professionals, a fact that was confirmed by the World Economic Forum in their 2020 Future of Jobs Report. That study listed 10 occupations with the highest demand for professionals. The results, shown in Table 1.2, found that data analysts and scientists are the most in-demand of any career field, closely followed by several other analytics-related fields.

TABLE 1.2   Highest-demand occupations

Rank	Occupation
1	Data analysts and scientists
2	AI and machine learning (ML) specialists
3	Big Data specialists
4	Digital marketing and strategy specialists
5	Process automation specialists
6	Business development professionals
7	Digital transformation specialists
8	Information security analyst
9	Software and applications developers
10	Internet of Things (IoT) specialists

The future is bright. There's no reason to anticipate a reduction in this demand any time soon. It's the right time to enter the exciting field of data analytics!

The Analytics Process

Analysts working with data move through a series of different steps as they seek to gain business value from their organization's data. Figure 1.3 illustrates the process they move through as they acquire new data, clean and manipulate that data, analyze it, create visualizations, and then report and communicate their results to business leaders.

FIGURE 1.3   The analytics process

Data Acquisition > Cleaning and Manipulation > Analysis > Visualization > Reporting and Communication

Data Acquisition

Analysts work with a wide variety of data, using data sources generated by the business itself or obtained from external sources. For example, data analysts might look at their own organization's sales data (an internal source) and augment it with census data (an external source) as they try to identify new potential markets for their firm's products and services.

In Chapter 2, "Understanding Data," you'll learn about the different data types, data structures, and file formats that analysts might encounter as they carry out data acquisition tasks. In Chapter 3, "Databases and Data Acquisition," you'll learn about the techniques used to collect this data and integrate it with existing systems as well as the use of relational databases to store, maintain, and query those datasets.

Cleaning and Manipulation

In an ideal world, we'd acquire data from internal and external sources and then simply pull it directly into our analysis. Unfortunately, the world of data is far from ideal, and you'll quickly discover (if you haven't already!) that datasets often contain errors, are missing crucial values, or come in a format that simply makes analysis difficult. Analysts spend a large portion of their time cleaning and manipulating data to get it ready for transformation. In fact, many analytics professionals estimate that cleaning and manipulation work consumes 80 percent of the time spent on most analytics projects!

In Chapter 4, "Data Quality," you'll learn more about the cleaning and manipulation work performed by data analysts. You'll discover the common reasons for cleansing and profiling datasets and different data manipulation methods. You'll also learn about the importance of data quality control and techniques you can use to improve the quality of your data.

WARNING

CompTIA uses the term *data mining* to refer to data acquisition, cleaning, and manipulation tasks. This is not, however, the commonly accepted definition of data mining. Most practicing data analysts use the term data mining to refer to the analysis tasks discussed in the next stage of the process. Analysts typically refer to the work of data acquisition, cleaning, and manipulation as *data wrangling* or *data munging*.

Analysis

Once you have clean datasets in hand, you're ready to begin analyzing your data. This work typically begins with a process known as exploratory data analysis (EDA), which uses simple statistical techniques to summarize a dataset and draw high-level conclusions. EDA creates hypotheses that analysts may further explore using the techniques of machine learning and artificial intelligence.

In Chapter 5, "Data Analysis and Statistics," you'll learn about the tools and techniques of data analysis. You'll learn how to use descriptive statistics to perform EDA and how to use inferential statistics to test hypotheses. You'll also learn about the processes used to continue analyses, including clarifying business questions, identifying data sources, and applying analytic techniques.

Visualization

The old adage "a picture is worth a thousand words" is as true in the world of analytics as it is in other aspects of life. The human mind excels at processing visual information and isn't so good at handling large quantities of numeric data.

You've already seen this at play once in this chapter. Table 1.1 presented a set of datapoints on the cost of storage. Looking at that table, you could tell that the cost of storage decreased over time, but you probably had to do a little thinking to reach that conclusion. A quick look at the same data visualized in Figure 1.2 likely led you to the same conclusion without all the mental gymnastics.

The storage dataset was fairly simple, however. Figure 1.4 shows you an excerpt from a 51-row dataset containing the average college tuition in each state. Can you quickly get a sense of the trend from state to state by looking at that data? It's probably not so easy for you.

Figure 1.5 presents the same data in a map-based visualization. Darker shades represent higher tuition costs. We'll bet that you can draw conclusions from this visualization much more quickly than you can from the raw data!

In Chapter 7, "Data Visualization with Reports and Dashboards," you'll learn about different types of data visualizations, including line charts, histograms, infographics, and more. You'll discover how to select a visualization method appropriate for your needs and use it to tell the story of your data.

Reporting and Communication

Although visualizations are very useful, they often can't stand alone. In most cases, you'll need to provide business leaders with multiple visualizations as well as supporting text to help communicate the story of your data. That's where *reports* and *dashboards* enter the picture. Reports provide the reader with textual analysis and supporting data in tabular and/or visualization form. They're an extremely common work product in the field of data analytics.

FIGURE 1.4   Table of college tuition data

	state	avg_tuition	region
1	AK	19610.00	alaska
2	AL	13736.33	alabama
3	AR	13637.44	arkansas
4	AZ	14760.17	arizona
5	CA	27036.34	california
6	CO	12900.64	colorado
7	CT	22108.86	connecticut
8	DC	36009.50	district of columbia
9	DE	14592.67	delaware
10	FL	16639.59	florida
11	GA	15381.37	georgia
12	HI	10884.00	hawaii
13	IA	26735.68	iowa
14	ID	12851.29	idaho
15	IL	24911.74	illinois
16	IN	22677.10	indiana
17	KS	19973.68	kansas

FIGURE 1.5   Visualization of college tuition data

Average College Tuition by State

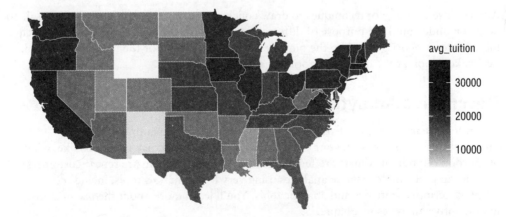

Reports, however, only present a point-in-time analysis. Business leaders often want to monitor business activities in real time using visualizations. Dashboards provide this real-time look at an organization's data using continuously updated visualizations.

Chapter 7 covers reporting and communication in more detail. You'll see examples of different types of reports and dashboards. You'll discover how to translate business requirements into appropriate reporting tools and how to design effective reports and dashboards.

The Analytics Process Is Iterative

While we describe the steps of the analytics process as a series of sequential actions, it's more accurate to think of them as a set of interrelated actions that may be revisited frequently while working with a dataset.

For example, an analyst reviewing a visualization may notice unusual data points that don't seem to belong in the dataset, causing them to return to the data cleaning stage and rerun their analysis with the newly cleaned dataset. Similarly, an analyst running an analysis might discover that their analysis would be enriched by adding another source of data, causing them to return to the data acquisition stage.

This process is meant to help you understand the different activities that take place during a data analysis effort and the approximate order in which they typically occur. You shouldn't view it as a rigid process, but rather as a rough guide.

Analytics Techniques

Analysts use a variety of techniques to draw conclusions from the data at their disposal. To help you understand the purpose of different types of analysis, we often group these techniques into categories based on the purpose of the analysis and/or the nature of the tool. Let's take a look at the major categories of analytics techniques.

Descriptive Analytics

Descriptive analytics uses statistics to describe your data. For example, if you perform descriptive analytics on your customer records, you might ask questions like, what proportion of your customers are female? And how many of them are repeat customers?

You can perform descriptive analytics using very basic analysis tools, including simple descriptive statistics and analytic tools. You'll learn more about the use of statistics in descriptive analytics in Chapter 5.

Predictive Analytics

Predictive analytics seek to use your existing data to predict future events. For example, if you have a dataset on how your customers respond to direct mail, you might use that dataset to build a model that predicts how individual customers will respond to a specific future mailing. That might help you tweak that mailing to improve the response rate by changing the day you send it, altering the content of the message, or even making seemingly minor changes like altering the font size or paper color.

Predictive analytics programs rely on the use of advanced statistical tools and specialized artificial intelligence, machine learning, and deep learning techniques.

Prescriptive Analytics

Prescriptive analytics seek to optimize behavior by simulating many scenarios. For example, if you want to determine the best way to allocate your marketing dollars, you might run different simulations of consumer response and then use algorithms to prescribe your behavior in that context. Similarly, you might use prescriptive analytics to optimize the performance of an automated manufacturing process.

Machine Learning, Artificial Intelligence, and Deep Learning

The work of analytics is intellectually and computationally demanding. Fortunately, you don't always have to do this work yourself; you can rely on automated techniques to help you unlock the hidden value in your data.

Machine learning uses algorithms to discover knowledge in your datasets that you can then apply to help you make informed decisions about the future. That's true regardless of the specific subject matter expertise where you're working, as machine learning has applications across a wide variety of fields. For example, here are some cases where machine learning commonly adds value:

- Segmenting customers and determining the marketing messages that will appeal to different customer groups
- Discovering anomalies in system and application logs that may be indicative of a cyber-security incident
- Forecasting product sales based on market and environmental conditions
- Recommending the next movie that a customer might wish to watch based on their past activity and the preferences of similar customers
- Setting prices for hotel rooms far in advance based on forecasted demand

Of course, those are just a few examples. Machine learning can bring value to almost every field where discovering previously unknown knowledge is useful—and we challenge you to think of a field where knowledge doesn't offer an advantage!

As we move through the world, we hear the terms *artificial intelligence, machine learning,* and *deep learning* being used almost interchangeably to describe any sort of technique where computers are working with data. Now that you're entering the world of data, it's important to have a more precise understanding of these terms.

Artificial intelligence (AI) includes any type of technique where you are attempting to get a computer system to imitate human behavior. As the name implies, you are trying to ask computer systems to artificially behave as if they were intelligent. Now, of course, it's not possible for a modern computer to function at the level of complex reasoning found in the human mind, but you can try to mimic some small portions of human behavior and judgment.

Machine learning (ML) is a subset of AI techniques. ML techniques attempt to apply statistics to data problems in an effort to discover new knowledge. Or, in other terms, ML techniques are AI techniques designed to learn.

Deep learning is a further subdivision of machine learning that uses quite complex techniques, known as neural networks, to discover knowledge in a particular way. It is a highly specialized subfield of machine learning that is most commonly used for image, video, and sound analysis.

Figure 1.6 shows the relationships between these fields.

FIGURE 1.6   The relationship between artificial intelligence, machine learning, and deep learning

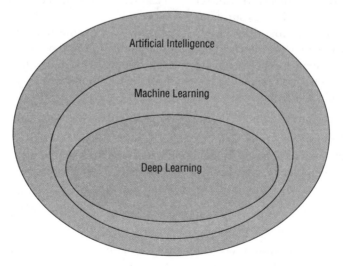

> **Exam Tip**
>
> You won't need to know the details of machine learning, artificial intelligence, or deep learning techniques when you take the CompTIA Data+ exam. It's important that data analysts understand these techniques, but they are beyond the scope of the test. Therefore, we won't dive into them more deeply in this book. If you're interested in learning more about machine learning, see the book *Practical Machine Learning in R* (Wiley, 2020) by Fred Nwanganga and Mike Chapple.

Data Governance

In the beginning of this chapter, we discussed the three major forces that have come together to create the Golden Age of Analytics: data, storage, and computing. In Figure 1.1, we illustrated how those three forces support modern analytics programs. However, there is one element of that figure that we haven't yet discussed. Notice that there is a slab of stone that supports the three pillars of analytics. This slab represents the important role of *data governance* in analytics programs. Without strong governance, analytics programs can't function effectively.

Data governance programs ensure that the organization has high-quality data and is able to effectively control that data. In Chapter 8, "Data Governance," you'll learn the major concepts of data governance and how organizations use *master data management (MDM)* programs to maintain and improve the quality of their data.

Analytics Tools

Software helps analysts work through each one of the phases of the analytics process. These tools automate much of the heavy lifting of data analysis, improving the analyst's ability to acquire, clean, manipulate, visualize, and analyze data. They also provide invaluable assistance in reporting and communicating results.

Some of these tools are well known to most computer users. For example, people are generally familiar with spreadsheet tools such as Microsoft Excel or Google Sheets. Figure 1.7 shows an example of the college dataset used to create Figures 1.4 and 1.5 loaded in Excel.

Other analytics tools require more advanced skills. For example, the R programming language is designed to provide analysts with direct access to their data, but it requires learning some basic coding skills. Figure 1.8 shows the RStudio integrated development environment with the code used to create Figure 1.5 loaded.

FIGURE 1.7 Data analysis in Microsoft Excel

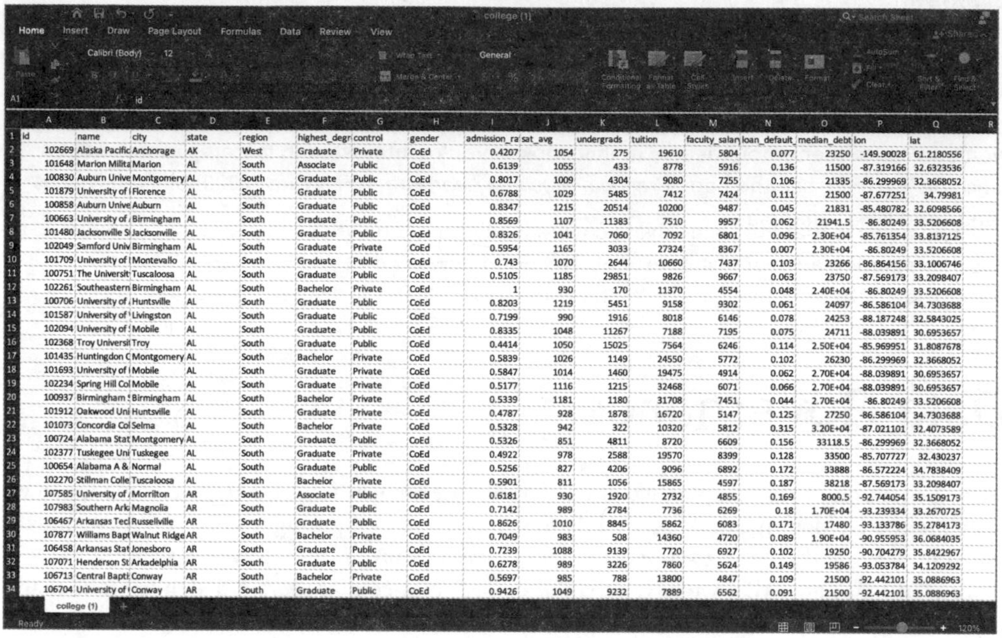

id	name	city	state	region	highest_degr	control	gender	admission_ra	sat_avg	undergrads	tuition	faculty_salary	loan_default_	median_debt	lon	lat
102669	Alaska Pacific	Anchorage	AK	West	Graduate	Private	CoEd	0.4207	1054	275	19610	5804	0.077	23250	-149.90028	61.2180556
101648	Marion Milita	Marion	AL	South	Associate	Public	CoEd	0.6139	1055	433	8778	5916	0.136	11500	-87.319166	32.6323536
100830	Auburn Unive	Montgomery	AL	South	Graduate	Public	CoEd	0.8017	1009	4304	9080	7255	0.106	21335	-86.299969	32.3668052
101879	University of	Florence	AL	South	Graduate	Public	CoEd	0.6788	1029	5485	7412	7424	0.111	21500	-87.677251	34.79981
100858	Auburn Unive	Auburn	AL	South	Graduate	Public	CoEd	0.8347	1215	20514	10200	9487	0.045	21831	-85.480782	32.6098566
100663	University of	Birmingham	AL	South	Graduate	Public	CoEd	0.8569	1107	11383	7510	9957	0.062	21941.5	-86.80249	33.5206608
101480	Jacksonville S	Jacksonville	AL	South	Graduate	Public	CoEd	0.8326	1041	7060	7092	6801	0.096	2.30E+04	-85.761354	33.8137125
102049	Samford Univ	Birmingham	AL	South	Graduate	Private	CoEd	0.5954	1165	3033	27324	8367	0.007	2.30E+04	-86.80249	33.5206608
101709	University of	Montevallo	AL	South	Graduate	Public	CoEd	0.743	1070	2644	10660	7437	0.103	23266	-86.864156	33.1006746
100751	The Universit	Tuscaloosa	AL	South	Graduate	Public	CoEd	0.5105	1185	29851	9826	9667	0.063	23750	-87.569173	33.2098407
102261	Southeastern	Birmingham	AL	South	Bachelor	Private	CoEd	1	930	170	11370	4554	0.048	2.40E+04	-86.80249	33.5206608
100706	University of	Huntsville	AL	South	Graduate	Public	CoEd	0.8203	1219	5451	9158	9302	0.061	24097	-86.586104	34.7303688
101587	University of	Livingston	AL	South	Graduate	Public	CoEd	0.7199	990	1916	8018	6146	0.078	24253	-88.187248	32.5843025
102094	University of	Mobile	AL	South	Graduate	Public	CoEd	0.8335	1048	11267	7188	7195	0.075	24711	-88.039891	30.6953657
102368	Troy Universi	Troy	AL	South	Graduate	Public	CoEd	0.4414	1050	15025	7564	6246	0.114	2.50E+04	-85.969951	31.8087678
101435	Huntingdon C	Montgomery	AL	South	Bachelor	Private	CoEd	0.5839	1026	1149	24550	5772	0.102	26230	-86.299969	32.3668052
101693	University of	Mobile	AL	South	Graduate	Private	CoEd	0.5847	1014	1460	19475	4914	0.062	2.70E+04	-88.039891	30.6953657
102234	Spring Hill Col	Mobile	AL	South	Graduate	Private	CoEd	0.5177	1116	1215	32468	6071	0.066	2.70E+04	-88.039891	30.6953657
100937	Birmingham	Birmingham	AL	South	Bachelor	Private	CoEd	0.5339	1181	1180	31708	7451	0.044	2.70E+04	-86.80249	33.5206608
101912	Oakwood Uni	Huntsville	AL	South	Graduate	Private	CoEd	0.4787	928	1878	16720	5147	0.125	27250	-86.586104	34.7303688
101073	Concordia Col	Selma	AL	South	Bachelor	Private	CoEd	0.5328	942	322	10320	5812	0.315	3.20E+04	-87.021101	32.4073589
100724	Alabama Stat	Montgomery	AL	South	Graduate	Public	CoEd	0.5326	851	4811	8720	6609	0.156	33118.5	-86.299969	32.3668052
102377	Tuskegee Uni	Tuskegee	AL	South	Graduate	Private	CoEd	0.4922	978	2588	19570	8399	0.128	33500	-85.707727	32.430237
100654	Alabama A &	Normal	AL	South	Graduate	Public	CoEd	0.5256	827	4206	9096	6892	0.172	33888	-86.572224	34.7838409
102270	Stillman Colle	Tuscaloosa	AL	South	Bachelor	Private	CoEd	0.5901	811	1056	15865	4597	0.187	38218	-87.569173	33.2098407
107585	University of	Morrilton	AR	South	Associate	Public	CoEd	0.6181	930	1920	2732	4855	0.169	8000.5	-92.744054	35.1509173
107983	Southern Ark	Magnolia	AR	South	Graduate	Public	CoEd	0.7142	989	2784	7736	6269	0.18	1.70E+04	-93.239334	33.2670725
106467	Arkansas Tec	Russellville	AR	South	Graduate	Public	CoEd	0.8626	1010	8845	5862	6083	0.171	17480	-93.133786	35.2784173
107877	Williams Bapt	Walnut Ridge	AR	South	Bachelor	Private	CoEd	0.7049	983	508	14360	4720	0.089	1.90E+04	-90.955953	36.0684035
106458	Arkansas Stat	Jonesboro	AR	South	Graduate	Public	CoEd	0.7239	1088	9139	7720	6927	0.102	19250	-90.704279	35.8422967
107071	Henderson St	Arkadelphia	AR	South	Graduate	Public	CoEd	0.6278	989	3226	7860	5624	0.149	19586	-93.053784	34.1209292
106713	Central Bapti	Conway	AR	South	Bachelor	Private	CoEd	0.5697	985	788	13800	4847	0.109	21500	-92.442101	35.0886963
106704	University of	Conway	AR	South	Graduate	Public	CoEd	0.9426	1049	9232	7889	6562	0.091	21500	-92.442101	35.0886963

FIGURE 1.8 Data analysis in RStudio

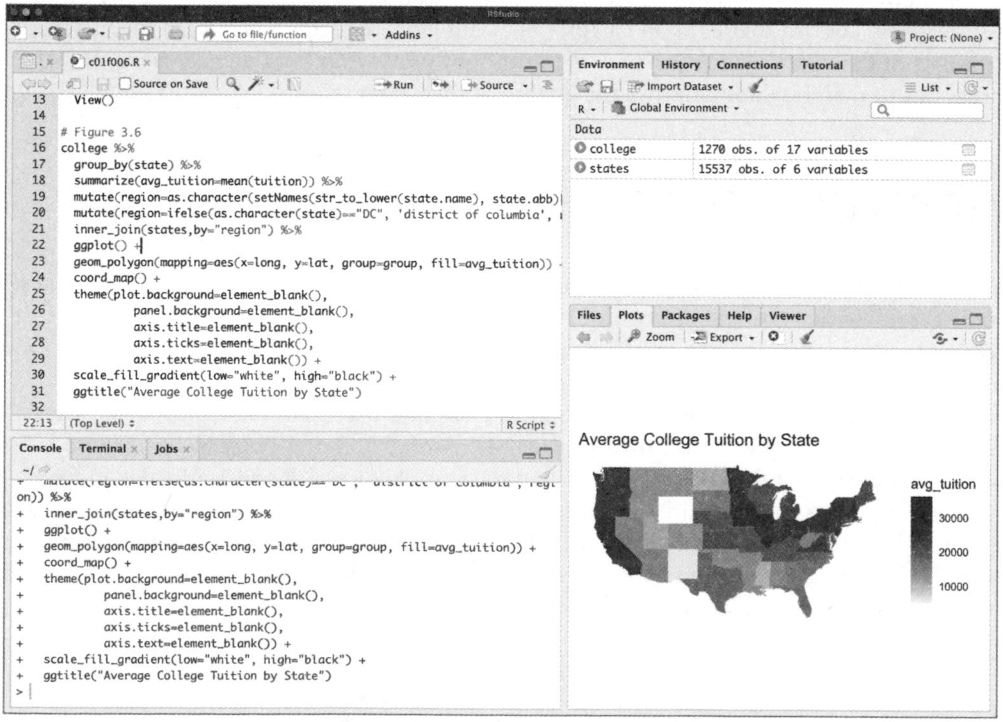

You'll likely work with several different tools in your work as a data analyst. Your choice of tools will depend on the work at hand, the standards used by your organization, and the software licenses available to you. We'll discuss many common analytics tools in Chapter 6, "Data Analytics Tools."

Exam Tip

The bad news is that the Data+ exam covers 20 different analytics tools that you'll need to understand to answer test questions. The good news is that you won't need deep knowledge of each of these tools. We'll explore everything that you need to know in Chapter 6.

Summary

Analytics programs allow businesses to access the untapped value locked within their data. Today, many organizations recognize the potential value of this work but are still in the early stages of developing their analytics programs. These programs, driven by the unprecedented availability of data, the rapidly decreasing cost of storage, and the maturation of cloud computing, promise to create significant opportunities for businesses and, in turn, for data professionals skilled in the tools and techniques of analytics.

As analysts develop analytic work products, they generally move through a series of stages. Their work begins with the acquisition of data from internal and external sources and continues with the cleaning and manipulation of that data. Once data is in a suitable form, data professionals apply analytic techniques to draw conclusions from their data, create visualizations to depict the story of their data, and develop reports and dashboards to effectively communicate the results of their work to business leaders.

Chapter

2

Understanding Data

THE COMPTIA DATA+ EXAM TOPICS COVERED IN THIS CHAPTER INCLUDE:

✓ **Domain 1.0: Data Concepts and Environments**

✓ **1.2. Compare and contrast different data types**

✓ **1.3. Compare and contrast common data structures and file formats**

We work with data every day in our business and personal lives. But how often do we stop and think about how our data is structured? Effective data analysts understand data in all its forms and how that data fits into their working environment. Knowledge of data includes understanding the various types of data that exist and the different options for storing that data in an enterprise environment. With a basic grounding in how to think about data, you will be well positioned to meaningfully contribute to the collection, organization, and analysis of data.

We will kick off this chapter by examining data types that categorize individual pieces of data and exploring considerations for dealing with the range of possible values for different data types. We will learn how these building blocks are combined to describe a unique object or event in the sections that follow. We will also explore different ways of organizing data and various file formats for facilitating data exchange, system interoperability, and ease of human consumption.

Exploring Data Types

To understand data types, it is best first to understand data elements. A *data element* is an attribute about a person, place, or thing containing data within a range of values. Data elements also describe characteristics of activities, including orders, transactions, and events. Consider the data in Table 2.1, which illustrates some simple information about domesticated animals. We can see that the data elements include the name, type, breed, date of birth, height, and weight for each animal in the table. The column headings name the data element, while each row is an example value for that element.

TABLE 2.1 Pet data

Pet Name	Animal Type	Breed Name	Date of Birth	Height (inches)	Weight (pounds)
Jack	Dog	Corgi	3/2/2018	10	26.3
Viking	Dog	Husky	5/8/2017	24	58
Hazel	Dog	Labradoodle	7/3/2016	23	61
Schooner	Dog	Labrador Retriever	8/14/2019	24.3	73.4

Pet Name	Animal Type	Breed Name	Date of Birth	Height (inches)	Weight (pounds)
Skippy	Dog	Weimaraner	10/3/2018	26.3	63.5
Alexander	Cat	American Shorthair	10/4/2017	9.3	10.4

Now that you understand what data elements are, let's explore how they relate to data types. A *data type* limits the values a data element can have. Consider the information in Table 2.1. Pet Name, Animal Type, and Breed Name are all words. Meanwhile, the Date of Birth column contains numbers and slashes that identify a specific date. Height and Weight are both numbers. Each of these groupings represents a particular data type.

Individual data types support structured, unstructured, and semi-structured data. Let's explore the differences between these categories.

Tabular Data

Tabular data is data organized into a table, made up of columns and rows. A table represents information about a single topic. Each *column* represents a uniquely named field within a table, also called a variable, about a single characteristic. The contents of each column contain values for the data element as defined by the column header. Consider the pet data in Table 2.1. The Pet Name column contains the names of a given animal.

Each *row* represents a record of a single instance of the table's topic. Looking at the row for Jack in Table 2.1, we see that he is a dog of breed Corgi, his birth date, and his height and weight information. All the information in that row is about Jack.

It is helpful to think of tabular data as rectangular data. It is easy to draw a rectangle around the data. The top of the rectangle is defined by columns, while rows define the left side of the rectangle.

The intersection of a row and column contains a specific value. Looking at the intersection of Jack and Breed Name in Table 2.1 tells us that Jack is a Corgi. If we want to identify Hazel's breed, we look at where her row intersects with the Breed Name column and see that she is a Labradoodle.

Spreadsheets, including Microsoft Excel, Google Sheets, and Apple Numbers, are practical tools for representing tabular data. A *relational database management system* (*RDMS*), commonly called a database, extends the tabular model. Instead of having all data in a single table, a database organizes related data across multiple tables. The connection between tables is known as a *relationship*. Oracle, Microsoft SQL Server, MySQL, and PostgreSQL are examples of database software. Tabular data is the concept that underpins both spreadsheets and relational databases.

We will explore databases in greater detail in Chapter 3, "Databases and Data Acquisition."

Structured Data Types

Structured data is tabular in nature, organized into rows and columns. Structured data is what typically comes to mind when looking at a spreadsheet. With clearly defined column headings, spreadsheets are easy to work with and understand. In a spreadsheet, cells are where columns and rows intersect.

Consider the dataset in Figure 2.1. It contains basic information about a group of people. When you read the column headings, you get a good sense of the kind of data that you're going to find in that column. For example, when you see the "Weight (pounds)" column, you expect to see numeric values. In the Address field, you expect to see text. Looking more closely, we see that the data values are consistent for each column. For example, all the height and weight information uses numbers instead of words. Taken as a whole, Figure 2.1 is an example of highly structured data, with defined columns, an expectation for what the rows will contain, and consistent columnar values in each row.

FIGURE 2.1   Person Data

First Name	Last Name	Date of Birth	Height (inches)	Weight (pounds)	Hair Color	Eye Color	Address	City	State	Zip Code
Chris	Stuzman	4/3/1976	78	183	brown	black	193 Main St	Stevens Point	Wisconsin	54481
Amy	Robinson	5/8/1985	72	134	black	hazel	388 Walnut St	Mobile	Alabama	36602
Tom	Henkel	8/23/1947	68	155	blond	green	3942 N. Beech S	Amarillo	Texas	79111
Cindy	Sturm	10/17/1991	66	159	brown	blue	881 Fir Rd	San Diego	California	92104
Dave	O'Leary	2/14/1983	70	196	red	blue	941 Hickory Ln	Fort Collins	Colorado	80526
Robin	Richardson	12/8/1986	64	167	grey	green	4024 W Division	Chicago	Illinois	60651

Let's explore some of the most common data types that give structured data its structure.

Character

The character data type limits data entry to only valid characters. Characters can include the alphabet that you might see on your keyboard, as well as numbers. Depending on your needs, multiple data types are available that can enforce character limits.

Alphanumeric is the most widely used data type for storing character-based data. As the name implies, alphanumeric is appropriate when a data element consists of both numbers and letters. Consider the Address field in Figure 2.1. To accurately represent a given street address, both the house number and the street name are required.

The alphanumeric data type is ideal for storing product stock-keeping units (SKUs). It is common in the retail clothing space to have a unique SKU for each item available for sale. If you sell jeans, you may stock products from Armani Jeans, Diesel, Lee Jeans, Levi's, and Wrangler. To keep track of all the manufacturer, size, color, and fit combinations in your inventory, you might use an SKU similar to the one depicted in Figure 2.2. Tracking inventory at the SKU level allows you to manage availability in your online and in-store systems, all courtesy of the alphanumeric data type.

FIGURE 2.2   SKU example

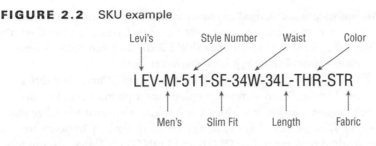

There are times when it is necessary to impose even stricter limits on character-related data to exclude numbers. Excluding numbers can be achieved using the *text* data type. Closely related to the alphanumeric data type, it is even more stringent. It is helpful to think of text as a subset of alphanumeric, only allowing the storage of alphabetic characters. One practical use of the text data type is to improve the overall data quality. For example, consider the "State" data element in Figure 2.1. If the system contains state names from the United States, it would be appropriate to select a text data type.

Consider a data entry example. Suppose you operate an online retail system. To deliver orders, you need address information for the intended recipients. This information comes from the customers themselves, since they can specify where orders should be shipped. Any time a person interacts with a computer, there is the potential for a data entry error. Suppose someone wanted to enter "Montana" for the state component of their address.

Take a look at the positioning of the O and 0 keys in Figure 2.3, depicting the U.S. QWERTY keyboard layout. These two keys are very close together. Many people press these keys with the fourth finger of their right hand, making a data entry error that much more likely. A person could supply the value "M0ntana" instead of the intended "Montana." With "State" as a text data type, trying to input the erroneous value would result in an error. However, with "State" implemented as alphanumeric, nothing would prevent that mistake from making its way into the database.

FIGURE 2.3   U.S. QWERTY keyboard layout

~ `	! 1	@ 2	# 3	$ 4	% 5	^ 6	& 7	* 8	(9	) 0	_ -	+ =	← Backspace
Tab	Q	W	E	R	T	Y	U	I	O	P	{ [	}]	| \\
Caps Lock	A	S	D	F	G	H	J	K	L	: ;	" '	Enter ↵	
Shift	Z	X	C	V	B	N	M	< ,	> .	? /	Shift		
Ctrl	Win Key	Alt						Alt	Win Key	Menu	Ctrl		

Each database software has its unique method of implementing character data types to handle the nuances related to character data. The most significant difference has to do with how much data a particular data element can contain. Table 2.2 shows a sampling of how the three most popular databases provide data types for character data.

All of the data types shown in Table 2.2 support alphanumeric data. Where they differ is on how much data they can handle. Before defining a column as alphanumeric, you need to determine how long your longest-possible text value will be. You also need to realize that while data types may have the same names, they are implemented differently by software vendors. There are also individual data types, like CLOB and LONGTEXT, that are vendor-specific. Finally, you need to be aware of the absolute limits imposed by the database you are using.

TABLE 2.2   Selected character data types and maximum size

Data type name	Oracle	Microsoft SQL Server	MySQL
char	2,000 bytes	8,000 bytes	255 bytes
varchar2	4,000 bytes	-	-
varchar	-	8,000 bytes	64 KB
CLOB	128 TB	-	-
varchar(max)	-	2 GB	-
LONGTEXT	-	-	4 GB

With spreadsheets, configuring a given cell or range of cells as a text-only data type takes more effort than when using a database. It is not possible to accomplish this with one of the native data types provided by the software. Instead, limiting to just text requires a formula. Figure 2.4 shows an example of how to use a formula to perform this level of validation in Microsoft Excel. Suppose a person tries to input a value containing numbers or symbols into a cell where the formula is active. Figure 2.5 illustrates the resulting error message.

FIGURE 2.4   Excel text-only formula

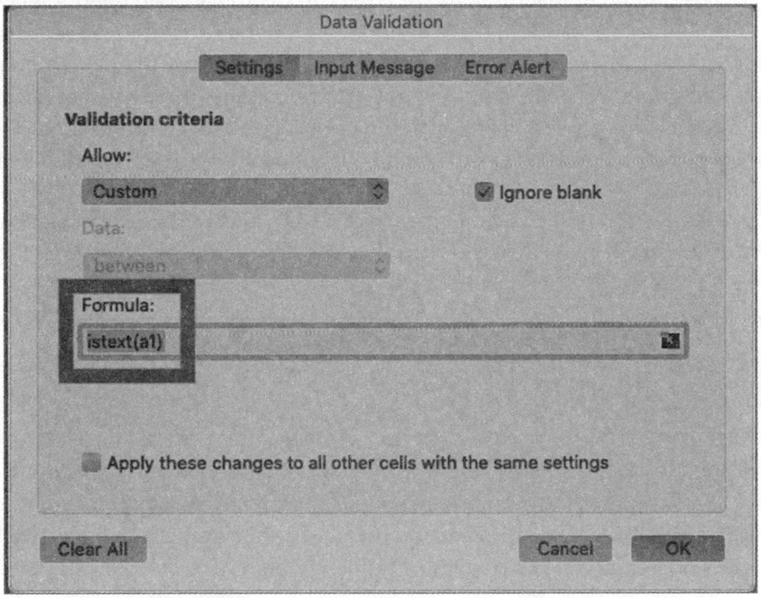

FIGURE 2.5   Text-only data validation restriction

Character Sets

When considering alphanumeric and text data types, you need to think about the character set you are using to input and store data when using a database. Databases use character sets to map, or encode, data and store it digitally. The ASCII encoding standard is based on the U.S. English alphabet. ASCII accommodates both the upper and lowercase English alphabet and numbers, mathematical operators, and symbols, as shown earlier in Figure 2.3.

Many languages include accent marks, extending the Latin alphabet. For example, Akrapovič is a Slovenian manufacturer. To store the č in Akrapovič, you need to encode that value appropriately. In addition, there are many languages, including Arabic, Chinese, Japanese, and Korean, which use symbols as opposed to extending the Latin alphabet. For example, قط is the Arabic word for "cat." Several encoding standards exist that accommodate non-Latin characters. One of the most common is Unicode Transformation Format-8 (UTF-8), which allows non-Latin characters to be input by a user and stored in a file or database.

It is necessary to realize that individual characters may consume multiple bytes, impacting the length of a character string you can store in a character data type.

Numeric

When numbers exclusively make up values for a data attribute, *numeric* becomes the data type of choice. This data type appears to be simple and obvious based on its name. As seen with the character data type, implementation nuances about numeric are essential to understand. Databases accommodate two types of numeric data types: *integer* and *numeric*.

Whole Numbers

The integer, and all its subtypes, are for storing whole numbers. As seen with the character family of data types, implementation differences exist across databases. Table 2.3 illustrates how Oracle, Microsoft, and MySQL support whole numbers.

Note that both the Microsoft and MySQL databases support the bit data type, which can be empty or store a 0 or a 1. In computer science, flags indicate whether something is on or off, or if a function has completed successfully. To show something is on, 1 or TRUE is used. For a value of off, 0 or FALSE is used. The bit data type is intended for storing the status of a flag.

Note also that the value ranges for smallint and shortinteger are identical. The same is true for int and integer, as well as bigint and longinteger. Although the data types have different names, their functionality is equivalent.

Rational Numbers

In all its variants, the numeric data type is for rational numbers that include a decimal point. As with the integer family of data types, each database vendor has its implementation nuances. Table 2.4 illustrates how Oracle, Microsoft, and MySQL support rational numbers.

TABLE 2.3   Selected integer data types and value range

Data type name	Oracle	Microsoft SQL Server	MySQL
bit	-	0 and 1	0 and 1
tinyint	-	0 to 255	0 to 255
smallint	-	-32,768 to 32,767	-32,768 to 32,767
shortinteger	-32,768 to 32,767	-	-
int	-	-2,147,483,648 to 2,147,483,647	-2,147,483,648 to 2,147,483,647
integer	-2,147,483,648 to 2,147,483,647	-	-
bigint	-	-9,223,372,036,854,775,808 to 9,223,372,036,854,775,807	-9,223,372,036,854,775,808 to 9,223,372,036,854,775,807
longinteger	-9,223,372,036,854,775,808 to 9,223,372,036,854,775,807	-	-

TABLE 2.4 Selected integer data types and value range

Data type name	Oracle	Microsoft SQL Server	MySQL
shortdecimal	−10^38 to 10^38, up to 7 significant digits	-	-
number	−10^125 to 10^125, up to 38 significant digits	-	-
decimal	−10^308 to 10^308, up to 15 significant digits	−10^38 to 10^38, up to 38 significant digits	Up to 65 digits in total, so the range depends on the number of digits assigned to the whole and fractional components

You must take several factors into account when dealing with rational numbers. In both SQL Server and MySQL, there is a data type called *numeric* that is functionally equivalent to the decimal data type. Realizing that data types are inconsistently named across databases, you need to consider the ultimate range of values a given data element handles. All the data types in Table 2.4 store numbers to a configurable number of significant digits. There are scientific use cases that require an even greater number of significant digits; additional numeric data type variants exist to accommodate that need.

Date and Time

Gathered together under the broad category of *date*, day of year and time of day are data elements that appear with great frequency. As illustrated in Table 2.5, databases have various data types for handling date- and time-related information. As seen with character and numeric data types, nuances exist across different databases. Selecting the appropriate date-related data type depends on the data you need to store.

TABLE 2.5 Selected date and time data types

Data type name	Oracle	Microsoft SQL Server	MySQL
date	YYYY-MM-DD	YYYY-MM-DD	YYYY-MM-DD
datetime2	-	YYYY-MM-DD hh:mm:ss.sss[.fractional seconds]	YYYY-MM-DD hh:mm:ss.sss[.fractional seconds]
time	-	hh:mm:ss.sss[.fractional seconds]	YYYY-MM-DD hh:mm:ss.sss[.fractional seconds]

Data type name	Oracle	Microsoft SQL Server	MySQL
timestamp	YYYY-MM-DD hh:mm:ss.sss[.fractional seconds]	-	-
year	-	-	YYYY

For example, suppose you operate a veterinary clinic and need to store birth date information for pets. In that case, you need to store the year, month, and day. With those three components of date, you can effectively administer medication and determine when to schedule annual veterinary appointments.

There are many occasions when it is more appropriate to include time, in addition to the day, month, and year. For instance, consider package tracking information for companies like FedEx, United Parcel Service, or DHL. Consumers want to know where a specific package is up to the minute. The company itself may need second-level details to optimize labor, infrastructure investments, and route planning.

Currency

Many people use spreadsheets to manage their finances. Organizations typically use enterprise-scale software for the same purpose, with the data residing in a database. While financial data is numeric, people prefer seeing the numbers displayed as a specific currency. For example, consider the Number, Dollar, and Euro columns in Figure 2.6. The column headings indicate what each column contains. The currency symbols in each cell tell the reader what the data represents, even if the column headings have scrolled off the screen.

Especially in this context, it is essential to differentiate between data formatting and data storage. Data storage contains the actual value for a given data element. Data formatting takes a given data value and then formats it for display purposes. Data formatting is common when dealing with currency and date data types.

The numeric data in all the columns of Figure 2.6 are numerically equivalent. Figure 2.7 illustrates a sampling of currencies available for formatting in a Google spreadsheet.

Of the databases mentioned in this chapter, only Microsoft SQL Server has data types specifically for storing currency. Table 2.6 illustrates these two data types. Both of these data types offer four digits of precision after the decimal point.

TABLE 2.6 Currency data types in Microsoft SQL Server

Data type name	Range of values
smallmoney	–214,748.3648 to 214,748.3647
money	–922,337,203,685,477.5808 to 922,337,203,685,477.5807

FIGURE 2.6 Numeric data formatted as different currencies

Number	Dollar	Euro
1.2	$1.20	€1.20
1.14	$1.14	€1.14
1.12	$1.12	€1.12
1.18	$1.18	€1.18
1.13	$1.13	€1.13
1.11	$1.11	€1.11
1.11	$1.11	€1.11
1.33	$1.33	€1.33
1.33	$1.33	€1.33
1.29	$1.29	€1.29
1.39	$1.39	€1.39
1.33	$1.33	€1.33
1.39	$1.39	€1.39
1.47	$1.47	€1.47
1.37	$1.37	€1.37
1.26	$1.26	€1.26
1.24	$1.24	€1.24
1.24	$1.24	€1.24
1.13	$1.13	€1.13
0.95	$0.95	€0.95
0.9	$0.90	€0.90
0.92	$0.92	€0.92

FIGURE 2.7 Currency formats in Google Sheets

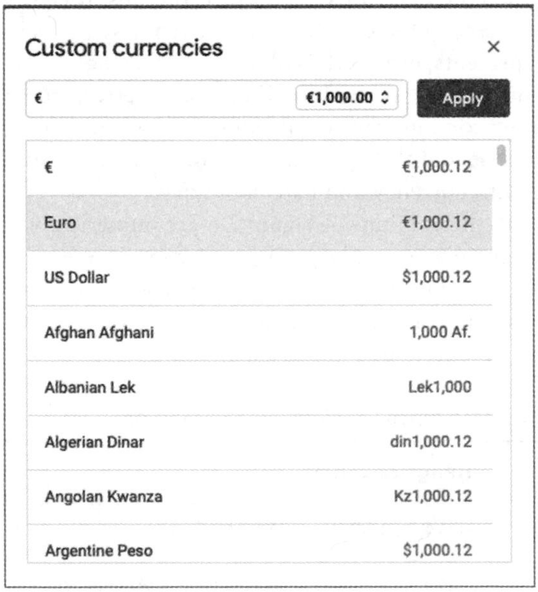

Custom currencies ✕

€   €1,000.00 ⌄   Apply

€	€1,000.12
Euro	€1,000.12
US Dollar	$1,000.12
Afghan Afghani	1,000 Af.
Albanian Lek	Lek1,000
Algerian Dinar	din1,000.12
Angolan Kwanza	Kz1,000.12
Argentine Peso	$1,000.12

While the currency data types exist, it is more common to use a numeric data type for storing currency data. Limiting a calculation to only four digits of precision after the decimal point can lead to incorrect rounding errors. Consider Figure 2.8, which illustrates retrieving values from a database. The money_table_example table contains columns defined as money for both sales price and price. The percentage column in the query result is calculated by taking the sales price divided by the price and then multiplying the result by 100. Figure 2.9 illustrates the same calculation in a spreadsheet, and Figure 2.10 shows the result of 18 divided by 22 in a calculator.

Recall that the money data type uses only four digits after the decimal. For this reason, the database incorrectly calculates the percentage as 81.81 instead of the spreadsheet's correct evaluation of 81.82.

FIGURE 2.8   Incorrect percentage due to money data type

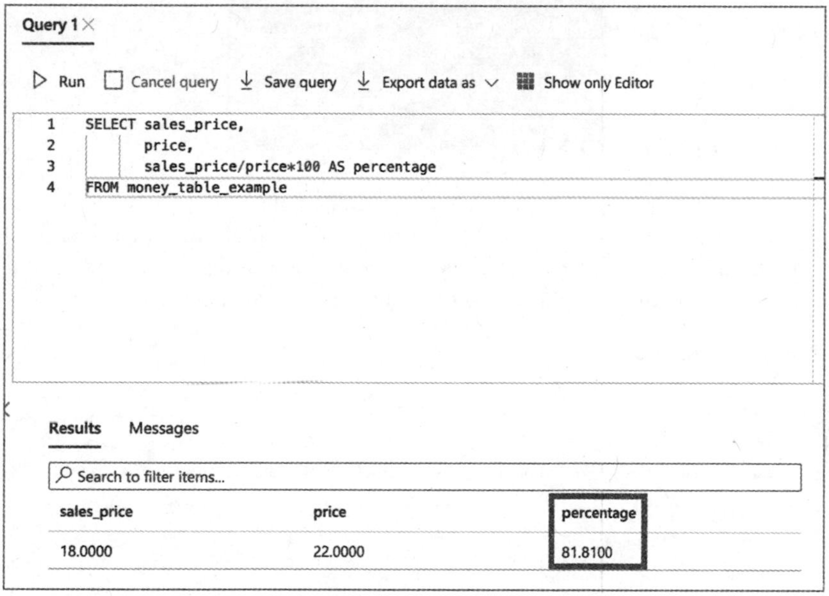

```
Query 1 ×

▷ Run   ☐ Cancel query   ↓ Save query   ↓ Export data as  ∨   ▦ Show only Editor

1    SELECT sales_price,
2         price,
3         sales_price/price*100 AS percentage
4    FROM money_table_example
```

Results   Messages

🔎 Search to filter items...

sales_price	price	percentage
18.0000	22.0000	81.8100

FIGURE 2.9   Correct percentage as calculated by a spreadsheet

Portion	Price	Percentage
$18.00	$22.00	81.82%

FIGURE 2.10   Unrounded calculation in a calculator

While SQL Server does support two currency-specific data type variants, most databases do not. As the rounding error in Figure 2.8 shows, it is best to use a numeric data type to store currency-related data. Figure 2.11 illustrates that the rounded results are mathematically accurate using the numeric data type for both sales_price and price.

FIGURE 2.11   Correct percentage when using a numeric data type

Query 1 ✕

▷ Run   ☐ Cancel query   ↓ Save query   ↓ Export data as ∨   ▦ Show only Editor

```
1   SELECT sales_price,
2        price,
3        round(sales_price/price*100,2) AS percentage
4   FROM numeric_table_example
```

Results   Messages

🔍 Search to filter items...

sales_price	price	percentage
18	22	81.8200000000000000

Exam Tip

As you prepare for the Data+ exam, you should recognize the difference between storing a data type and formatting it to facilitate human interpretation. Take care not to automatically infer a data type based on formatting.

Strong and Weak Typing

Data types define values placed in columns. *Strong typing* is when technology rigidly enforces data types. Databases, discussed in Chapter 3, use strong typing. A database column defined as numeric only accepts numerical values. You will get an error if you attempt to enter characters into a numeric column.

Weak typing loosely enforces data types. Spreadsheets use weak typing to help make it easier for people to accomplish their work. Spreadsheets default to an "automatic" data type and accommodate practically any value. When a person specifies a data type, it is loosely enforced compared to a database. For example, with a numeric spreadsheet cell, the software does not stop you from entering and storing characters.

Software that uses weak typing can be helpful. That said, be mindful that you may experience unexpected and perhaps incorrect results.

Unstructured Data Types

While much of the data we use to record transactions is highly structured, most of the world's data is *unstructured*. Unstructured data is any type of data that does not fit neatly into the tabular model. Examples of unstructured data include digital images, audio recordings, video recordings, and open-ended survey responses. Analyzing unstructured data creates a wealth of information and insight. Many people have camera-enabled smartphones, and using video for conversations and meetings is commonplace. To capture and analyze unstructured data, we make use of data types designed explicitly for that purpose.

Consider the pet data depicted in Table 2.1. Suppose the veterinary office wants to augment their records to include digital images of the animals. To accommodate that requirement, we need to make use of an unstructured data type.

Binary

Binary data types are one of the most common data types for storing unstructured data. It supports any type of digital file you may have, from Microsoft Excel spreadsheets to digital photographs. When considering which binary data type to use, file size tends to be the limiting factor. You need to select a data type that is as large as the largest file you plan on storing.

The most common types of unstructured data are audio, image, and video data. Spreadsheets are consumer applications designed to manage highly structured data, but they're often not very good at storing binary data. Figure 2.12 illustrates the result of trying to integrate images into the pet information spreadsheet in Excel. While it is possible to place images within the spreadsheet, it is impossible to store the images within a cell. However, Google Sheets does allow the storing of binary data within a cell, as shown in Figure 2.13.

FIGURE 2.12   Images in Excel

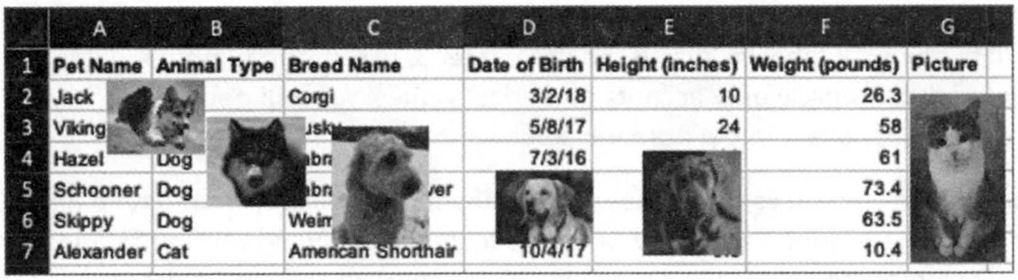

FIGURE 2.13   Binary data in a Google spreadsheet

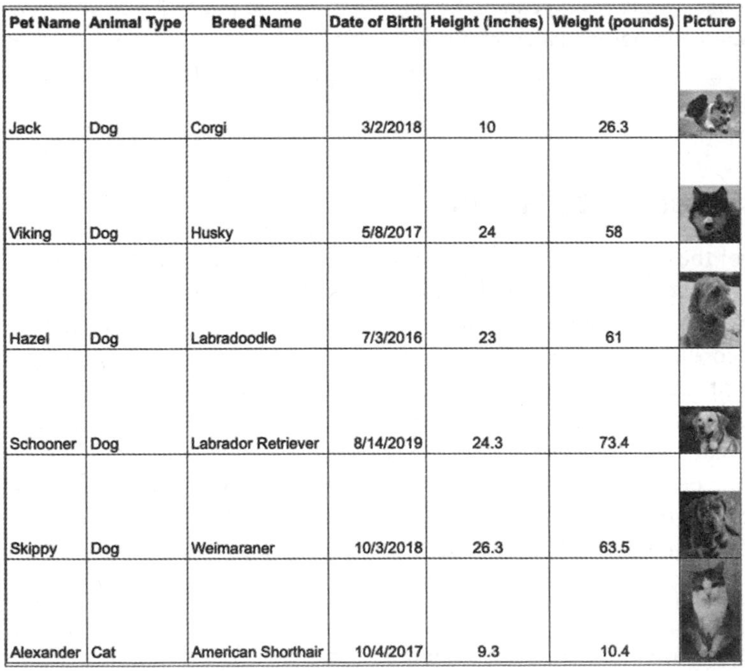

Pet Name	Animal Type	Breed Name	Date of Birth	Height (inches)	Weight (pounds)	Picture
Jack	Dog	Corgi	3/2/2018	10	26.3	
Viking	Dog	Husky	5/8/2017	24	58	
Hazel	Dog	Labradoodle	7/3/2016	23	61	
Schooner	Dog	Labrador Retriever	8/14/2019	24.3	73.4	
Skippy	Dog	Weimaraner	10/3/2018	26.3	63.5	
Alexander	Cat	American Shorthair	10/4/2017	9.3	10.4	

Databases offer a much more sophisticated collection of data types for storing binary data, as Table 2.7 illustrates. Note that the maximum size is per row, not per table. Once again, we see the inconsistency in naming, as well as supported size.

TABLE 2.7   Selected binary data types and maximum sizes

Data type name	Oracle	Microsoft SQL Server	MySQL
tinyblob	-	-	255 bytes
mediumblob	-	-	16 MB
binary	-	8,000 bytes	64 MB
varbinary	-	-	64 MB
varbinary(max)	-	2 GB	-
longblob	-	-	4 GB
BLOB	128 TB	-	64 KB

Audio

Audio data can come from a variety of sources. Whenever you interact with a customer service agent and hear "this call may be recorded for quality assurance purposes," your conversation is probably being recorded and stored for later analysis. The impact of capturing, storing, and analyzing audio data has led to the development of *avalanche detection systems*. These systems listen for and detect the acoustic characteristics of an avalanche. With real-time notification capabilities, these systems reduce the time it takes for emergency services to respond and alert hikers to treacherous conditions.

In order to ingest audio data into a system and make it available for processing, data is first captured via a microphone. The data is then digitized and stored. Audio can be stored in its raw form, which consumes the most storage space. Alternatively, it can be encoded with a compression algorithm to reduce the amount of space required. Regardless of if it is in raw or compressed form, storing audio requires a data type designed to handle raw binary data.

Images

Image data can come from a variety of sources. People take more than 1 trillion photographs every calendar year, fueled by the ubiquity of camera-enabled smartphones and relatively low storage costs. Each digital picture is a piece of unstructured data. Examining Figure 2.14, it is easy for a human to identify the contents of the photograph. However, it is a binary file to a computer, ultimately stored as a series of ones and zeros. Applying artificial intelligence algorithms for image processing over a set of digital photos allows people to look for the objects they contain. Figure 2.15 illustrates the search results for the word "motorcycle" in a digital image library.

FIGURE 2.14   Photograph of racing motorcycles

FIGURE 2.15   Motorcycle search results

Image data has applicability across several industries. For example, dentists use digital X-rays to augment a person's dental record. Magnetic resonance imaging scans, used for soft tissue investigations, are added to a person's health record. Insurance companies provide mobile applications to upload photographs of accident scenes. As the use of image data grows, understanding how it is stored is vital for the modern data analyst.

Resolution is the most significant factor that governs how much space is required to store an image. The greater the resolution, the more detail an image contains, and the more storage space it needs. Similar to compressing audio data, there are a variety of ways to encode and store images. Storing images in a database requires a data type designed to handle raw binary data, such as varbinary or BLOB.

Video

Video data is growing at a similar pace to image data. In the consumer space, people upload videos to YouTube, Instagram, and TikTok every day. Police officers wear body cameras to create a video record of enforcement situations. Image processing algorithms examine videos to detect everything from traffic congestion to intruders in the home.

As is the case with audio data, the resolution has a significant impact on the storage a video consumes. Video duration is also another factor that impacts storage size. Consider Table 2.8, which approximates the space required for storing a still image, one minute of audio data, and one minute of video data as recorded on a modern smartphone. We see that every minute of video is equivalent to over 50 individual images, or more than 200 minutes of audio.

TABLE 2.8   Approximate storage needs

	Still image	Audio (1 minute)	Video (1 minute)
Space consumed (KB)	2,048	503	102,400

Large Text

There are times when it is appropriate to store a significant amount of text data. It is the combination of words into sentences that result in classifying large text as unstructured data. You may need to explore text data to detect nuance, humor, sarcasm, and inferential meaning. For example, you may need to keep the complete transcript of a legal proceeding, public address, or verbose open-ended survey responses. What differentiates large text from the text and alphanumeric data types is size. When considering Table 2.9, keep in mind that 2 GB of character data is approximately 1 million pages of text.

TABLE 2.9   Selected binary data types and maximum sizes

Data type name	Oracle	Microsoft SQL Server	MySQL
varchar(max)	-	2 GB	-
longtext	-	-	4 GB
CLOB	128 TB	-	-

Once again, note that data type names differ across vendor products. For example, Table 2.2 shows that Oracle has the varchar2 text data type. Oracle currently implements varchar as a synonym for varchar2. However, Microsoft's implementation of varchar is vastly different. In Oracle, since the varchar data type is a synonym of varchar2, it is limited to 4,000 bytes. Meanwhile, Microsoft's implementation of varchar supports up to 2 GB. To handle larger amounts of text, Oracle created the proprietary CLOB data type.

Exam Tip

As you prepare for the Data+ exam, you should be familiar with the different types of structured and unstructured data that you might encounter. Be prepared to evaluate a situation and select the most appropriate data type to store a piece of data.

Categories of Data

We try to fit data into structured and unstructured categories. The reality is that the world is not black and white, and not all data fits neatly into structured and unstructured categories. Semi-structured data represents the space between structured spreadsheets and unstructured videos.

As illustrated in Table 2.1, a veterinary practice may be interested in collecting structured data about the animals under its care. When mapping data attributes to data types, there are additional considerations regarding the actual values to be stored.

Quantitative vs. Qualitative Data

Regardless of structure, data is either *quantitative* or *qualitative*. Quantitative data consists of numeric values. Data elements whose values come from counting or measuring are quantitative. In Table 2.1, the Height and Weight columns are quantitative. Quantitative data answers questions like "How many?" and "How much?"

Qualitative data consists of frequently text values. Data elements whose values describe characteristics, traits, and attitudes are all qualitative. In Table 2.1, Pet Name, Animal Type, and Breed Name are all qualitative. Qualitative data answers questions like "Why?" and "What?"

Discrete vs. Continuous Data

Numeric data comes in two different forms: *discrete* and *continuous*. A helpful way to think about discrete data is that it represents measurements that can't be subdivided. You may intuitively think of discrete data as using whole numbers, but that doesn't have to be the case. For example, if a fundraising organization sells chickens in half-chicken increments, you can buy 1.5 chickens. However, you can't buy .25 chickens.

Another way to think about it is that discrete data is useful when you have things you want to count. For example, a veterinary clinic may be interested in the number of dogs and cats under its care. Figure 2.16 shows the aggregation of the pet from Table 2.1. The Total data element is an example of discrete data, as it contains the value 5 for Dog and 1 for Cat. A veterinary practice would not care for 5.5 dogs or 2.25 cats.

FIGURE 2.16   Discrete data example

Animal Type	Total
Dog	5
Cat	1

Instead of counting, when you measure things like height and weight, you are collecting continuous data. While whole numbers represent discrete data, continuous data typically need a decimal point. Two dogs in Table 2.1 have their height recorded to the tenth of an inch. Similarly, weight is recorded to the tenth of an inch for three dogs and one cat. Figure 2.17 shows the continuous measure of average height and weight information by animal.

FIGURE 2.17   Continuous data example

Animal Type	Total	Average Height	Average Weight
Dog	5	21.52	56.44
Cat	1	9.3	10.4

Both the Average Height and Average Weight calculations for dogs result in numbers to the hundredths. These averages will change as the animals' weight changes and as the veterinarian's practice grows and adds animals. In addition, the degree of precision in terms of weight measurement could change. For example, the vet could start recording weight information to the hundredths instead of the tenths. The Height and Weight attributes from Table 2.1, as well as the Average Height and Average Weight from Figure 2.17, are examples of continuous data elements.

Qualitative data is discrete, but quantitative data can be either discrete or continuous data. For example, age is a continuous variable, but you may treat a person's age in years as discrete. A good rule of thumb is that discrete applies when counting while continuous applies when measuring.

Exam Tip

As you prepare for the Data+ exam, make sure you can distinguish between qualitative and quantitative data, as well as discrete and continuous data.

Categorical Data

In addition to quantitative, numeric data, there is categorical data. Text data with a known, finite number of categories is categorical. When considering an individual data element, it is possible to determine whether or not it is categorical. Let's continue to identify each data element of the pet dataset in Table 2.1. Animal Type is a good example of categorical data. As represented, this column separates the data into two categories: dog and cat. As additional dogs or cats enter into care, they fall within the existing categories.

That said, the range of accepted values for a given category can change over time. For instance, suppose the veterinarian branches out beyond small animal care and starts caring for horses. It is possible to expand the range of acceptable values in a category to accommodate this change.

You can also use categories to enforce data validation when someone is first entering data. Category enforcement has the effect of improving data quality. For example, suppose the veterinarian decides to only care for cats and dogs. To streamline operations, the veterinarian has a website built so that clients can schedule appointments online. Suppose the intent is to limit online appointments only for dogs and cats. In that case, the website can implement a dropdown menu where the only options for the animal type are "dog" and "cat." If someone had a mouse, hamster, or gerbil, the validation check prevents the scheduling of an appointment.

Dimensional Data

Dimensional modeling is an approach to arranging data to facilitate analysis. Dimensional modeling organizes data into fact tables and dimension tables. Fact tables store measurement data that is of interest to a business. A veterinary practice may want to answer some questions about appointments. A table holding appointment data would be called a fact table.

Dimensions are tables that contain data about the fact. For appointment data, the veterinarian's office manager may want to understand who was at an appointment and if any procedures were performed. In Figure 2.18, the Appointments table is the fact table. The Veterinarians, Owners, Procedures, and Pets tables are all dimensions that can answer questions about appointments.

FIGURE 2.18   Dimension illustration

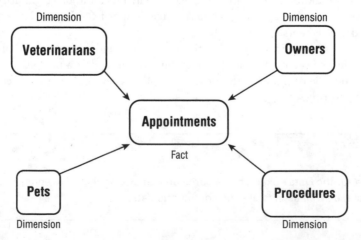

Dimensional data contains groupings of individual attributes about a given subject. For example, taken as a whole, the pets dataset from Table 2.1 can be called the "pets" dimension. You can imagine that the "owners" dimension in Figure 2.18 contains biographic information about a pet's owner, identifying who was present at an appointment. When combined with data from additional dimensions, data elements from each dimension add detail about the facts in the fact table. We will explore dimensional modeling in greater detail in Chapter 3.

Common Data Structures

In order to facilitate analysis, data needs to be stored in a consistent, organized manner. When considering structured data, several concepts and standards inform how to organize data. On the other hand, unstructured data has a wider variety of storage approaches.

Analysts need to be able to perform their roles as efficiently as possible. It is common to use multiple tools to analyze data. Improved integration and interoperability between tools makes it easier for analysts to be productive. As a result, several concepts have become standardized. Let's explore the similarities and differences in how structured and unstructured data is defined and organized.

Structured Data

Tabular data is structured data, with values stored in a consistent, defined manner, organized into columns and rows. Data is *consistent* when all entries in a column contain the same type of value. This method of organization facilitates aggregation. For example, you can add each value in the Weight column in Table 2.1 to get the total weight for all animals. Structured data also makes summarization easy, since you can compute the average height for each animal in Table 2.1. It is common to perform summarization across groups. Figure 2.17 illustrates summarization at the categorical level.

However, structured data does not translate directly to data quality. For example, suppose a new dog named Thor became a patient. When Thor's data was input into the system, a person transposed the Pet Name and Animal Type values, as highlighted in Figure 2.19. Since both Pet Name and Animal Type are character data types, nothing from a structural standpoint prevents this mistake. However, if you were to perform the same summarization as in Figure 2.16, the result would be what is represented by Figure 2.20. A person looking at the summary in Figure 2.20 would immediately know that something is amiss from a data quality standpoint, as "Thor" is not a type of animal.

FIGURE 2.19   Data entry error

	A	B	C	D	E	F
1	Pet Name	Animal Type	Breed Name	Date of Birth	Height (inches)	Weight (pounds)
2	Jack	Dog	Corgi	3/2/2018	10	26.3
3	Viking	Dog	Husky	5/8/2017	24	58
4	Hazel	Dog	Labradoodle	7/3/2016	23	61
5	Schooner	Dog	Labrador Retriever	8/14/2019	24.3	73.4
6	Skippy	Dog	Weimaraner	10/3/2018	26.3	63.5
7	Alexander	Cat	American Shorthair	10/4/2017	9.3	10.4
8	Dog	Thor	German Shepherd	10/3/2020	28	95

FIGURE 2.20   Data entry error identified in a summary

Animal Type	Total
Dog	5
Cat	1
Thor	1

Just as there is an expectation that the values in a given column are consistent, it is a convention that each row contains data about a single record. In Figure 2.19, each row contains data about a single animal. Once again, nothing structural prevents a person from incorrectly putting data about Thor into Alexander's row. However, the intent is that each row's data pertains to a single animal.

It is a best practice to specify a *key* that uniquely identifies all values for a given row. In Figure 2.19, no column enforces uniqueness across rows. Consider this possible, though unlikely, scenario: a Labradoodle named Hazel, born on 7/3/2016, measuring 23 inches tall and weighing 61 pounds, becomes a new patient. Since all of her information is identical to an existing animal, nothing in the structure exists to differentiate the two. Figure 2.21 illustrates how to address this storage issue. The Pet ID column has a data type of integer and contains a unique number for each row. With Pet ID as the key, we can differentiate between the Hazel in rows 3 and 8.

FIGURE 2.21   Pet ID as a key

A	B	C	D	E	F	G
Pet ID	Pet Name	Animal Type	Breed Name	Date of Birth	Height (inches)	Weight (pounds)
1	Jack	Dog	Corgi	3/2/2018	10	26.3
2	Viking	Dog	Husky	5/8/2017	24	58
3	Hazel	Dog	Labradoodle	7/3/2016	23	61
4	Schooner	Dog	Labrador Retriever	8/14/2019	24.3	73.4
5	Skippy	Dog	Weimaraner	10/3/2018	26.3	63.5
6	Alexander	Cat	American Shorthair	10/4/2017	9.3	10.4
7	Thor	Dog	German Shepherd	10/3/2020	28	95
8	Hazel	Dog	Labradoodle	7/3/2016	23	61

Unstructured Data

Unstructured data is qualitative, describing characteristics about an event or an object. Images, phrases, audio or video recordings, and descriptive text are all examples of unstructured data. There is very little that is common about different kinds of unstructured data. Since the data is highly variable, its organizational and storage needs are different from structured data. Unstructured data also represents a significant opportunity. A Forbes study shows that over 90 percent of businesses need to manage and derive value from unstructured data.

Machine data is a common source of unstructured data. Machine data has various sources, including Internet of Things devices, smartphones, tablets, personal computers, and servers. As machines operate, they create digital footprints of their activity. This data is unstructured and can identify machine-to-machine interaction. Although some may think of machine data as digital exhaust, it is a treasure trove just waiting to be exploited by organizations.

A wide variety of technologies has emerged to facilitate the storage of unstructured data. Operationally, these technologies are similar to how a key in a tabular dataset identifies its associated values. With unstructured data, the key is a unique identifier, whereas the value is the unstructured data itself.

Consider the log entry shown in Figure 2.22. As an example of machine data, it represents a single entry within a log file generated when accessing a specific image on the Internet. The log entry contains a mix of seemingly random strings, time stamps, IP addresses, URLs, and browser metadata.

FIGURE 2.22 Unstructured data: log entry

```
a67c0359188d9f84bc33da6007b9f3697a5ad6b733826d1fc1457fd0cf6f376e global_sbn [02/
Feb/2021:18:46:56 +0000] 129.74.45.248 - FCDBECB76E3AE654 REST.GET.OBJECT lp_ima
ge-1.jpeg "GET /lp_image-1.jpeg HTTP/1.1" 304 - - 172032 10 - "https://s3.consol
e.aws.amazon.com/s3/object/global_sbn?region=us-east-1&prefix=lp_image-1.jpeg" "
Mozilla/5.0 (Macintosh; Intel Mac OS X 10_15_7) AppleWebKit/537.36 (KHTML, like
Gecko) Chrome/88.0.4324.96 Safari/537.36" - u+g8xLT4ji5dgMlB9VdXVXr5X2I2vFOnWb22
g9LUgyp+1TIzC4pGoOn8kUJTOcAYM1e1VUPYL6s= - ECDHE-RSA-AES128-GCM-SHA256 - global_
sbn.s3.amazonaws.com TLSv1.2
```

Object storage facilitates the storage of unstructured data. The key-value concept underpins the design of object storage. The key is a unique identifier, and the value is the unstructured data itself. In Figure 2.23, the key is the filename, and the value is the contents of the file itself. Note that in this figure, each file is of a different type. The word document.docx is a Microsoft Word file, textfile.txt contains plain-text data, and the png image.png and lp_image-8.jpeg objects are digital images.

To access the contents of a file, you need to know its key. Figure 2.24 illustrates how an individual key serves as a reference to its unstructured data.

FIGURE 2.23   Files in object storage

Name	▽	Type	▽	Last modified	▽	Size	▽	Storage class	▽
📄 word document.docx		docx		April 23, 2021, 14:24:32 (UTC-04:00)		72.3 KB		Standard	
📄 textfile.txt		txt		April 23, 2021, 14:22:58 (UTC-04:00)		2.1 KB		Standard	
📄 spreadsheet.xlsx		xlsx		April 23, 2021, 14:22:33 (UTC-04:00)		52.0 KB		Standard	
📄 png image.png		png		April 23, 2021, 14:24:45 (UTC-04:00)		7.1 KB		Standard	
📄 pdf document.pdf		pdf		April 23, 2021, 14:24:15 (UTC-04:00)		104.5 KB		Standard	
📄 lp_image-8.jpeg		jpeg		February 2, 2021, 13:39:36 (UTC-05:00)		172.3 KB		Standard	

FIGURE 2.24   Keys and values in object storage

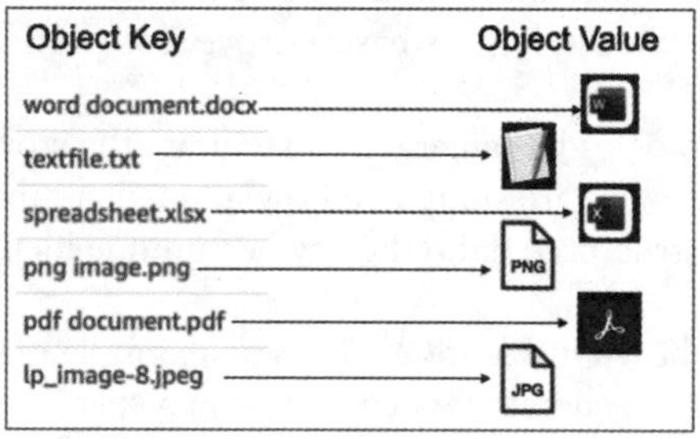

Semi-structured Data

Semi-structured data is data that has structure and that is not tabular. Email is a well-known example of semi-structured data. Every email message has structural components, including recipient, sender, subject, date, and time. However, the body of an email is unstructured text, while attachments could be anything type of file.

The need to make semi-structured data easier to work with has led to the emergence of semi-structured formatting options. These formatting options use separators or tags to provide some context around a data element. Let's explore common file formats for transporting semi-structured data.

Common File Formats

Common file formats facilitate data exchange and tool interoperability. Several file formats have emerged as standards and are widely adopted. As a modern data analyst, you will need to recognize all of these formats and be familiar with common use cases for each type.

Text Files

Text files are one of the most commonly used data file formats. As the name implies, they consist of plain text and are limited in scope to alphanumeric data. One of the reasons text files are so widely adopted is their ability to be opened regardless of platform or operating system without needing a proprietary piece of software. Whether you are using a Microsoft Windows desktop, an Apple MacBook, or a Linux server, you can easily open a text file. Text files are also commonly referred to as flat files.

When machines generate data, the output is commonly stored in a text file. For example, the unstructured log entry, as illustrated in Figure 2.22, is an excerpt taken from a plain-text file.

A unique character known as a *delimiter* facilitates transmitting structured data via a text file. The delimiter is the character that separates individual fields. A delimiter can be any character. Over the years, the comma and tab grew into a widely accepted standard. Various software packages support reading and writing delimited files using the comma and the tab. In addition, many coding languages have libraries that make it easy to write comma- or tab-delimited files. When a file is comma-delimited, it is known as a *comma-separated values* (*CSV*) file. Similarly, when a file is tab-delimited, it is called a *tab-separated values* (*TSV*) file.

Suppose you have the pet data from Table 2.1 in a Google spreadsheet. Figure 2.25 illustrates how it is possible to download the data as either a comma- or tab-delimited file. Microsoft Excel also supports CSV and TSV as options.

FIGURE 2.25 Exporting as CSV or TSV

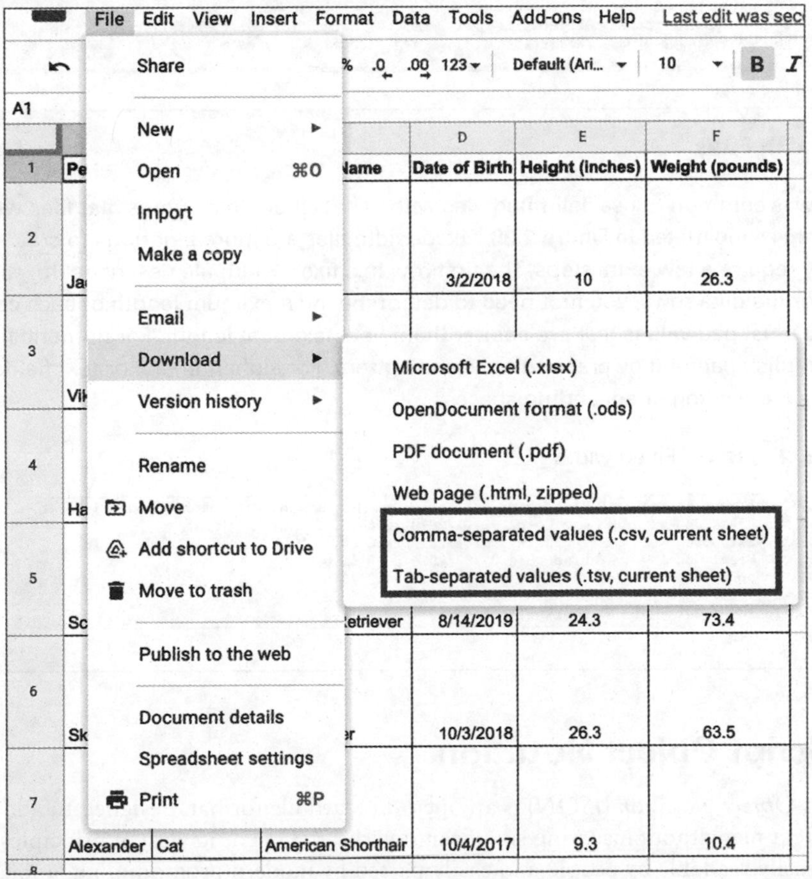

Note that the columns in Figure 2.26 do not line up with each other. The width of each column is variable, only as long as it needs to be to store the data in each row.

FIGURE 2.26 Contents of a CSV file

```
Pet Name,Animal Type,Breed Name,Date of Birth,Height (inches),Weight (pounds)
Jack,Dog,Corgi,3/2/2018,10,26.3
Viking,Dog,Husky,5/8/2017,24,58
Hazel,Dog,Labradoodle,7/3/2016,23,61
Schooner,Dog,Labrador Retriever,8/14/2019,24.3,73.4
Skippy,Dog,Weimaraner,10/3/2018,26.3,63.5
Alexander,Cat,American Shorthair,10/4/2017,9.3,10.4
```

You may think that all CSV files represent structured data. Consider Figure 2.27, containing an excerpt from playback-related events from a Netflix viewer. Every column header except for Playtraces is structured. However, note the contents of the Playtraces field within the red rectangle. It contains quite a bit of text that appears to have a structure of its own.

FIGURE 2.27 Semi-structured CSV

```
Profile Name,Title Description,Device,Country,Playback Start Utc Ts,Playtraces
Jackson,"The Office (U.S.): Season 8: ""Jury Duty""",Sony,Sony Android TV 2019 M1 Smart TV,US,2020-11-05 04:22:29
,"[{""eventType"":""start"",""sessionOffsetMs"":0,""mediaOffsetMs"":1000},{""eventType"":""playing"",""sessionOff
setMs"":2217,""mediaOffsetMs"":1000},{""eventType"":""paused"",""sessionOffsetMs"":76295,""mediaOffsetMs"":73833}
,{""eventType"":""repos"",""sessionOffsetMs"":76296,""mediaOffsetMs"":87500},{""eventType"":""playing"",""session
OffsetMs"":76857,""mediaOffsetMs"":87500},{""eventType"":""stopped"",""sessionOffsetMs"":1184351,""mediaOffsetMs"
":1194036}]"
```

Fixed-Width Files

Before it was common to use delimited files with variable-length columns, flat files were fixed-width, as illustrated in Figure 2.28. Fixed-width files are more laborious to create, since they require a few extra steps. The first row in a fixed-width file describes the column names. For the data rows, you first need to determine the maximum length of each column. Then, you must pad values that are shorter than that maximum length. For numeric fields, you accomplish padding by prepending a leading zero. For alphanumeric or text fields, this is done by prepending or appending spaces.

FIGURE 2.28   Fixed-width file

```
Pet_ID Pet_Name Animal_Type Breed_Name Date_of_Birth Height_(inches) Weight_(pounds) Picture
0001    Jack Dog            Corgi 03/02/2018 10.0 26.3
0002    Viking Dog          Husky 05/08/2017 24.0 58.0
0003    Hazel Dog           Labradoodle 07/03/2016 23.0 61.0
0004 Schooner Dog Labrador Retriever 08/14/2019 24.3 73.4
0005    Skippy Dog          Weimaraner 10/03/2018 26.3 63.5
0006 Alexander Cat American Shorthair 10/04/2017 09.3 10.4
```

JavaScript Object Notation

JavaScript Object Notation (JSON) is an open standard file format, designed to add structure to a text file without incurring significant overhead. One of its design principles is that JSON is easily readable by people and easily parsed by modern programming languages.

Languages such as Python, R, and Go have libraries containing functions that facilitate reading and writing JSON files.

Consider Figure 2.29, which illustrates data about the first three pets from Table 2.1, formatted as JSON. As a person, it is easy to see that the information corresponding to an individual pet is within curly braces, with name-value pairs corresponding to the data elements and values.

FIGURE 2.29   Pet data JSON example

```
 1 [
 2   {
 3     "Pet ID": 1,
 4     "Pet Name": "Jack",
 5     "Animal Type": "Dog",
 6     "Breed Name": "Corgi",
 7     "Date of Birth": "3/2/2018",
 8     "Height (inches)": 10,
 9     "Weight (pounds)": 26.3
10   },
11   {
12     "Pet ID": 2,
13     "Pet Name": "Viking",
14     "Animal Type": "Dog",
15     "Breed Name": "Husky",
16     "Date of Birth": "5/8/2017",
17     "Height (inches)": 24,
18     "Weight (pounds)": 58
19   },
```

To illustrate how a machine processes this same information, Figure 2.30 shows how the entire pet data, formatted as JSON, is read using the Python programming language. Figure 2.31 illustrates reading the same file using the R programming language. Note that R, which facilitates statistical analysis of data, has a summary command, the results of which illustrate some summary statistics about the pet data. The summary statistics are convenient, as it shows six dogs and only one cat in this dataset. It also shows the quartile breakdowns for height and weight.

Extensible Markup Language (XML)

Extensible Markup Language (XML) is a markup language that facilitates structuring data in a text file. While conceptually similar to JSON, XML incurs more overhead because it makes extensive use of tags. *Tags* describe a data element and enclose each value for each data element. While these tags help readability, they add a significant amount of overhead.

Consider Figure 2.32, which illustrates an XML representation for a single pet. Note that for each data element, there is an open tag that defines the element, followed by its value and a closing tag. Compared with the JSON in Figure 2.29, XML results in a file roughly double in size. Although this is insignificant for small files, the impact is much more profound when dealing with data in the gigabyte and terabyte range.

FIGURE 2.30   Reading JSON in Python

```
# Import the json package in order to read files formatted as JSON
import json

# Read in each line in the JSON file.
with open('./c2pets.json') as f:
  pets = json.load(f)

# Print out the entire data structure
print(pets)

[{'Pet ID': 1, 'Pet Name': 'Jack', 'Animal Type': 'Dog', 'Breed Name': 'Corgi', 'Date of Birth': '3/2/2018', 'H
eight (inches)': 10, 'Weight (pounds)': 26.3}, {'Pet ID': 2, 'Pet Name': 'Viking', 'Animal Type': 'Dog', 'Breed
Name': 'Husky', 'Date of Birth': '5/8/2017', 'Height (inches)': 24, 'Weight (pounds)': 58}, {'Pet ID': 3, 'Pet
Name': 'Hazel', 'Animal Type': 'Dog', 'Breed Name': 'Labradoodle', 'Date of Birth': '7/3/2016', 'Height (inches
)': 23, 'Weight (pounds)': 61}, {'Pet ID': 4, 'Pet Name': 'Schooner', 'Animal Type': 'Dog', 'Breed Name': 'Labr
ador Retriever', 'Date of Birth': '8/14/2019', 'Height (inches)': 26.3, 'Weight (pounds)': 73.4}, {'Pet ID': 5,
'Pet Name': 'Skippy', 'Animal Type': 'Dog', 'Breed Name': 'Weimaraner', 'Date of Birth': '10/3/2018', 'Height (
inches)': 26.3, 'Weight (pounds)': 63.5}, {'Pet ID': 6, 'Pet Name': 'Alexander', 'Animal Type': 'Cat', 'Breed N
ame': 'American Shorthair', 'Date of Birth': '10/4/2017', 'Height (inches)': 9.3, 'Weight (pounds)': 10.4}, {'P
et ID': 7, 'Pet Name': 'Thor', 'Animal Type': 'Dog', 'Breed Name': 'German Shepherd', 'Date of Birth': '10/3/20
20', 'Height (inches)': 28, 'Weight (pounds)': 95}]

# Print the information for the first pet only
pets[0]

{'Pet ID': 1,
 'Pet Name': 'Jack',
 'Animal Type': 'Dog',
 'Breed Name': 'Corgi',
 'Date of Birth': '3/2/2018',
 'Height (inches)': 10,
 'Weight (pounds)': 26.3}
```

FIGURE 2.31   Reading JSON in R

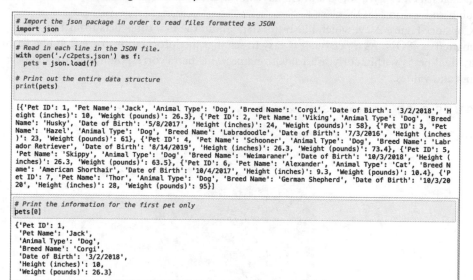

FIGURE 2.32   Representing a single animal in XML

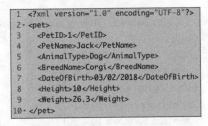

```
 1  <?xml version="1.0" encoding="UTF-8"?>
 2  <pet>
 3      <PetID>1</PetID>
 4      <PetName>Jack</PetName>
 5      <AnimalType>Dog</AnimalType>
 6      <BreedName>Corgi</BreedName>
 7      <DateOfBirth>03/02/2018</DateOfBirth>
 8      <Height>10</Height>
 9      <Weight>26.3</Weight>
10  </pet>
```

In 1999, XML was the data format of choice and facilitated *Asynchronous JavaScript and XML (Ajax)* web development techniques. AJAX allowed client applications, written in HTML, to retrieve data from a server asynchronously. Without having to wait for a server response, the speed with which dynamic web pages operated increased. With JSON as a lighter-weight alternative to XML, it is becoming increasingly popular when interacting asynchronously between a web browser and a remote server.

HyperText Markup Language (HTML)

HyperText Markup Language (HTML) is a markup language for documents designed to be displayed in a web browser. HTML pages serve as the foundation for how people interact with the World Wide Web. Similar to XML, HTML is a tag-based language. Figure 2.33 illustrates the creation of a table in HTML containing the data for a single pet. Figure 2.34 illustrates how a browser processes an HTML of fully populated pet data to display it to people.

FIGURE 2.33   Representing a single animal in HTML

```
 1  <!DOCTYPE html>
 2  <html>
 3  <table class="table table-bordered table-hover table-condensed">
 4  <thead><tr><th title="Field #1">Pet ID</th>
 5  <th title="Field #2">Pet Name</th>
 6  <th title="Field #3">Animal Type</th>
 7  <th title="Field #4">Breed Name</th>
 8  <th title="Field #5">Date of Birth</th>
 9  <th title="Field #6">Height (inches)</th>
10  <th title="Field #7">Weight (pounds)</th>
11  </tr></thead>
12  <tbody><tr>
13  <td align="right">1</td>
14  <td>Jack</td>
15  <td>Dog</td>
16  <td>Corgi</td>
17  <td>3/2/2018</td>
18  <td align="right">10</td>
19  <td align="right">26.3</td>
20  </tr>
21  </tbody></table>
22  </html>
```

FIGURE 2.34   HTML table in a browser

Pet ID	Pet Name	Animal Type	Breed Name	Date of Birth	Height (inches)	Weight (pounds)
1	Jack	Dog	Corgi	3/2/2018	10	26.3
2	Viking	Dog	Husky	5/8/2017	24	58
3	Hazel	Dog	Labradoodle	7/3/2016	23	61
4	Schooner	Dog	Labrador Retriever	8/14/2019	26.3	73.4
5	Skippy	Dog	Weimaraner	10/3/2018	26.3	63.5
6	Alexander	Cat	American Shorthair	10/4/2017	9.3	10.4
7	Thor	Dog	German Shepherd	10/3/2020	28	95

Most people interact with HTML as interpreted by a web browser. HTML has become increasingly sophisticated over the years, with the ability for developers to create web pages that dynamically display content, adjust to different screen sizes, and play videos. Among the many tags that HTML supports is the image tag. It would be possible to display a picture for each pet in the table using image tags. Figure 2.35 illustrates the code that makes this happen.

FIGURE 2.35   Displaying an image in an HTML table

```
1   <!DOCTYPE html>
2 • <html>
3 • <table class="table table-bordered table-hover table-condensed">
4 • <thead><tr><th title="Field #1">Pet ID</th>
5   <th title="Field #2">Pet Name</th>
6   <th title="Field #3">Animal Type</th>
7   <th title="Field #4">Breed Name</th>
8   <th title="Field #5">Date of Birth</th>
9   <th title="Field #6">Height (inches)</th>
10  <th title="Field #7">Weight (pounds)</th>
11  <th title="Field #8">Picture</th>
12 •</tr></thead>
13 •<tbody><tr>
14  <td align="right">1</td>
15  <td>Jack</td>
16  <td>Dog</td>
17  <td>Corgi</td>
18  <td>3/2/2018</td>
19  <td align="right">10</td>
20  <td align="right">26.3</td>
21  <td><img src="https://global_sbn.s3.amazonaws.com/jack.jpeg"> </td>
22 •</tr>
```

Summary

When dealing with data, you need to think through the data values you are working with, because doing so influences your choice of data type. When using structured data, you may be working with dates, numbers, text, currency, or alphanumeric data. Whether the data is discrete, continuous, or categorical, choosing the appropriate data type can help boost data quality. There are also data types for storing unstructured data, such as images, audio, and video.

If you are working with structured data, you should start thinking about it in a tabular fashion. Getting structured data into unique rows and consistent columns is the first step on the path to preparing data for analysis. Structured data fits well into CSV files, a popular format for exchanging data via flat files.

When you have to incorporate additional metadata or represent a complex data structure, you need capabilities beyond what a flat file provides. Formatting the data as JSON or XML is a viable alternative.

The modern analyst frequently works with data sources over the Internet. Understanding that HTML is the standard for structuring web pages is crucial to developing the ability to interact with data over the Internet programmatically.

Exam Essentials

Consider the values of what you will store before selecting data types.   Data types are used to store different kinds of values. When dealing with numeric information, the best option is a numeric data type that can accommodate decimals. For sequences of whole numbers, an integer data type is a good choice. Be wary of using currency-specific data types—that can lead to calculation errors. For text values, the alphanumeric data type is the optimal choice. When dealing with dates, you will want to consider whether you need to store the time as well. For binary data, including audio, video, and images, you should use a BLOB data type.

Know that you can format data after storing it.   While data types determine how data gets stored, formatting data governs how data will be displayed to a person. You may wish to store numeric data to many decimal places but round to the hundredths for display purposes. Similarly, numeric data can be formatted and displayed as a currency. Dates are possibly the most commonly formatted data type, since the same information may need to be displayed differently depending on cultural norms.

Consider the absolute limits of values that you will use before selecting data types.   When selecting data types, consider the range of values that a data element can contain. Suppose the values need to fall within a given, defined range. In that case, you must select a data element that can support discrete data. If the data element's range is unknown, a data element that supports continuous data is necessary.

Explain the differences between structured and unstructured data.   Individual data elements fall along the structured data continuum. At one end, there is highly structured, rectangular data. Structured data is organized into columns and rows. Each column has a consistent data type, and each row contains data about one data subject. Unstructured data does not fit neatly into a column. Looking for similarities or differences in unstructured data requires more advanced analytical techniques than structured data.

Understand the differences in common file formats.   Common file formats make it easy for people to read a file's contents and facilitate interoperability between tools. Delimiters separate variable-length fields in a file. The comma and the resultant CSV file are among the most commonly used formats for exchanging text files. To provide additional metadata about data values and support more complex data structures, XML and JSON were developed. JSON is a preferred format, given its low overhead, especially when compared with XML.

Review Questions

1. Enzo is building a database that will store flight information for his travel agency. He is adding a field to a table that will contain flight numbers. A flight number is a combination of a two-character airline designator and a one-to-four-digit number. For example, United Airlines flight 769 between Chicago and San Francisco has flight number UA 769. What data type would be most appropriate for this field?

   A. Date

   B. Numeric

   C. Text

   D. Alphanumeric

2. Madeline is building a medical transcription system, which transcribes physician voice reports so they can be easily read by other healthcare professionals. Which of the following data types is the most appropriate for her to select in order to store the raw recordings?

   A. Alphanumeric

   B. Numeric

   C. BLOB

   D. Date

3. Rupert is working on implementing a general ledger system that can accommodate financial records in excess of $1 million. Which of the following data types is the most appropriate for him to select in order to store financial transactions?

   A. Alphanumeric

   B. Smallmoney

   C. Money

   D. Numeric

4. Hazel needs to store video recordings for subjects participating in a psychological experiment. There are 300 participants in the experiment, and each session is 45 minutes long. Presuming the video is captured using a modern smartphone at a rate of 102,400 KB per minute, which of the following data types does Hazel need to select if she is storing these videos in a database?

   A. Varbinary

   B. BLOB

   C. CLOB

   D. Numeric

5. Alexander is doing research on literary works and wants to store the title, complete text, and community-sourced rating in a database. The longest book included in his study is *Atlas Shrugged* by Ayn Rand, coming in at 1,168 pages. Presuming that Alexander is working in an Oracle database, which of the following data types should he choose?

    A. BLOB

    B. CLOB

    C. varchar

    D. Numeric

6. Barnali is analyzing defects at a manufacturing plant. In order to inform her work, she tracks the number of defective control arms that come down the assembly line on an hourly basis. What kind of data is represented by the number of defects?

    A. Discrete

    B. Continuous

    C. Categorical

    D. Alphanumeric

7. Haroon is choosing a pair of running shoes. In the past, he has found a size 10 to be too small and size 10.5 to be uncomfortable. While he would like to be able to order a size 10.25, it is simply not available as shoes are sold in half-size increments. What kind of data is represented by shoe size?

    A. Discrete

    B. Continuous

    C. Categorical

    D. Alphanumeric

8. Amdee is measuring her feet to help her figure out what shoe size to order. At 9.75 inches, that places her between a U.S. size 8 and a U.S. size 8.5 shoe. What kind of data does Amdee's measured foot size represent?

    A. Discrete

    B. Continuous

    C. Categorical

    D. Alphanumeric

9. Connor is aggregating temperature information from 5,000 Internet of Things temperature sensors at disparate locations around his farm. What type of measure is temperature, and what is an appropriate data type to contain these values?

    A. Discrete; integer

    B. Discrete; numeric

    C. Continuous; integer

    D. Continuous; numeric

10. Zahara is conducting a survey to collect opinions about a recent theatrical release. She is capturing this via an open-ended text response field on a web form. What category of data does this represent?

  A. Quantitative

  B. Qualitative

  C. Categorical

  D. Dimensional

11. Jed wants to track his expenditures in a spreadsheet containing check number, date, recipient, and amount. What kind of data is Jed working with?

  A. Unstructured

  B. Semi-structured

  C. Structured

  D. Machine

12. Amy is interested in exploring the Netflix viewing history, including Profile Name, Title Description, Device, Country, Playback Start Times, and Playtraces, for her household. Navigating to the account export screen, which option should she select in order to facilitate analysis using the Python programming language?

  A. CSV

  B. Text file

  C. HTML

  D. XML

13. Zeke is experimenting with home automation. Reading the application programming interface (API) guide, he sees that commands can be issued in the following syntax:

```
{
    "commands": [
        {
            "component": "main",
            "capability": "switch",
            "command": "off",
            "arguments": []
        }
    ]
}
```

Which data format does the API require?

  A. JSON

  B. TSV

  C. CSV

  D. XML

14. Maura is a data engineer tasked with a new system integration. She has been given the following sample file to help her understand how to parse files of a similar type:

```
{
    "VIN": "WP0ZZZ99Z5S73824",
    "Manufacturer": "Porsche",
    "Model": "Carrera S",
    "Horsepower": "443",
    "Torque": "390"
}
```

Which data format does the API require?

A. JSON

B. TSV

C. CSV

D. XML

15. Chris is a financial analyst who wants to use Microsoft Excel to perform what-if analysis on data extracted from his corporate accounting system. To make the data extract easy to import, which of the following file formats should he specify?

A. CSV

B. JSON

C. XML

D. YAML

16. Claire is a web developer working on an interactive website. While she is programming in JavaScript, which of the following file types is essential to test her work in a web browser?

A. CSV

B. JSON

C. HTML

D. XML

17. Claire has just received a spreadsheet of streaming media use data, and one of the columns contained the following data:

```
[{"eventType":"start","sessionOffsetMs":0,"mediaOffsetMs":0},{"eventType"
:"playing","sessionOffsetMs":3153,"mediaOffsetMs":0},{"eventType":
"stopped","sessionOffsetMs":4818,"mediaOffsetMs":559}]
```

While the spreadsheet is displaying this data as a single piece of text, Claire feels like there is structure to the data. Is Claire correct, and if so, how are the contents of the column formatted?

A. No; it is plain text.

B. No; it is machine data.

C. Yes; it is JSON.

D. Yes; it is plain text.

18. Jorge is transferring data from a mainframe to his laptop so that he can upload it into a Google spreadsheet for analysis. Looking at the file from the mainframe, he sees that it uses ^% as a delimiter. In order to make it easy to load into the Google spreadsheet, what should Jorge do?

   A. Nothing, the file will load just fine.

   B. Nothing, you cannot transfer data from a mainframe to a laptop.

   C. Use software on the mainframe instead of a Google spreadsheet.

   D. Convert the ^% into a comma or a tab.

19. Eleanora has been tasked with analyzing web server logs to better understand where website visitors are coming from. Every time a person visits a website, an entry containing multiple items, including IP address, destination page, and current time, is automatically made in the log. What type of data is this?

   A. Machine data

   B. Undefined data

   C. Automatic data

   D. Web data

20. Dave is a graphic designer who wants to build a website to show off his portfolio. For each item in his portfolio, he wants to show the client name, date of commission, and a thumbnail image of the artwork. While he can accomplish this by building out a table in HTML, what category of data best describes what he wants to do?

   A. Unstructured

   B. Semi-structured

   C. Structured

   D. Machine

Chapter 3

Databases and Data Acquisition

THE COMPTIA DATA+ EXAM TOPICS
COVERED IN THIS CHAPTER INCLUDE:

- ✓ Domain 1.0: Data Concepts and Environments
- ✓ 1.1. Identify basic concepts of data schemas and dimensions
- ✓ Domain 2.0: Data Mining
- ✓ 2.1. Explain data acquisition concepts
- ✓ 2.4 Explain common techniques for data manipulation and query optimization

In Chapter 2, "Understanding Data," you learned how organizations rely on structured and unstructured data to meet their business needs. The vast majority of transactional systems generate structured data, and we need technology that will help us store all of that data. Databases are the foundational technology that allows us to keep our data organized and easy to retrieve when we need it.

We collect data from many sources to derive insights. For example, a financial analyst wants to understand why some retail outlets are more profitable than others. The analyst might look at the individual records for each store, but that's difficult to do if there are thousands of items and hundreds of stores. Answering the business questions here requires summarizing the data for each store. Databases make it easy to answer this question.

In this chapter, you will examine the two main database categories: relational and nonrelational. You will learn several different approaches for designing databases to store structured data. Building on this foundation, you will learn about common database design practices. You will proceed to dive into the details of working with databases. You will examine tools and techniques that will help you answer questions using data. You will wrap up this chapter by exploring ways to improve the efficiency of how you ask questions. Equipped with this knowledge, you will have a clear understanding of database structure, how data flows between systems, and how to minimize the time needed to get actionable insights.

Exploring Databases

There are many different database options to choose from when an organization needs to store data. While many database products exist, they belong in one of two categories: *relational* and *nonrelational*. One of the oldest and most mature databases is the relational database. Relational databases excel at storing and processing structured data. As you discovered in Chapter 2, much of the world's data is unstructured. The need to interact with unstructured data is one of the reasons behind the rise of nonrelational databases.

Although databases fall into two categories, many of the systems we interact with daily produce tabular data. Because tabular data is highly structured, most of this chapter goes deeper into relational databases, their design, and how to use them.

The Relational Model

In 1969, IBM's Edgar F. Codd developed the relational model for database management. The relational model builds on the concept of tabular data. In the relational model, an *entity* contains data for a single subject. When creating an IT system, you need to consider all the entities required to make your system work. You can think of entities as nouns because they usually correspond to people, places, and things.

Imagine a veterinary clinic that has to store data about the animals it treats and the people who own those animals. The clinic needs one entity for data about animals and a separate entity for data about people to accomplish this goal. Figure 3.1 shows the structure of the Animal and Person entities.

An *entity instance* identifies a specific example of an entity. Considering the Animal entity in Figure 3.1, an entity instance is a particular animal. Looking at Table 3.1, all of the information about Jack represents an entity instance.

TABLE 3.1   Animal data

Animal_ID	Animal_Name	Animal_Type	Breed_Name	Date_of_Birth	Height (inches)	Weight (pounds)
1	Jack	Dog	Corgi	3/2/2018	10	26.3
2	Viking	Dog	Husky	5/8/2017	24	58
3	Hazel	Dog	Labradoodle	7/3/2016	23	61
4	Schooner	Dog	Labrador Retriever	8/14/2019	24.3	73.4
5	Skippy	Dog	Weimaraner	10/3/2018	26.3	63.5
6	Alexander	Cat	American Shorthair	10/4/2017	9.3	10.4

For both entities in Figure 3.1, the bolded word in the header is the entity's name. For example, suppose you want to know where to look for data about a specific person. The Person entity in Figure 3.1 is a clear choice since it stores data about people.

Understanding that the header corresponds to the name of an entity, look at the rows of the Person entity. Each row represents an individual attribute associated with a person. Suppose you want to enhance the Person entity to accommodate a mobile phone number. You would just edit the Person entity to include a mobile phone attribute.

FIGURE 3.1   The (a) Animal entity and (b) Person entity in a veterinary database

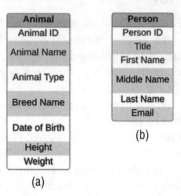

(a)

(b)

Each of these entities becomes a separate table in the database, with a column for each attribute. Each row represents an instance of the entity. The power of the relational model is that it also allows us to describe how entities connect, or relate, to each other. The veterinary clinic needs to associate animals with people. Animals do not have email addresses, cannot schedule appointments, and cannot pay for services. Their owners, on the other hand, do all of these things. There's a relationship between animals and people, and we can include this relationship in our database design, as shown in Figure 3.2.

FIGURE 3.2   Relationship connecting Animal and Person

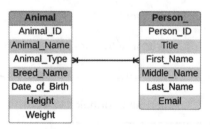

The *entity relationship diagram* (ERD) is a visual artifact of the data modeling process. It shows the connection between related entities. The line in Figure 3.2 illustrates that a *relationship* exists between the Animal and Pet entities. A relationship is a connection between entities. The symbols adjacent to an entity describe the relationship.

Cardinality refers to the relationship between two entities, showing how many instances of one entity relate to instances in another entity. You specify cardinality in an ERD with various line endings. The first component of the terminator indicates whether the relationship between two entities is optional or required. The second component indicates whether an entity instance in the first table is associated with a single entity instance in the related table or if an association can exist with multiple entity instances. Figure 3.3 illustrates the possible combinations for representing relationships.

FIGURE 3.3 ERD line endings

Relationship Description	Cardinality Symbol
Optional relationship, at most one instance	
Required relationship, at most one instance	
Optional relationship, potentially many instances	
Required relationship, potentially many instances	

With an understanding of ERD line endings, let's apply it to Figure 3.2. Reading the diagram aloud from left to right, you say, "An individual animal belongs to at least one and possibly many people." Reading from right to left sounds like, "A specific person has at least one and possibly many animals."

A *unary relationship* is when an entity has a connection with itself. For example, Figure 3.4 illustrates a unary relationship where a single manager has multiple employees.

FIGURE 3.4 Unary relationship

With an understanding of ERD line endings, let's apply it to Figure 3.2. Reading the diagram

A *binary relationship* connects two entities, as seen in Figure 3.2. A *ternary relationship* connects three entities. For example, you might use a ticket entity to connect a venue, a performing artist, and a price.

Binary relationships are the most common and easy to explore, whereas unary and ternary are comparatively complex and rare.

As you think about a database that would support an actual veterinary clinic, you're probably realizing that it would need to store more information than we've already discussed. For example, we'd need to store addresses, appointments, medications, and procedures. Database designers would continue to add entities and relationships to the diagram until it meets all of the veterinary clinic's business needs, such as the one shown in Figure 3.5.

FIGURE 3.5   Entity relationship diagram

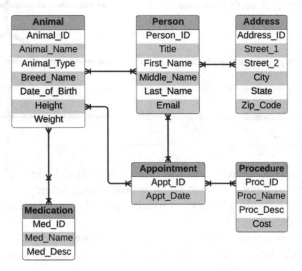

Apart from being a helpful picture, the entity relationship diagram also serves as a relational database's blueprint. The ability to read ERDs helps you understand the structure of a relational database. ERDs are particularly useful when formulating how to retrieve information from the database that is spread across multiple tables because the diagrams allow you to visualize the connections between entities.

Relational Databases

Relational databases are pieces of software that let you make an operational system out of an ERD. You start with a relational model and create a physical design. Relational entities correspond to database tables, and entity attributes correspond to table columns. When creating a database table, the ordering of columns does not matter because you can specify the column order when retrieving data from a table. When an attribute becomes a column, you assign it a data type. Completing all of this work results in a diagram known as a *schema*. You can think of a schema as an ERD with the additional details needed to create a database. For example, the relational model in Figure 3.2 becomes the schema in Figure 3.6.

FIGURE 3.6   Database schema

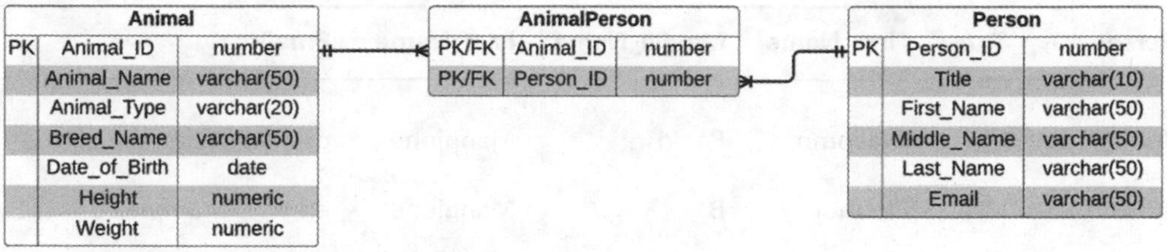

Note that the two entities in Figure 3.2 become three tables in Figure 3.6. The new AnimalPerson table is necessary because you need to resolve a many-to-many relationship with an *associative table*. An associative table is both a table and a relationship. Recall that an animal can belong to more than one person, and a person can have more than one animal. An associative table lets you identify the relationship between a specific animal and a particular person with a minimum amount of data duplication. Let's examine the tables and their data in more detail to see the Animal, AnimalPerson, and Person tables in action.

With the schema design complete, you can build the tables. Once you have the tables, you can load them with data. Table 3.1 shows what the Animal entity from Figure 3.1 looks like with data.

Similarly, the Person entity from Figure 3.1 corresponds to Table 3.2. The first column in both Table 3.1 and Table 3.2 is an identifier with a numeric data type. In both cases, these identifier columns (Animal_ID and Person_ID) are the *primary key* for the table. A primary key is one or more attributes that uniquely identify a specific row in a table. It is best to use a *synthetic primary key*, which is simply an attribute whose only purpose is to contain unique values for each row in the table. In Table 3.1, Animal_ID is a synthetic primary key, and the number 3 is arbitrarily assigned to Hazel. The number 3 has no meaning beyond its ability to uniquely identify a row. Nothing about Hazel's data changes if her Animal_ID was 7 instead of 3. Taking another look at Figure 3.6, note how PK denotes the primary key for the Animal, AnimalPerson, and Person tables.

Note that within a given table, the actual sequencing of the rows does not matter. For example, you might want to retrieve data from Table 3.2 alphabetically by first or last name. Using SQL, you can easily specify the order in which you want to bring data back from a table.

TABLE 3.2   Person Data

Person_ID	Title	First_Name	Middle_Name	Last_Name	Email
10000	Mr	Paul		Tupy	pault@example.com
10001	Ms	Emma	M	Snyder	esnyder@example.com
10002	Ms	Giustina	Marguerite	Rossi	gmrossi@example.com

TABLE 3.2   Person Data *(continued)*

Person_ID	Title	First_Name	Middle_Name	Last_Name	Email
10003	Mr	Giacomo	Paolo	Mangione	gpman@example.com
10004	Mrs	Eleonora	B	Mangione	eman@example.com
10005	Ms	Leila	Abir	Abboud	leila@example.com
10006	Mr	Chris	Thomas	Bregande	christb@example.com

You can imagine the data in Tables 3.1 and 3.2 existing as separate tabs in a spreadsheet. Suppose both Hazel and Alexander belong to the Mangione family. There is nothing in the data that connects an animal to a person. To link the two tables, you need a *foreign key*. A foreign key is one or more columns in one table that points to corresponding columns in a related table. Frequently, a foreign key references another table's primary key. Looking at the AnimalPerson table in Figure 3.6, FK denotes a foreign key. The Person_ID in the AnimalPerson table points to the Person_ID in the Person table. You can't put a row in the AnimalPerson table if the Person_ID doesn't exist in the Person table. Similarly, you can't use an Animal_ID in AnimalPerson if it doesn't exist in the Animal table.

Every row in a relational database must be unique. In Table 3.1, each row contains data about a specific animal, whereas each row in Table 3.2 refers to a particular person. Since the Mangione family has multiple animals, we need an associative table to describe the relationship between Animal and Person. Table 3.3 shows data from the AnimalPerson table in Figure 3.6.

TABLE 3.3   AnimalPerson table

Animal_ID	Person_ID
3	10003
3	10004
6	10003
6	10004

Suppose you want to send an email reminder about an upcoming appointment for a pet. Figure 3.7 shows an email template with placeholder values.

FIGURE 3.7 Email template

> Dear <Title> <Last_Name>,
>
>
> This is a reminder to let you know that your <Animal_Type> <Animal_Name> is due for an annual appointment. Please schedule one at your convenience.
>
>
> Regards,
>
> Your Friendly Family Vet

To populate the email template, you need the person's title, last name, and email address from Table 3.2 and the corresponding pet's name and animal type from Table 3.1. To pull data from a relational database table, you perform a *query*. You compose queries using a programming language called *Structured Query Language* (*SQL*).

Your query needs to perform a *database join* to retrieve the data to substitute in the email reminder. A join uses data values from one table to retrieve associated data in another table, typically using a foreign key.

The first row in Table 3.3 represents the relationship between Mr. Mangione and Hazel. To send Mr. Mangione an email, you take 10003, the value for Person_ID in the first row of Table 3.3, and join it to Table 3.2. Using 10003, you retrieve Mr. Mangione's title, last name, and email address. To retrieve Hazel's information, you perform a similar join. You get 3 for Animal_ID from Table 3.3 and look up Hazel's information in Table 3.1. The result is the email that gets sent, shown in Figure 3.8. Note that if you send an email for each row in Table 3.3, both Mr. and Mrs. Mangione get emails about Hazel the Dog and Alexander the Cat.

FIGURE 3.8 Reminder appointment email

> Dear Mr. Mangione,
>
>
> This is a reminder to let you know that your Dog Hazel is due for an annual appointment. Please schedule one at your convenience.
>
>
> Regards,
>
> Your Friendly Family Vet

Foreign keys enforce *referential integrity*, or how consistent the data is in related tables. Consider Figure 3.9, which shows why referential integrity is crucial to enforcing data quality. Suppose you try to add a row to the middle table, specifying 6 for the Animal_ID and 99999 as the Person_ID. The foreign key on Animal_ID checks the table to the left to ensure a row exists with the Animal_ID of 6. The new record passes this check because there is a record with Animal_ID 6 for the cat named Alexander. When a similar check happens on Person_ID, there is no row corresponding to the Person_ID 99999 in the table on the right. Therefore, adding the new row fails, and the relationship between the tables is maintained.

FIGURE 3.9   Referential integrity illustration

Animal ID	Animal Name	Animal Type	Breed Name	Date of Birth	Height (inches)	Weight (pounds)
1	Jack	Dog	Corgi	3/2/2018	10	26.3
2	Viking	Dog	Husky	5/8/2017	24	58
3	Hazel	Dog	Labradoodle	7/3/2016	23	61
4	Schooner	Dog	Labrador Retriever	8/14/2019	24.3	73.4
5	Skippy	Dog	Weimaraner	10/3/2018	26.3	63.5
6	Alexander	Cat	American Shorthair	10/4/2017	9.3	10.4

Animal ID	Person ID
3	10003
3	10004
6	10003
6	10004
6	~~99999~~

Person ID	Title	First Name	Middle Name	Last Name	Email
10000	Mr	Paul		Tupv	pault@example.com
10001	Ms	Emma	M	Snyder	esnyder@example.com
10002	Ms	Giustina	Marguerita	Rossi	gmrossi@example.com
10003	Mr	Giacomo	Paolo	Mangione	gpman@example.com
10004	Mrs	Eleonora	B	Mangione	eman@example.com
10005	Ms	Leila	Abir	Abboud	leila@example.com
10006	Mr	Chris	Thomas	Bregande	christb@example.com

In Table 3.3, the Animal_ID column is a foreign key that points to the Animal_ID primary key in Table 3.1. Looking at the first data row in Table 3.3, Animal_ID 3 refers to Hazel. Similarly, the Person_ID column points to the Person_ID column in Table 3.2, with 10003 identifying Giacomo Mangione. The combination of both Animal_ID and Person_ID is what makes each row in Table 3.3 unique. Taken together, Animal_ID and Person_ID represent a *composite primary key*. As the name implies, a composite primary key is a primary key with more than one column. While Figure 3.2 describes a relational model, Figure 3.6 shows modifications necessary to create tables for storing data.

Relational databases are complicated to operate at scale. A *database administrator* (DBA) is a highly trained person who understands how database software interacts with computer hardware. A DBA looks after how the database uses the underlying storage, memory, and processor resources assigned to the database. A DBA also looks for processes that are slowing the entire database down.

Address Referential Integrity Example

Let's explore another example of how foreign keys enforce referential integrity. Suppose an organization has an order management system that stores customers' information and addresses, as shown in Figure 3.10.

FIGURE 3.10   Customer ERD

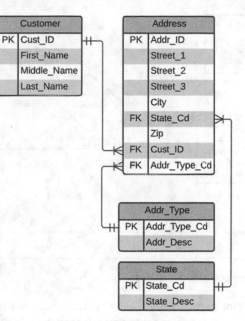

With an understanding of cardinality, you can read that ERD in Figure 3.10 and see that:

- A specific customer can have many addresses, while a particular address belongs to a single customer.

- A specific address has a single address type, while a particular address type can apply to many different addresses.

- A specific address has a single state, while a particular state can exist in many different addresses.

Implementing the relationships from an ERD enforces data constraints. For example, Figure 3.10 shows that an individual address must have a relationship with a state. You use foreign keys to implement data constraints in a database, like the relationship connecting Address with State. The FK designation for the State_Cd attribute on the Address entity in Figure 3.10 indicates that State_Cd is a foreign key. With a foreign key constraint in place, the database will not allow you to insert an address unless it exists in the State table, as shown in Figure 3.11.

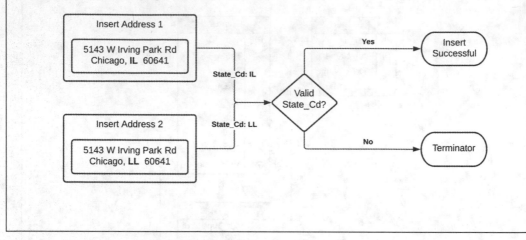

FIGURE 3.11   Foreign key data constraint

Relational Database Providers

From a software standpoint, there are many relational database options. Oracle is one of the most mature database platforms and was first released in 1979. Over time, Microsoft developed SQL Server, and the open source community created offerings including MySQL, MariaDB, and PostgreSQL. Amazon Web Services (AWS) developed Aurora, which is compatible with MySQL and PostgreSQL. Aurora is unique because it takes advantage of AWS's underlying cloud platform and is easy to scale.

Nonrelational Databases

A nonrelational database does not have a predefined structure based on tabular data. The result is a highly flexible approach to storing data. However, the data types available in relational databases are absent. As a result, you need to know more about the data itself to interact with it. Data validation happens in code, as opposed to being done in the database. Examples of nonrelational databases include *key-value*, *document*, *column family*, and *graph*.

Key-Value

A key-value database is one of the simplest ways of storing data. Data is stored as a collection of keys and their corresponding values. A key must be globally unique across the entire database. The use of keys differs from a relational database, where a given key identifies an individual row in a specific table. There are no structural limits on the values of a key. A key can be a sequence of numbers, alphanumeric strings, or some other combination of values.

The data that corresponds with a key can be any structured or unstructured data type. Since there are no underlying table structures and few limitations on the data that can be stored, operating a key-value database is much simpler than a relational database. It also can scale to accommodate many simultaneous requests without impacting performance. However, since the values can contain multiple data types, the only way to search is to have the key.

One reason for choosing a key-value database is when you have lots of data and can search by a key's value. Imagine an online music streaming service. The key is the name of a song, and the value is the digital audio file containing the song itself. When a person wants to listen to music, they search for the name of the song. With a known key, the application quickly retrieves the song and starts streaming it to the user.

Document

A document database is similar to a key-value database, with additional restrictions. In a key-value database, the value can contain anything. With a document database, the value is restricted to a specific structured format. For example, Figure 3.12 is an example of using JSON as the document format.

FIGURE 3.12   JSON person data

```
{
  "firstName": "George",
  "lastName": "Villeneuve",
  "address": {
    "streetAddress": "123 Sample St",
    "city": "Chicago",
    "state": "IL",
    "postalCode": "60601"
  },
  "phoneNumbers": [
    {
      "type": "mobile",
      "number": "312-555-1234"
    },
    {
      "type": "office",
      "number": "312-555-6789"
    }
  ]
}
```

With a known, structured format, document databases have additional flexibility beyond what is possible with key-value. While searching with a known document key yields the fastest results, searching using a field within the document is possible. Suppose you are storing social network profiles. The document key is the profile name. The document itself is a JSON object containing details about the person, as Figure 3.6 shows. With a document database, it is possible to retrieve all profiles that match a specific zip code. This searching ability is possible because the database understands the document's structure and can search based on data within the document.

Column Family

Column-family databases use an index to identify data in groups of related columns. A relational database stores the data in Table 3.2 in a single table, where each row contains the Person_ID, Title, First_Name, Middle_Name, Last_Name, and Email columns. In a column-family database, the Person_ID becomes the index, while the other columns are stored independently. This design facilitates distributing data across multiple machines, which enables handling massive amounts of data. The ability to handle large data volumes is due to the technical implementation details of how these databases organize and store. From a design standpoint, column-family databases optimize performance when you need to examine the contents of a column across many rows.

The main reason for choosing a column-family database is its ability to scale. Suppose you need to analyze U.S. stock transactions over time. With daily trade volumes of over 6 billion records, processing that amount of data on a single database server is not feasible. It is in situations like this where column-family databases shine.

Graph

Graph databases specialize in exploring relationships between pieces of data. Consider Figure 3.6, which shows the tables required to indicate which animals belong to which people. Figure 3.13 illustrates how a graph models data from Tables 3.1 and 3.2. Each animal and person represents a *node* in the graph. Each node can have multiple *properties*. Properties store specific attributes for an individual node. The arrow connecting nodes represents a *relationship*.

FIGURE 3.13 Data in a graph

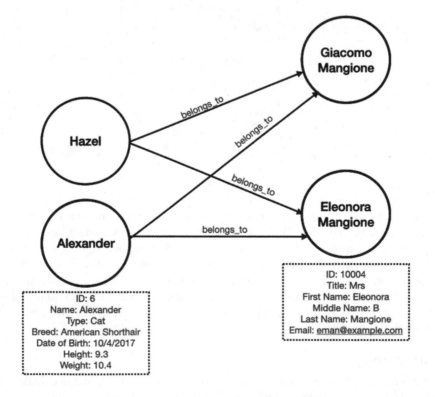

Relational models focus on mapping the relationships between entities. Graph models map relationships between actual pieces of data. In Figure 3.6, you have to use three tables to represent the same data in Figure 3.13. Since fewer objects are involved, graphs allow you to follow very quickly.

Graphs are an optimal choice if you need to create a recommendation engine, as graphs excel at exploring relationships between data. For example, when you search for a product on an e-commerce website, the results are frequently accompanied by a collection of related items. Understanding the connection between products is a challenge that graphs solve with ease.

Database Use Cases

Different business needs require different database designs. While all databases store data, the database's structure needs to match its intended purpose. Business requirements impact the design of individual tables and how they are interconnected. Transactional and reporting systems need different implementation approaches to serve the people who use them efficiently. Databases tend to support two major categories of data processing: *Online Transactional Processing (OLTP)* and *Online Analytical Processing (OLAP)*.

Online Transactional Processing

OLTP systems handle the transactions we encounter every day. Example transactions include booking a flight reservation, ordering something online, or executing a stock trade. While the number of transactions a system handles on a given day can be very high, individual transactions process small amounts of data. OLTP systems balance the ability to write and read data efficiently.

Based on the data in Table 3.1, Table 3.2, and Table 3.3, suppose Giacomo Mangione wants to book an annual visit appointment for his cat Alexander. Suppose both Giacomo and Alexander already exist in the database that supports the appointment system, as shown in Figure 3.14.

To book an appointment, Giacomo logs in to the vet clinic's website. When Giacomo logs in, the system retrieves his information from the Person table. Using the Animal_IDs corresponding to his Person_ID in the AnimalPerson table, the system displays a list of Giacomo's animals. Selecting Alexander from the list, Giacomo specifies a date and time of his choosing. Giacomo's input represents all the data necessary to create an appointment record, which Table 3.4 illustrates.

TABLE 3.4   Appointment booking

Appt_ID	AnmlPers_ID	Date	Time
53	10003	5/5/2022	13:00

FIGURE 3.14   Vet clinic transactional schema

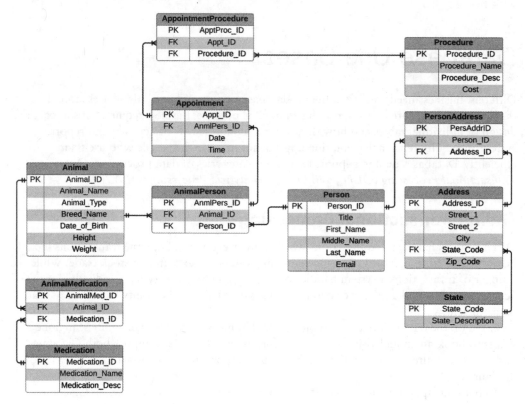

In Table 3.4, the AnmlPers_ID identifies Giacomo and Alexander. The Appt_ID is a system-generated synthetic key while Giacomo supplies the Date and Time. To retrieve the rest of the details about the person and the animal, you need to join the tables together using the foreign key to primary key relationship.

For this appointment, Alexander is due for a complete blood count and blood chemistry panel. The details about each procedure are in the Procedure table in Figure 3.14. The AppointmentProcedure table provides the link between a given appointment and all of the procedures performed during that appointment.

Normalization

Normalization is a process for structuring a database in a way that minimizes duplication of data. One of the principles is that a given piece of data is stored once and only once. As a result, a normalized database is ideal for processing transactions.

First normal form (*1NF*) is when every row in a table is unique and every column contains a unique value. Consider Figure 3.15, where there are separate rows for Giacomo and Eleonora. While Giacomo and Eleonora have the same home address, appending Eleonora's name in the Person_Name column to Giacomo's in the first row would violate 1NF. However, since each row is unique, Figure 3.15 is in 1NF.

FIGURE 3.15   Data in first normal form

Person_ID (PK)	Person_Name	Addr_Code	Addr_Desc	Street	City	State_Code	State_Desc
10003	Giacomo	H	Home	123 State St.	Chicago	IL	Illinois
10003	Giacomo	W	Work	51 Work St.	Chicago	IL	Illinois
10004	Eleonora	H	Home	123 State St.	Chicago	IL	Illinois

Second normal form (*2NF*) starts where 1NF leaves off. In addition to each row being unique, 2NF applies an additional rule stating that all nonprimary key values must depend on the entire primary key. To get to 2NF, the table from Figure 3.15 evolves into the tables in Figure 3.16. Note that the Person_Address table has a composite primary key composed of Person_ID and Addr_ID. The values of both Addr_Code and Addr_Desc are associated with the composite primary key.

Suppose Eleonora starts working from home and updates the Addr_Desc for her row with the value "Work." That causes data corruption, as the Addr_Code corresponds to the Addr_Desc. Addr_Desc depends on Addr_Code, and with that change, "H" would mean both "Home" and "Work."

FIGURE 3.16   Data in second normal form

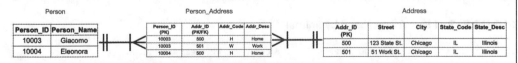

Third normal form (*3NF*) builds upon 2NF by adding a rule stating all columns must depend on only the primary key. Evolving Figure 3.16 into 3NF results in Figure 3.17. If Eleonora starts working from home, the only value that needs to change is Addr_Code in the

Person_Address table. The description for each type of address is in the Addr_Code table. Similarly, the description for each state code is in the State_Code table. The result is that there is little redundancy in the data's storage location and that keys enforce the relationships between tables. Databases in 3NF are said to be highly normalized.

FIGURE 3.17   Data in third normal form

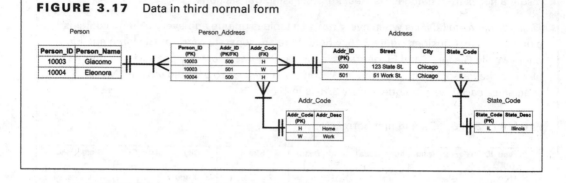

Online Analytical Processing

OLAP systems focus on the ability of organizations to analyze data. While OLAP and OLTP databases can both use relational database technology, their structures are fundamentally different. OLTP databases need to balance transactional read and write performance, resulting in a highly normalized design. Typically, OLTP databases are in 3NF.

On the other hand, databases that power OLAP systems have a denormalized design. Instead of having data distributed across multiple tables, denormalization results in wider tables than those found in an OLTP database. It is more efficient for analytical queries to read large amounts of data for a single table instead of incurring the cost of joining multiple tables together.

Imagine you want to create a summary of the clinic's interaction history with a family's pets, as shown in Figure 3.18. Using the normalized OLTP database from Figure 3.14, you need to retrieve data from the Procedure, AppointmentProcedure, Appointment, AnimalPerson, and Animal tables. The greater the number of joins, the more complex the query. The more complex the query, the longer it takes to retrieve results.

FIGURE 3.18   Yearly spend by animal

Animal ID	Name	Breed	Visit Year	Total Spend
3	Hazel	Labradoodle	2022	30
3	Hazel	Labradoodle	2021	30
3	Hazel	Labradoodle	2020	50
3	Hazel	Labradoodle	2019	30
3	Hazel	Labradoodle	2018	175
3	Alexander	Domestic Shorthair	2022	50
3	Alexander	Domestic Shorthair	2021	30
6	Alexander	Domestic Shorthair	2020	100
6	Alexander	Domestic Shorthair	2019	30
6	Alexander	Domestic Shorthair	2018	30

Consider the table in Figure 3.19, whose structure easily supports the data in Figure 3.18. It is possible to create the summary in Figure 3.18 using the OLTP database from Figure 3.14. However, the CostSummary table in Figure 3.19 greatly simplifies that operation.

FIGURE 3.19   CostSummary table

CostSummary	
PK	Animal_ID
PK	Visit_Year
	Name
	Breed
	Total_Spend

Schema Concepts

The design of a database schema depends on the purpose it serves. Transactional systems require highly normalized databases, whereas a denormalized design is more appropriate for analytical systems. A *data warehouse* is a database that aggregates data from many transactional systems for analytical purposes. Transactional data may come from systems that power the human resources, sales, marketing, and product divisions. A data warehouse facilitates analytics across the entire company.

A *data mart* is a subset of a data warehouse. Data warehouses serve the entire organization, whereas data marts focus on the needs of a particular department within the organization. For example, suppose an organization wants to do analytics on their employees to understand retention and career evolution trends. To satisfy that use case, you can create a data mart focusing on the human resources subject area from the data warehouse.

A *data lake* stores raw data in its native format instead of conforming to a relational database structure. Using a data lake is more complex than a data warehouse or data mart, as it requires additional knowledge about the raw data to make it analytically useful. Relational databases enforce a structure that encapsulates business rules and business logic, both of which are missing in a data lake.

For data warehouses and data marts, several design patterns exist for modeling data. It is crucial to realize that the structure of a database schema impacts analytical efficiency, particularly as the volume of data grows. In addition to a schema's design, it is vital to consider the life cycle. Life-cycle considerations include where data comes from, how frequently it changes, and how long it needs to persist.

Star

The *star schema* design to facilitate analytical processing gets its name from what the schema looks like when looking at its entity relationship diagram, as Figure 3.20 illustrates. Star schemas are denormalized to improve read performance over large datasets.

FIGURE 3.20 Star schema example

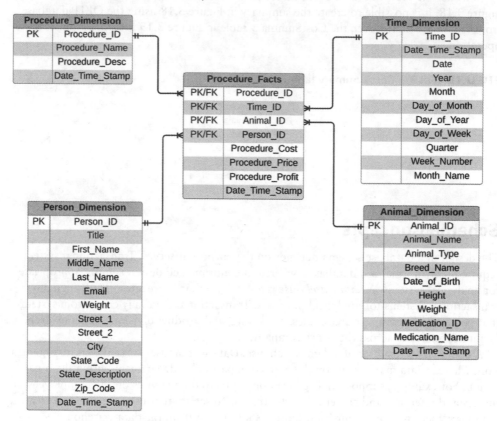

At the center of the star is a *fact table*. Fact tables chiefly store numerical facts about a business. In Figure 3.20, the schema design centers on reporting on the cost and profitability of procedures. Qualitative data, including names, addresses, and descriptions, is stored in a series of *dimension tables* that connect to the main fact table.

Consider Figure 3.20, which has the Procedure_Facts table at the center of the star. This table makes it straightforward to calculate overall profitability. If you want to explore profitability for cats, you need to join the Procedure_Facts table to the Animal_Dimension. Similarly, you can join in the Procedure_Dimension table to understand profitability by procedure name. The Time_Dimension is unique in that it makes it easy to look at profitability by day of week, quarter, month, or any other time-related attribute.

With a fact table surrounded by dimension tables, the queries to answer questions are simple to write and understand. Suppose you want to understand the aggregate cost of all procedures performed on dogs. In Figure 3.21, the OLTP Query shows how to answer that question using the transactional schema from Figure 3.14. The Star Schema Query provides the same answer, using the schema in Figure 3.20.

FIGURE 3.21   OLTP and OLAP query example

OLTP Query

```
Select SUM(procedure_cost)
FROM procedure
INNER JOIN appointmentprocedure
ON procedure.procedure_id = appointmentprocedure.procedure_id
INNER JOIN appointment
ON appointmentprocedure.appt_id = appointment.appt_id
INNER JOIN animalperson
ON appointment.anmlpers_id = animalperson.anmlpers_id
INNER JOIN animal
ON animalperson.animal_id = animal.animal_id
WHERE animal_type = 'Dog'
```

Star Schema Query

```
Select SUM(procedure_cost)
FROM procedure_facts
INNER JOIN animal_dimension
ON procedure_facts.animal_id = animal_dimension.animal.id
WHERE animal_type = 'Dog'
```

Even if you have never seen SQL before, you can appreciate that the four INNER JOIN statements in the OLTP Query indicate that you need five tables to get the result. In contrast, the single INNER JOIN in the Star Schema Query requires two tables. Now imagine that you want to get procedure cost by animal type and zip code. Crafting that query using the schema in Figure 3.14 requires you to bring in the Person, PersonAddress, and Address tables. Using the star schema from Figure 3.20, you only need to add the Person_ Dimension table.

When data moves from an OLTP design into a star schema, there is a significant amount of data duplication. As such, a star schema consumes more space than its associated OLTP design to store the same data. These additional resource needs are one of the factors that makes data warehouses expensive to operate.

Snowflake

Another design pattern for data warehousing is the *snowflake schema*. As its name implies, the schema diagram looks like a snowflake. Snowflake and star schemas are conceptually similar in that they both have a central fact table surrounded by dimensions. Where the approaches differ is in the handling of dimensions. With a star, the dimension tables connect directly to the fact table. With a snowflake, dimensions have subcategories, which gives the snowflake design its shape. A snowflake schema is less denormalized than the star schema.

Recall that in a star schema, dimensions are one join away from the fact table. With a snowflake schema, you may need more than one join to get the data you are looking for. Consider the Day, Quarter, and State lookup tables in Figure 3.22. The data for State_ Description is in the State table. In Figure 3.20, State_Description exists in the Person_ Dimension.

FIGURE 3.22 Snowflake example

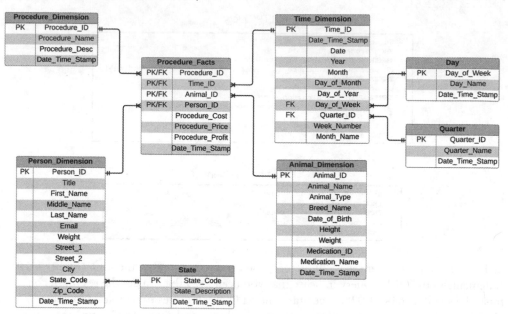

Recall that as the number of tables in a schema grows, queries become more complicated. For example, suppose you want to get procedure cost on a quarter-by-quarter basis and include Quarter_Name in the output. Using a star schema, you need two tables to answer this question. With the snowflake from Figure 3.22, you need three.

A snowflake schema query is more complex than the equivalent query in a star schema. Part of the trade-off is that a snowflake schema requires less storage space than a star schema. Consider where State_Description exists in Figure 3.20 and Figure 3.22. When State_Description is in a separate lookup table, it also consumes much less storage space. Imagine that there are 1 billion rows in the Person_Dimension table. In a star schema, the State_Description is stored 1 billion times. With a snowflake schema, you only end up storing State_Description 50 times—once for each of the 50 U.S. states.

Data warehouses often use snowflake schemas, since many different systems supply data to the warehouse. Data marts are comparatively less complicated, because they represent a single data subject area. As such, data marts frequently use a star-schema approach.

Exam Tip

As you prepare for the Data+ exam, keep in mind that the amount of storage a database needs decreases as a function of the degree of normalization. OLTP databases are highly normalized, whereas OLAP databases are denormalized.

Dimensionality

Dimensionality refers to the number of attributes a table has. The greater the number of attributes, the higher the dimensionality. A *dimension table* provides additional context around data in fact tables. For example, consider the Person_Dimension table in Figure 3.22, which contains details about people. If you need additional data about people, add columns to Person_Dimension.

It is crucial to understand the types of questions an analyst will need to answer when designing dimension tables. For example, a vice president of sales may want to examine profitability by geographical region and time of year. They may want to zoom in and look at product sales by day to gauge the effectiveness of a marketing campaign. They may also want to better understand trends by product and product family.

One dimension you will frequently encounter is time. It is necessary to answer questions about when something happened or when something was true. For example, to understand historical profitability, you need to keep track of pricing at the product level over time. One way to accomplish this is to add a start and end date to each product's price.

Consider Table 3.5, reflecting the price history for a 17 mm socket in a product dimension table. This table illustrates one approach to handling time. The last price change went into effect on January 1, 2021. The value for this date goes in the End_Date column for the $7.39 price and the Start_Date column for the $6.29 price. With this approach, it is easy to identify a 17 mm socket price on any given day after its original on-sale date.

TABLE 3.5   Product dimension

Product_ID	Product_Name	Price	Start_Date	End_Date
53	17 mm socket	5.48	1993-01-01 00:00:00	2003-01-01 00:00:00
53	17 mm socket	5.89	2003-01-01 00:00:00	2013-01-01 00:00:00
53	17 mm socket	5.99	2013-01-01 00:00:00	2020-05-03 00:00:00
53	17 mm socket	6.23	2020-05-03 00:00:00	2020-05-31 00:00:00
53	17 mm socket	8.59	2020-05-31 00:00:00	2020-10-31 00:00:00
53	17 mm socket	7.39	2020-10-31 00:00:00	2021-01-01 00:00:00
53	17 mm socket	6.29	2021-01-01 00:00:00	9999-12-31 23:59:59

Imagine a time-specific dimension that allows grouping by various time increments, including the day of the year, day of the week, month, and quarter. Using time stamp data types for both the Start_Date and End_Date columns in Table 3.5 makes it easy to calculate the average price for all sockets regardless of the level of time detail.

One of the criteria to consider is how quickly a dimension changes over time. Consider a geographic dimension table containing the 50 U.S. states. Ever since Hawaii became the 50th state in 1959, the number of states has remained constant. Looking forward, it is unlikely that additional states will enter the union with great frequency. In this context, geography is an example of a *slowly changing dimension*. However, other geographic attributes change more quickly. For example, a person's street address is more likely to change than the number of states in the United States.

Regardless of the speed at which a dimension changes, you need to handle both current and historical data.

Handling Dimensionality

There are multiple ways to design dimensions. Table 3.5 illustrates the start and end date approach. An understanding of this method is required to write a query to retrieve the current price. Another method extends the snowflake approach to modeling dimensions. You have a product dimension for the current price and a product history table for maintaining price history. One advantage of this approach is that it is easy to retrieve the current price while maintaining access to historical information.

Another approach is to use an indicator flag for the current price. This approach requires another column, as shown in Table 3.6. The indicator flag method keeps all pricing data in a single place. It also simplifies the query structure to get the current price. Instead of doing date math, you look for the price where the Current flag equals "Y."

TABLE 3.6   Current flag

Product_ID	Product_Name	Price	Start_Date	End_Date	Current
53	17 mm socket	8.59	2020-05-31 00:00:00	2020-10-31 00:00:00	N
53	17 mm socket	7.39	2020-10-31 00:00:00	2021-01-01 00:00:00	N
53	17 mm socket	6.29	2021-01-01 00:00:00	9999-12-31 23:59:59	Y

It is also possible to use the effective date approach to handling price changes. Consider Table 3.7, which illustrates this approach. In the table, each row has the date on which the given price goes into effect. The assumption is that the price stays in effect until there is a price change, at which point a new row is added to the table.

TABLE 3.7   Effective date

Product_ID	Product_Name	Price	Effective_Date
53	17 mm socket	8.59	2020-05-31 00:00:00
53	17 mm socket	7.39	2020-10-31 00:00:00
53	17 mm socket	6.29	2021-01-01 00:00:00

There is additional complexity with the effective date approach because queries have to perform date math to determine the price. Looking at the table, the price of 8.59 went into effect on May 31, 2020. The price changes on October 31, 2020. To retrieve the price on October 3, 2020, we know that October 3 falls after May 31 and before October 31. As such, the price on May 31 is current on October 3. While it is possible to code this logic in SQL, it complicates the queries.

Data Acquisition Concepts

To perform analytics, you need data. Data can come from internal systems you operate, or you can obtain it from third-party sources. Regardless of where data originates, you need to get data before analyzing it to derive additional value. In this section, we explore methods for integrating data from systems you own. We also explore strategies for collecting data from external systems.

Integration

Data from transactional systems flow into data warehouses and data marts for analysis. Recall that OLTP and OLAP databases have different internal structures. You need to retrieve, reshape, and insert data to move data between operational and analytical environments. You can use a variety of methods to transfer data efficiently and effectively.

One approach is known as *extract, transform, and load (ETL)*. As the name implies, this method consists of three phases.

- **Extract:** In the first phase, you extract data from the source system and place it in a staging area. The goal of the extract phase is to move data from a relational database into a flat file as quickly as possible.

- **Transform:** The second phase transforms the data. The goal is to reformat the data from its transactional structure to the data warehouse's analytical design.

- **Load:** The purpose of the load phase is to ensure data gets into the analytical system as quickly as possible.

Extract, load, and transform (ELT) is a variant of ETL. With ELT, data is extracted from a source database and loaded directly into the data warehouse. Once the extract and load phases are complete, the transformation phase gets under way. One key difference between ETL and ELT is the technical component performing the transformation. With ETL, the data transformation takes place external to a relational database, using a programming language like Python. ELT uses SQL and the power of a relational database to reformat the data.

ELT has an advantage in the speed with which data moves from the operational to the analytical database. Suppose you need to get massive amounts of transactional data into an analytical environment as quickly as possible. In that case, ELT is a good choice, especially at scale when the data warehouse has a lot of capacity. Whether you choose ETL or ELT is a function of organizational need, staff capabilities, and technical strategy.

ETL Vendors

Whether you choose ETL or ELT for loading your data warehouse, you don't have to write transformations by hand. Many products support both ETL and ELT. Before you pick one, carefully evaluate the available free and paid options to determine the one that best fits your needs and system architecture goals.

An *initial load* occurs the first time data is put into a data warehouse. After that initial load, each additional load is a *delta load*, also known as an *incremental load*. A delta load only moves changes between systems. Figure 3.23 illustrates a data warehouse that launches in January and uses a monthly delta load cycle. The initial load happens right before the data warehouse becomes available for use. All of the transactional data from January becomes the delta load that initiates on the first of February. Figure 3.23 illustrates a monthly delta-load approach that continues throughout the year.

FIGURE 3.23   Delta load example

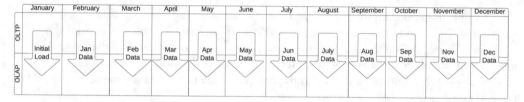

The frequency with which delta loads happen depends on business requirements. Depending on how fresh the data needs to be, delta loads can happen at any interval. Hourly, daily, and weekly refreshes are typical.

When moving data between systems, you have to balance the speed and complexity of the overall operation. Suppose you operate nationally within the United States and start processing transactions at 7 in the morning and finish by 7 in the evening. The 12 hours between 7 p.m. and 7 a.m. represent the *batch window*, or time period available, to move data into your data warehouse. The duration of a batch window must be taken into account when designing a delta load strategy.

Exam Tip

You need to understand the time available for performing delta loads into your data warehouse. Regardless of how long your batch window is, think carefully about moving current data into the data warehouse without losing history.

Data Collection Methods

Augmenting data from your transactional systems with external data is an excellent way to improve the analytical capabilities of your organization. For example, suppose you operate a national motorcycle rental fleet and want to determine if you need to rebalance your fleet across your existing locations. You also want to evaluate whether it is profitable to expand to a new geographic region, as well as predict the best time and place to add motorcycles to your fleet.

Your internal data is a good place to start when analyzing how to grow your business. To improve the accuracy of your analysis, you want to include data about the weather, tourism, and your competitors. This additional data can come from various sources, including federal and state open data portals, other public data sources, and private purveyors of data.

Application Programming Interfaces (APIs)

An *application programming interface (API)* is a structured method for computer systems to exchange information. APIs provide a consistent interface to calling applications, regardless of the internal database structure. Whoever calls an API has no idea whether a transactional or analytical data store backs it. The internal data structure does not matter as long as the API returns the data you want. APIs can be transactional, returning data as JSON objects. APIs can also facilitate bulk data extraction, returning CSV files.

APIs represent a specific piece of business functionality. Let's return to our motorcycle rental business. Say a repeat customer logs into the website. The web application looks up their profile information, including their name and most frequently visited locations, to personalize their experience. To provide excellent customer service, you want that same information to be available to customer service agents who answer phone calls.

In the top half of Figure 3.24, the SQL to extract customer profile information exists in both the web application and customer service system. This code duplication makes maintenance a challenge—when the SQL needs to change, it has to happen in two places.

The bottom half of Figure 3.24 illustrates the benefit of using an API. Instead of directly embedding SQL in two places, you wrap it in a single `GetProfile` API. You can easily connect the API to the customer-facing web server and internal-facing customer service system. Suppose you have another application that needs to extract profile information. In that case, all you have to do is connect it to the `GetProfile` API.

Web Services

Many smartphone applications need a network connection, either cellular or Wi-Fi, to work correctly. The reason is that much of the data these applications need is not on the smartphone itself. Instead, data is found in private and public data sources and is accessible via a *web service*. A web service is an API you can call via *Hypertext Transfer Protocol (HTTP)*, the language of the World Wide Web.

FIGURE 3.24   Internal API example

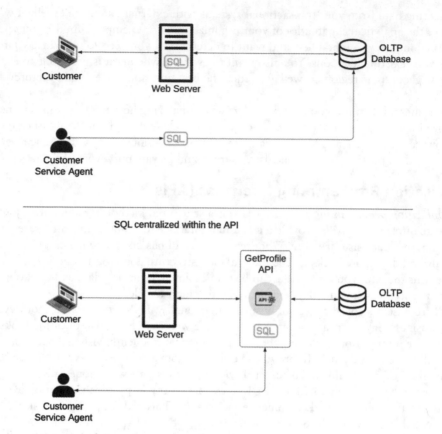

While a web service is an API, an API does not have to be a web service. Consider the customer service system from Figure 3.24. You might need to install it on each customer service agent's computer, the same way you install Microsoft Excel or PowerPoint, instead of making it a web application. If this is the case, the application accesses the API directly, not as a web service.

Suppose you want to get weather-related data. The National Centers for Environmental Information (NCEI) is a U.S. federal agency within the National Oceanic and Atmospheric Administration (NOAA) office. The NCEI is an authoritative source for weather data. It makes that data available to the public via a web service–enabled API.

Many APIs, like those available from the NCEI, require an *API key*. If you imagine an API as the door behind which data treasures exist, an API key is what unlocks the door. API providers generate a unique API key for each calling application. Centralized creation and distribution of API keys allow the provider to understand who is using the API and to turn off individual keys' access in the event of abuse.

Open data providers like NCEI make API keys available for free. You register for an API using an email address. After registering, you receive your unique API key in an email. Other data purveyors charge for API access. For example, Google has excellent APIs for static and dynamic map information. In addition to having to register for an API, you incur a nominal charge for each API call. The more you use an API, the more you have to pay. Other API providers take a tiered approach, where you get a limited number of API calls for free, after which you have to pay.

Web Scraping

Some of the data you want may not be available internally as an API or publicly via a web service. However, data may exist on a website. As seen in Chapter 2, data can present itself in an HTML table on a web page. If data exists in a structured format, you can retrieve it programmatically. Programmatic retrieval of data from a website is known as *web scraping*.

You can use software bots to scrape data from a website. Many modern programming languages, including Python and R, make it easy to create a web scraper. Instead of using an API or a web service, a web scraper reads a web page similar to a browser, such as Chrome, Safari, or Edge. Web scrapers read and parse the HTML to extract the data the web pages contain.

The search results for some websites span multiple web pages. Your web scraper has to account for pagination to ensure that you are not leaving any data behind. The scraper must understand how many result pages exist and then iterate through them to harvest the data.

WARNING   Keep in mind that programmatically scraping a website may violate its terms of service. If you persist in programmatically collecting data in violation of a website's terms, the website provider may block your ability to access the site.

Human-in-the-Loop

There are times when the data you seek exists only in people's minds. For example, you can extract the most popular and profitable motorcycling destination from your existing internal data. You can get weather information from an API packaged as a web service. You can glean insight into competitive pricing by scraping your competitors' websites. Even with all of these data sources, you may still want insight into how customers feel about the services you provide.

Surveys

One way to collect data directly from your customers is by conducting a *survey*. The most simplistic surveys consist of one question and indicate customer satisfaction. For example,

Figure 3.25 illustrates a survey collection approach in the airline industry. As people board their aircraft, they walk past a small machine with two buttons on it. In response to the question, the people press either the happy face or the unhappy face. Although single-question surveys don't provide any depth as to why people feel positively or negatively, they provide an overall indicator of satisfaction.

FIGURE 3.25   Single question survey

Surveys can be much more complicated than a single question. For example, suppose you want a comprehensive understanding of customer satisfaction. In that case, you design a sophisticated survey that presents people with different questions depending on their answers. Complex survey logic lets you gather additional detail as to why a person has a particular opinion.

You can design surveys to achieve your data collection goals and your audience. You can tailor a survey to collect data on how your employees feel about the effectiveness of their manager, or more broadly, about your organization's approach to pay and benefits. You may want feedback on a customer appreciation event or training session. As long as you know the objective of a survey, you can design one to accomplish your goals.

As you can imagine, survey design is an entire discipline. As you design a survey, you want to keep in mind how you will analyze the data you collect. Numeric data is easy to analyze using a variety of statistical methods. Free-response questions result in unstructured text data, which is more challenging to interpret. You need to clearly understand what is essential to your organization and what decisions you will make using the output to develop and administer an impactful survey.

Survey Tools

Instead of designing a custom application to collect survey data, several survey products let you design complex surveys without worrying about building a database. Qualtrics is a powerful tool for developing and administering surveys. Figure 3.26 shows what it is like to build a survey in Qualtrics.

FIGURE 3.26   Qualtrics survey build

Edit question	Tools ⌄ Saved Jun 25, 2021 at 3:31 PM Published	🔍	Preview	Publish

Question type

☰ Multiple choice ⌄

Laptop Preferences   iQ Score: Great

▾ **Answer type**

🔘 Allow one answer

◯ Allow multiple answers

▾ **Choices**

Number of choices

− 4 +

Use suggested choices ⬤

▾ **Format**

List ⌄

Alignment

Vertical ⌄

Add choice group

▾ **Response requirements**

Add requirements ⬤

Add validation ⬤

▾ **Question behavior**

↳ Display logic

↷ Skip logic

↳ Carry forward choices

⤭ Choice randomization

×→ Recode values

⬤ Default choices

▾ Default Question Block

☐ **Q1**   •••

What is your budget when considering a new laptop?

◯ <1000

◯ 1000-1500

◯ 1501-2000

◯ >2000

＋ Add page break

Q2

What screen size do you prefer?

◯ Small

◯ Medium

◯ Large

Q3

Amount of RAM?

◯ 8GB

◯ 16GB

◯ 32GB

Q4

HDD size

◯ 256

◯ 512

◯ 1024

What makes Qualtrics so compelling is its API, which you can use to integrate survey response data into a data warehouse for additional analysis.

Observation

Observation is the act of collecting primary source data, from either people or machines. Observational data can be qualitative or quantitative. Collecting qualitative observational data leads to unstructured data challenges.

Imagine observing a person as they perform their work and interact with their colleagues. When you take this approach, it is hard to account for nonverbal communication. You also may struggle to collect data about what people do subconsciously. Returning to our motorcycle rental business, imagine a mechanic going through a post-rental examination. He may augment the post-ride checklist with his experience and intuition. For example, he may decide to change the brake pads and tighten the clutch lever if he perceives the motorcycle was subject to abuse. That may lead him to intuitively look at particular areas of the vehicle for indications of abuse before signing off on the security deposit return.

Asking someone to write down everything they do or the number of times they do something can introduce bias into the data. Developing methods for observation is one way to record what is happening in an environment accurately. Of course, you need to account for the bias of the observer.

Quantitative observations are much easier to collect and interpret. For example, suppose you are trying to establish the defect rate on a production line. You can count the number of vehicles that come off the line, as well as how many fail post-production quality checks.

Sampling

Regardless of the data acquisition approach, you may end up with more data than is practical to manipulate. Imagine you are doing analytics in an Internet-of-Things environment, in which 800 billion events occur daily. Though it is possible, ingesting and storing 800 billion records is a challenging task. Manipulating 800 billion records takes a lot of computing power.

Suppose you want to analyze one day's worth of data. In that case, the 800 billion records represent the total *population*, or the number of events, available. Since manipulating 800 billion records is unwieldy, you might collect a *sample*, or subset, of the overall population. Once you have collected sample data, you can use statistical methods to make generalizations about the entire population. For more detail on these methods, see Chapter 5, "Data Analysis and Statistics."

Working with Data

Determining an appropriate database structure, identifying data sources, and loading a database takes a considerable amount of effort. To turn a database design into an operational database ready to accept data, you use the *Data Definition Language* (*DDL*) components of SQL. DDL lets you create, modify, and delete tables and other associated database objects.

With all of that work complete, the foundation is in place to derive impactful insights. To generate insights, a productive analyst must be comfortable using the *Data Manipulation*

Language (*DML*) capabilities of SQL to insert, modify, and retrieve information from databases. While DDL manages the structure of a database, DML manages the data in the database.

The DML components of SQL change very slowly. As long as relational databases exist, you will need to understand SQL to work with them. It is worth learning SQL, as the foundational knowledge of DML operations will serve you well.

Data Manipulation

When manipulating data, one of four possible actions occurs:

- Create new data.
- Read existing data.
- Update existing data.
- Delete existing data.

The acronym *CRUD* (*Create, Read, Update, Delete*) is a handy way to remember these four operations.

SQL uses verbs to identify the type of activity a specific statement performs. For each CRUD activity, there is a corresponding DML verb, as Table 3.8 illustrates. These verbs are known as *keywords*, or words that are part of the SQL language itself.

TABLE 3.8 Data manipulation in SQL

Operation	SQL Keyword	Description
Create	INSERT	Creates new data in an existing table
Read	SELECT	Retrieves data from an existing table
Update	UPDATE	Changes existing data in an existing table
Delete	DELETE	Removes existing data from an existing table

Reading and manipulating data is commonplace on the path to creating insights. To that end, we will focus on options that affect reading data. Before jumping in, it is helpful to understand the syntax of a query.

FIGURE 3.27 SQL SELECT statement

```
SELECT <what>
FROM   <source>
```

Figure 3.27 illustrates the basic structure of a SQL query that reads from a database. SELECT, FROM, and WHERE are all reserved words that have specific meaning in SQL.

The SELECT clause identifies the columns from the table(s) that are retrieved. If you want to list the name and animal type from Table 3.1, the SELECT portion of the query will look like this:

```
SELECT Animal_Name, Breed_Name
```

The FROM clause in a query identifies the source of data, which is frequently a database table. Both the SELECT and FROM clauses are required for a SQL statement to return data, as follows:

```
SELECT Animal_Name, Breed_Name
FROM  Animal
```

As the queries in Figure 3.21 illustrate, it is possible to specify more than one location for data by joining tables together.

SQL Considerations

The keywords in SQL are case-insensitive. However, the case-sensitivity of column names and values depend on the database configuration.

Consider the following query:

```
Select Animal_Name, Breed_Name from Animal
```

The previous query returns the same results as this query:

```
SELECT Animal_Name, Breed_Name FROM Animal
```

SQL can also span multiple lines. For example, rewriting the previous query as follows will return identical results:

```
SELECT Animal_Name, Breed_Name
FROM  Animal
```

How a query appears is a function of organizational conventions. Factors that influence convention include database configuration, query efficiency, and how easy it is for people to read and understand the query.

Filtering

Examining a large table in its entirety provides insight into the overall population. To answer questions that an organization's leadership has typically requires a subset of the overall data. Filtering is a way to reduce the data down to only the rows that you need.

To filter data, you add a WHERE clause to a query. Note that the column you are filtering on does not have to appear in the SELECT clause. To retrieve the name and breed for only the dogs from Table 3.1, you modify the query as follows:

```
SELECT Animal_Name, Breed_Name
FROM  Animal
WHERE Animal_Type = 'Dog'
```

Filtering and Logical Operators

A query can have multiple filtering conditions. You need to use a logical operator to account for complex filtering needs. For example, suppose you need to retrieve the name and breed for dogs weighing more than 60 pounds. In that case, you can enhance the query using the AND logical operator, as follows:

```
SELECT Animal_Name, Breed_Name
FROM  Animal
WHERE Animal_Type = 'Dog'
AND  Weight > 60
```

The AND operator evaluates the Animal_Type and Weight filters together, only returning records that match both criteria. OR is another frequently used logical operator. For example, suppose you want to see the name and breed for all dogs and any animals that weigh more than 10 pounds regardless of the animal type. The following query delivers the answer to that question:

```
SELECT Animal_Name, Breed_Name
FROM  Animal
WHERE Animal_Type = 'Dog'
OR   Weight > 10
```

Complex queries frequently use multiple logical operators at the same time. It is good to use parentheses around filter conditions to help make queries easy for people to read and understand.

Data warehouses often contain millions, billions, or even trillions of individual data records. Filtering data is essential to making effective use of these massive data stores.

Sorting

When querying a database, you frequently specify the order in which you want your results to return. The ORDER BY clause is the component of a SQL query that makes sorting possible. Similar to how the WHERE clause performs, you do not have to specify the columns you are using to sort the data in the SELECT clause.

For example, suppose you want to retrieve the animal and breed for dogs over 60 pounds, with the oldest dog listed first. The following query delivers the answer:

```
SELECT  Animal_Name, Breed_Name
FROM    Animal
```

```
WHERE   Animal_Type = 'Dog'
AND     Weight > 60
ORDER BY Date_of_Birth ASC
```

If you want to return the youngest dog first, you change the ORDER BY clause as follows:

```
SELECT   Animal_Name, Breed_Name
FROM     Animal
WHERE    Animal_Type = 'Dog'
AND      Weight > 60
ORDER BY Date_of_Birth DESC
```

The ASC keyword at the end of the ORDER BY clause sorts in ascending order whereas using DESC with ORDER BY sorts in descending order. If you are sorting on multiple columns, you can use both ascending and descending as appropriate. Both the ASC and DESC keywords work across various data types, including date, alphanumeric, and numeric.

Date Functions

As seen in Table 3.5 and Table 3.6, date columns are frequently found in OLAP environments. Date columns also appear in transactional systems. Storing date information about an event facilitates analysis across time. For example, you may be interested in first-quarter sales performance or outstanding receivables on a rolling 60-day basis. Fortunately, there is an abundance of functions that make working with dates easy.

The most important thing to note is that you have to understand the database platform you are using and how that platform handles dates and times. Since each platform provider uses different data types for handling this information, you need to familiarize yourself with the functions available from your provider of choice.

Logical Functions

Logical functions can make data substitutions when retrieving data. Remember that a SELECT statement only retrieves data. The data in the underlying tables do not change when a SELECT runs. Consider Table 3.9, which enhances Table 3.1 by adding a Sex column. Looking at the values for Sex, we see that this column contains code values. To understand the description for each code value in a sound relational model, the Sex column from Table 3.9 is a foreign key pointing to the Sex column in Table 3.10.

TABLE 3.9 Augmented animal data

Animal_ID	Animal_Name	Animal_Type	Breed_Name	Sex	Date_of_Birth	Height (inches)	Weight (pounds)
1	Jack	Dog	Corgi	M	3/2/2018	10	26.3
2	Viking	Dog	Husky	M	5/8/2017	24	58
3	Hazel	Dog	Labradoodle	F	7/3/2016	23	61
4	Schooner	Dog	Labrador Retriever	M	8/14/2019	24.3	73.4
5	Skippy	Dog	Weimaraner	F	10/3/2018	26.3	63.5
6	Alexander	Cat	American Shorthair	M	10/4/2017	9.3	10.4

TABLE 3.10   Sex Lookup Table

Sex	Sex_Description
M	Male
F	Female

Suppose you want to retrieve the name and sex description for each animal, as Table 3.11 illustrates. One way to accomplish this is by joining the two tables together, retrieving the Animal_Name from Table 3.9 and Sex_Description from Table 3.10.

TABLE 3.11   Desired Query Results

Animal_Name	Sex
Jack	Male
Viking	Male
Hazel	Female
Schooner	Male
Skippy	Female
Alexander	Male

When writing SQL, there are frequently many ways to write a query and create the same results. Another way to generate the output in Table 3.10 is by using the IFF logical function. The IFF function has the following syntax:

```
IFF(boolean_expression, true_value, false_value)
```

As you can see from the syntax, the IFF function expects the following three parameters:

- **Boolean Expression:** The expression must return either TRUE or FALSE.

- **True Value:** If the Boolean expression returns TRUE, the IFF function will return this value.

- **False Value:** If the Boolean expression returns FALSE, the IFF function will return this value.

The following query, using the IFF function, generates the results in Table 3.11:

```
SELECT  Animal_Name, IFF(Sex = 'M', 'Male', 'Female')
FROM    Animal
```

Note that with the `IFF` approach, the values for Male and Female come from the function parameters, not from the source table (Table 3.9). Suppose the description in the underlying table gets modified. In that case, the results of the `IFF` query will not reflect the modified data.

Table 3.12 shows the results of the following query, which also uses the `IFF` function:

```
SELECT  Animal_Name, IFF(Sex = 'M', 'Boy', 'Girl')
FROM    Animal
```

TABLE 3.12   Modified IFF query results

Animal_Name	Sex
Jack	Boy
Viking	Boy
Hazel	Girl
Schooner	Boy
Skippy	Girl
Alexander	Boy

`IFF` is just one example of a logical function. When using logical functions, you need to balance their convenience with the knowledge that you are replacing data from the database with the function's coded values. The ability to do this type of substitution is a real asset when dividing data into categories.

Aggregate Functions

Summarized data helps answer questions that executives have, and aggregate functions are an easy way to summarize data. Aggregate functions summarize a query's data and return a single value. While each database platform supports different aggregation functions, Table 3.13 describes functions that are common across platforms. Be sure to familiarize yourself with the functions available in your platform of choice.

TABLE 3.13   Common SQL aggregate functions

Function	Purpose
COUNT	Returns the total number of rows of a query.
MIN	Returns the minimum value from the results of a query. Note that this works on both alphanumeric and numeric data types.
MAX	Returns the maximum value from the results of a query. Note that this works on both alphanumeric and numeric data types.
AVG	Returns the mathematic average of the results of a query.
SUM	Returns the sum of the results of a query.
STDDEV	Returns the sample standard deviation of the results of a query.

You can also use aggregate functions to filter data. For example, you may want a query that shows all employees who make less than the average corporate salary. Aggregate functions also operate across subsets of data. For instance, you can calculate total sales by month with a single query.

System Functions

Each database platform offers functions that expose data about the database itself. One of the most frequently used system functions returns the current date. The current date is a component of transactional records and enables time-based analysis in the future. The current date is also necessary for a system that uses an effective date approach.

System functions also return data about the database environment. For example, whenever a person or automated process uses data from a database, they need to establish a *database session*. A database session begins when a person/program connects to a database. The session lasts until the person/program disconnects. For example, a poorly written query can consume most of the resources available to the database. When that happens, a database administrator can identify and terminate the problematic session.

Query Optimization

Writing a SQL query is straightforward. Writing a SQL query that efficiently does what you intend can be more difficult. There are several factors to consider when creating well-performing SQL.

Parametrization

Whenever a SQL query executes, the database has to *parse* the query. Parsing translates the human-readable SQL into code the database understands. Parsing takes time and impacts how long it takes for a query to return data. Effective use of parameterization reduces the number of times the database has to parse individual queries.

Suppose you operate a website and want to personalize it for your customers. Login details serve as parameters to the query to retrieve your information for display. After logging in, a customer sees a welcome message identifying them by name.

Figure 3.28 provides an example of the web server creating a hard-coded query. Examining the WHERE filter in the query, we see that it matches the string "Gerald." When Gerald logs in, the database parses the query, executes it, and returns Gerald's information.

In this situation, when Gina logs in, the WHERE filter looks specifically for "Gina." Since "Gerald" is different from "Gina," the database treats this as a new query and parses it. The time it takes to parse becomes problematic at scale. Imagine 1,000 people all logging in at the same time. The database sees each of these queries as unique and ends up parsing 1,000 times.

FIGURE 3.28 Hard-coded SQL query

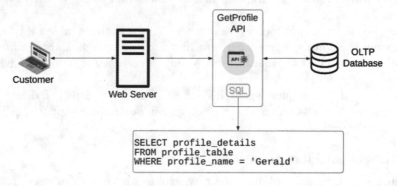

Figure 3.29 illustrates how to address this potential performance problem using parameterization. Instead of looking specifically for an exact string match for every customer, the query uses a variable called &customer_name. The code in the web server populates the variable with the appropriate customer name. To the database, this appears as a single query. While the value of &customer_name changes for every customer, the database parses it only once.

FIGURE 3.29 Parameterized SQL query

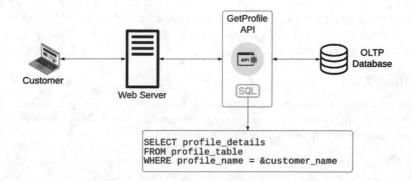

Indexing

When retrieving data from a table, the database has to scan each row until it finds the ones that match the filters in the WHERE clause. The process of looking at each row is called a *full table scan*. A full table scan is like flipping through every page in a book to find a specific piece of data. For small tables, full table scans happen quickly. As data volumes increase, scanning the entire table takes a long time and is not efficient. To speed up query performance, you need a *database index*.

A database index works like the index in the back of a book. Instead of looking at each page in a book to find what you are looking for, you can find a specific page number in the index and then go to that page.

A database index can point to a single column or multiple columns. When running queries on large tables, it is ideal if all of the columns you are retrieving exist in the index. If that is not feasible, you at least want the first column in your SELECT statement to be covered by an index.

If a query is running slowly, look at the indexes on the underlying tables. If you think a new index would help improve query performance, discuss it with a database administrator. The administrator will look at other factors that impact performance and will have the permissions to create an index if necessary.

While indexing improves query speed, it slows down create, update, and delete activity. An indexing strategy needs to match the type of system the database supports, be it transactional or reporting.

Data Subsets and Temporary Tables

When dealing with large data volumes, you may want to work with a subset of records. For example, suppose an organization has 1,000,000 customers. Each of those customers places 200 orders per year, and there are 10 years of data in the data warehouse. In this situation, the Order table in the data warehouse would have 2 billion rows. If you want to explore trends for a specific customer's order history, it would not be efficient to query the main Order table.

It is possible to create a temporary table to make the data more manageable. Temporary tables can store the results of a query and are disposable. Temporary tables automatically get removed when the active session ends. Using temporary tables is an effective method of creating subsets for ad hoc analysis.

For example, you can establish a database session, create a temporary table with the order history for a single customer, run queries against that temporary table, and disconnect from the database. When the session disconnects, the database automatically purges any temporary tables created during the session.

Execution Plan

An *execution plan* shows the details of how a database runs a specific query. Execution plans are extremely helpful in troubleshooting query performance issues. They provide additional information about how a query is spending its time.

For example, an execution plan can tell you if a slow-running query uses a full table scan instead of an index scan. In this case, it could be that the query is poorly written and not using the existing indexes. It also could be that a column needs a new index.

Looking at execution plans is an integral part of developing efficient queries. It is worth understanding the nuances of how to interpret execution plans for the database platform you use. If you need help understanding an execution plan, get in touch with your local database administrator.

Summary

Databases are technology platforms for processing and storing data. There are two primary types of databases: relational and non-relational. Relational databases are ideal when you have tabular data, while there are numerous non-relational offerings when you need more flexibility than the structure a relational database imposes.

Using a relational database as a technology platform, you can build transactional or analytical databases to address the business need. Transactional (OLTP) and analytical (OLAP) databases require different schema design approaches. Since a transactional database needs to balance reading and writing data, it follows a highly normalized schema design.

On the other hand, analytical databases prioritize reading data and follow a denormalized approach. The star and snowflake schema designs are two approaches to structuring data for analysis. Both methods implement dimensional modeling, which organizes quantitative data into facts and qualitative data into dimensions.

There are multiple ways to acquire data for analysis. For example, most data warehouses source data from transactional systems. To copy data from a transactional system, you can use an ETL or ELT approach. ETL leverages technology external to a relational database to transform data, while ELT uses the power of a relational database to do the transformation. Depending on the rate of change and data volume, you can take a complete refresh or delta load approach.

You can also acquire data from external sources. APIs are integration components that encapsulate business logic and programmatically expose data. It is common to interact with APIs to source data for both transactional and analytical purposes. You may also find yourself needing to scrape data from a website or pull data from a public database.

There are times when you need primary source data that you can't obtain programmatically. In that case, you may end up conducting a survey or observing people and processes.

Once you have data in a relational database, you need to be comfortable manipulating it. Structured Query Language (SQL) is the standard for relational data manipulation. With SQL queries, you can filter, sort, compare, and aggregate data.

There are times when you will be working with large volumes of data that impact performance. There are several approaches you can take to mitigate performance issues. When writing frequently executed queries, make sure you use parametrization to reduce the database's parsing load. Reducing the number of records you're working with is another viable approach, which you can achieve by subsetting the data and using temporary tables. If you have queries taking more time than you expect, work with a database administrator to review the query's execution plan and ensure you have the appropriate indexing strategy.

Exam Essentials

Describe the characteristics of OLTP and OLAP systems.   The two main categories of relational databases are transactional (OLTP) and analytical (OLAP). Transactional systems use highly normalized schema design, which allows for database reads and writes to perform well. Analytical systems are denormalized and commonly have a star or snowflake schema. Remember that a star design simplifies queries by having a main fact table surrounded by dimensions. A snowflake design is more normalized than a star. While this approach reduces storage requirements, the queries are more complex than in a star schema.

Describe approaches for handling dimensionality.   It is crucial to keep track of how data changes over time to perform historical analysis. Although an effective date approach is valid, the SQL queries to retrieve a value at a specific point in time are complex. A table design that adds start date and end date columns allows for more straightforward queries. Enhancing the design with a current flag column makes analytical queries even easier to write.

Understand integration and how to populate a data warehouse.   The more data an organization has, the more impactful the analysis it can conduct. The extract, transform, and load (ETL) process copies data from transactional to analytical databases. Suppose an organization wants to use the power of a relational database to reformat the data for analytical purposes. In that case, the order changes to extract, load, and transform. Regardless of the approach, remember that a delta load migrates only changed data.

Differentiate between data collection methods.   Data can come from a variety of sources. An organization may scrape websites or use publicly available databases to augment its data. While web scraping may be the only way to retrieve data, it is better if a published application programming interface exists. An API is more reliable since its structure makes for a consistent interface. If you want to capture the voice of the customer, a survey is a sound approach. Collecting data through observation is a great way to validate business processes and collect quantitative data.

Describe how to manipulate data and optimize queries.   Analytical databases store massive amounts of data. Manipulating the entire dataset for analysis is frequently infeasible. To efficiently analyze data, understand that SQL has the power to filter, sort, and aggregate data. When focusing on a particular subject, creating a subset is an ideal approach. Although it is possible to create permanent tables to house subsets, using a temporary table as part of a query is viable for ad hoc analysis. When an analytical query performs poorly, use its execution plan to understand the root cause. It is wise to work with a database administrator to understand the execution plan and ensure that indexes exist where they are needed.

Review Questions

1. Claire operates a travel agency and wants to automatically recommend accommodation, rental car, and entertainment packages based on her customers' interests. What type of database should Claire select?

   A. Relational

   B. Graph

   C. Key-value

   D. Column-family

2. Evan needs to retrieve information from two separate tables to create a month-end credit card summary. What should he use to join the tables together?

   A. Primary key

   B. Foreign key

   C. Synthetic primary key

   D. Referential integrity

3. Taylor wants to investigate how manufacturing, marketing, and sales expenditures impact overall profitability for her company. Which of the following systems is most appropriate? Choose the best answer.

   A. OLTP

   B. OLAP

   C. Data warehouse

   D. Data mart

4. J. R. needs to move data into his data warehouse. One of his primary concerns is how fast data can get into the warehouse. As he thinks about approaches for transferring data, which of the following is the *best* option?

   A. Initial load

   B. Delta load

   C. ETL

   D. ELT

5. Riley is designing a data warehouse and wants to make writing queries that track customer satisfaction over time as simple as possible. What could she add to her table design to accomplish her goal? Choose the best answer.

   A. Current flag

   B. Start date

   C. Middle date

   D. End date

6. Richard is designing a data warehouse and wants to minimize query complexity. What design pattern should he follow?

    A. Avalanche

    B. Star

    C. Snowflake

    D. Quasar

7. Razia is working on understanding population trends by county across the United States. Considering the rate of change, which of the following *best* describes county name?

    A. Static dimension

    B. Slowly changing dimension

    C. Rapidly changing dimension

    D. Fluid dimension

8. Zaiden is debating between a snowflake and a star schema design for a data warehouse. Which of the following is not a factor in his selection?

    A. Storage space

    B. Query complexity

    C. Number of records in the fact table

    D. Degree of normalization

9. Madeline wants to collect data about how her competitor prices products. She can see this information after logging in to her competitor's website. After some initial struggles, Madeline creates a web scraper to harvest the data she needs. What does she need to do next? Choose the best answer.

    A. Check the terms of service.

    B. Load the data into an OLTP database.

    C. Load the data into an OLAP database.

    D. Figure out how to parse JSON.

10. Maurice manages an organization of software developers with deep expertise in Python. He wants to make use of this expertise to move data between transactional systems and the data warehouse. In what phase are Python skills most relevant?

    A. Extract

    B. Transform

    C. Load

    D. Purge

11. Ellen is collecting data about a proprietary manufacturing process and wants to control for any bias that workers may have. What type of data collection approach is most appropriate?

    A. Survey

    B. Sample

    C. Public database

    D. Observation

12. George wants to integrate data from his city's open data portal. Reading the website, he sees that he can download the data he wants as a CSV file. After manually downloading the file, he writes the code to transform the data and load it into his database. Presuming the data changes once a month, what can George do to ensure he has the most up-to-date data from the city? Choose the best answer.

    A. Manually check the city's website every day.

    B. Contact the city and encourage the development of an API.

    C. Automate the process that downloads, transforms, and uploads the CSV file.

    D. Nothing, George has already successfully loaded the data.

13. Martha is designing a nightly ETL process to copy data from an order processing system into a data warehouse. What should she do to replicate the data she needs efficiently without losing historical data? Choose the best answer.

    A. Complete purge and load

    B. Delta load

    C. ELT

    D. Use an ETL product

14. Bob manages a production line and is worried that defects are not being accurately reported. What is the best way for him to obtain the true number of defects?

    A. Survey the production staff.

    B. Test a sample of finished goods.

    C. Observe the final quality check process.

    D. Use historical data to establish a trend.

15. Barb wants to understand which product costs the least. What aggregate function can she use in her SQL query to get this answer?

    A. COUNT

    B. MAX

    C. MIN

    D. AVG

16. Elena is an analyst at a multinational corporation. She wants to focus her analysis on transactions that took place in Italy. What is the first thing she should do to make efficient use of resources?

    A. Filter out transactions for all countries except Italy.

    B. Filter out transactions for Italy.

    C. Aggregate transactions across the European Union.

    D. Subset the data to a specific Italian province.

17. Jeff is an analyst at a company that operates in the United States. He wants to understand profitability trends by region, state, and county. What should he do next? Choose the best answer.

    A. Aggregate data at the county level.

    B. Aggregate data by region, state, and county.

    C. Use effective date logic to determine current profitability.

    D. Make sure there is an index on the county column.

18. Gretchen is trying to create a list of purchases in chronological order. What clause does she need to add to her SQL query?

    A. SELECT

    B. FROM

    C. WHERE

    D. ORDER BY

19. Brandon is trying to understand why the personalization features of his website performs poorly under heavy load. Looking at the query that retrieves customer profile information, he sees that the web application is hard-coding the customer's identifying number into each query, then using the Customer_ID column to retrieve profile data. Looking at the execution plan, Brandon sees that the query is performing optimally. What does he need to do to resolve the performance issue? Choose the best answer.

    A. Check to ensure there is an index to the Customer_ID column.

    B. Review the execution plan for the query with a DBA.

    C. Remove the personalization features due to the performance problems.

    D. Change the application code to use query parameters instead of hard-coding.

20. Julie wants to retrieve the total number of rows in a table. Which aggregation function should she use in her SQL query?

    A. STDDEV

    B. COUNT

    C. SUM

    D. MAX

Data Quality

THE COMPTIA DATA+ EXAM TOPICS COVERED IN THIS CHAPTER INCLUDE:

✓ **Domain 2.0: Data Mining**

✓ **2.2. Identify common reasons for cleansing and profiling datasets**

✓ **2.3. Given a scenario, execute data manipulation techniques**

✓ **Domain 5.0: Data Governance, Quality, and Controls**

✓ **5.2. Given a scenario, apply data quality control concepts**

In Chapter 3, "Databases and Data Acquisition," you learned about sources of data and the design differences between transactional and analytical databases. With this knowledge of data sources and retrieval methods under your belt, we can now consider issues that impact data quality.

Businesses need high-quality data to create the kinds of analysis that organizations rely on for decision making. While the data we use in these analyses isn't ever perfect, understanding the limitations of each dataset you use will help you identify any data transformation work that you must complete before proceeding with analysis.

In this chapter, we will explore the reasons why data needs transformation. With a scenario providing context, we will explore the data manipulation techniques that best prepare data for analysis. Zooming out, we will walk through data quality scenarios and examine methods for resolving data quality issues.

Data Quality Challenges

Analysts are often eager to jump straight to analyzing data. As discussed in Chapter 3, "Databases and Data Acquisition," data warehouses aggregate multiple data sources and provide a platform for conducting analysis. However, each data source has its own unique quality issues that need resolution before finding its way into a data warehouse. Whether designing an *extract, transform, and load (ETL)* process or digging into a new set of data warehouse tables, an analyst needs to examine each data source and resolve any underlying quality issues. Let's explore some common reasons for cleaning and profiling datasets.

Duplicate Data

Duplicate data occurs when data representing the same transaction is accidentally duplicated within a system. Suppose you want to open a spreadsheet on your local computer. To open the spreadsheet, you locate the file and double-click it. This method of opening documents establishes muscle memory that associates double-clicking with the desired action.

Suppose you are shopping online for flights between Chicago and San Francisco. Once you identify a flight that meets your scheduling needs, you proceed to a web page to complete your purchase. Unintentionally, you double-click the purchase button. Instead of purchasing one ticket for your upcoming travels, you create two. The first is intentional, whereas the second is a duplicate.

Humans are primarily responsible for creating duplicate data. System architects work diligently to prevent duplicate data from being created. The best way to resolve duplicate data is to prevent its creation in the first place. One common approach to stopping duplicate data before it gets into a system is a visual warning to alert users. If you've ever purchased something online, you probably have come across a warning, such as "Please wait while your transaction is being processed. Clicking Purchase Now again may result in a duplicate charge on your credit card."

Having multiple data sources for the same data elements is also a source of duplicate data. Consider the scenario in Figure 4.1 where Allison wants to update her billing address. She speaks with Jackson, who inputs her address information into the Sales database. After some time, Allison moves and wants to update her billing address. This time, she speaks with Rachel. Instead of updating Allison's existing billing information, Rachel adds a new billing address. At this point, Allison has duplicate data in the Sales system.

To resolve duplicate data issues, the company has a duplicate resolution process. This process looks for customers with multiple billing addresses, validates the correct address, and updates the Sales database by removing the duplicate record.

FIGURE 4.1   Duplicate data resolution process

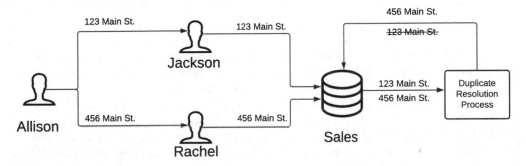

Redundant Data

While duplicate data typically comes from accidental data entry, redundant data happens when the same data elements exist in multiple places within a system. Frequently, data redundancy is a function of integrating multiple systems.

For example, multiple source systems that perform different business functions and use shared data elements create the conditions for data redundancy. When a record changes in one system, there is no guarantee that its new value changes in another system. Since there is no certainty of data synchronization, a data element can have conflicting values across systems. When integrating multiple data sources, dealing with redundant data is a persistent challenge.

Figure 4.2 illustrates two transactional systems feeding a single data warehouse. In this illustration, the Sales ETL Job connects to the sales database and copies data into the warehouse. Independently, the Accounting ETL Job copies accounting data into the warehouse.

Suppose a salesperson enters a customer's address information into the Sales system. After the customer places an order, an accounting clerk enters the same address information into the Accounting system for billing purposes. Now that the same information exists in two places, the potential for a data redundancy problem exists.

FIGURE 4.2   Illustration of multiple data sources

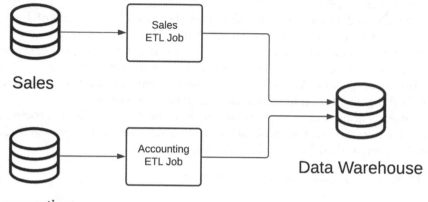

Suppose the salesperson processes an address change after talking with a customer. The Sales system would have the new address, making the Accounting system out of date. Different systems have different addresses for the same customer.

The customer's address in the data warehouse depends on how the ETL jobs function. Recall from Chapter 3 that ETL jobs can be either a full load, replacing data entirely, or a delta load, moving only changes between systems. If they perform a full reload and the Accounting ETL Job processes before Sales, the old address ends up in the warehouse. If the ETL jobs perform delta loads, the new address ends up in the warehouse since its value in the Sales system is more recent than in the Accounting system. Either way, the address data in the transactional systems contain different values.

There are several options for resolving redundant data. One approach synchronizes changes to shared data elements between the Accounting and Sales systems. However, technical or political realities can make synchronizing source systems unfeasible.

Figure 4.3 illustrates how an integrated ETL approach addresses this redundant data problem while maintaining accurate historical data. This integrated ETL process takes a delta load approach. When an address changes, the ETL job sets the effective end date for the old address and inserts a new row for the current address. The additional ETL logic ensures that the warehouse contains the correct values. While the data discrepancy between the Sales and Accounting systems still needs resolution, the analyst has the proper customer address in the data warehouse.

FIGURE 4.3   Resolving redundancy with an integrated ETL process

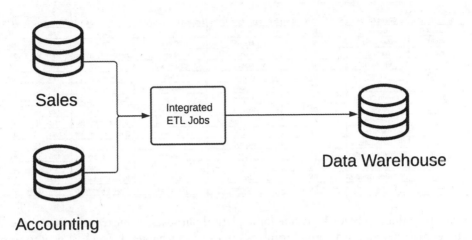

Another root cause of data redundancy is an inappropriate database design. For example, consulting companies bill clients by the hour. To that end, consultants need to keep track of client projects, employees, and job roles. Figure 4.4 illustrates a poorly designed transactional table for storing billing information.

FIGURE 4.4   Redundant data

	A	B	C	D	E	F	G	H
1	Project Number	Client Name	Employee Number	Employee First Name	Employee Last Name	Job Class	Bill Rate	Billable Hours
2	42523	Bosch	68	Isabel	Diehl	DBA	175	40
3	95003	Tenneco	68	Isabel	Diehl	DBA	175	35
4	95003	Tenneco	68	Isabel	Diehl	DevOps Engineer	215	28
5	42523	Bosch	69	Roland	Clem	Developer	128	150
6	37724	Johnson Controls	80	Igor	Stravinsky	Developer	128	304
7	37724	Johnson Controls	492	Johann	Bach	Senior Developer	200	58
8	95003	Tenneco	69	Roland	Clem	Developer	128	103
9	95003	Tenneco	73	Ferdinand	Kamienski	Project Manager	190	40
10	95003	Tenneco	39	Bruce	Logan	DevOps Engineer	215	67
11	30243	ZF Friedrichshafen	69	Roland	Clem	Developer	128	43
12	30243	ZF Friedrichshafen	80	Igor	Stravinsky	Developer	128	64
13	30243	ZF Friedrichshafen	492	Johann	Bach	Senior Developer	200	86
14	30243	ZF Friedrichshafen	39	Bruce	Logan	DevOps Engineer	215	57
15	30243	ZF Friedrichshafen	73	Ferdinand	Kamienski	Project Manager	190	40

Examining Figure 4.4 more closely, there are multiple redundant data issues. Rows 2, 3, and 4 illustrate Isabel Diehl's billable hours and job roles on the Bosch and Tenneco projects. The only meaningful difference between these rows is the Project Number, Client Name, Job Class, and Billable Hours. The other data elements are all redundant.

For example, suppose Isabel changes her last name and works on a new project, as Figure 4.5 shows. Since this is a transactional table, Isabel's last name should change in rows 2, 3, and 4. Similarly, if the consulting organization wants to increase the bill rate for a developer, rows 6, 7, 9, 12, and 13 all have to change.

FIGURE 4.5 Name change issue

Project Number	Client Name	Employee Number	Employee First Name	Employee Last Name	Job Class	Bill Rate	Billable Hours
42523	Bosch	68	Isabel	Diehl	DBA	175	40
95003	Tenneco	68	Isabel	Diehl	DBA	175	35
95003	Tenneco	68	Isabel	Diehl	DevOps Engineer	215	28
69937	Akrapovič	68	Isabel	Chanteaux	DBA	175	35
42523	Bosch	69	Roland	Clem	Developer	128	150
37724	Johnson Controls	80	Igor	Stravinsky	Developer	128	304
37724	Johnson Controls	492	Johann	Bach	Senior Developer	200	58
95003	Tenneco	69	Roland	Clem	Developer	128	103
95003	Tenneco	73	Ferdinand	Kamienski	Project Manager	190	40
95003	Tenneco	39	Bruce	Logan	DevOps Engineer	215	67
30243	ZF Friedrichshafen	69	Roland	Clem	Developer	128	43
30243	ZF Friedrichshafen	80	Igor	Stravinsky	Developer	128	64
30243	ZF Friedrichshafen	492	Johann	Bach	Senior Developer	200	86
30243	ZF Friedrichshafen	39	Bruce	Logan	DevOps Engineer	215	57
30243	ZF Friedrichshafen	73	Ferdinand	Kamienski	Project Manager	190	40

While the table in Figure 4.5 is fine for analytical purposes, it illustrates why transactional databases are often in third normal form, as discussed in Chapter 3. The best way to resolve a data redundancy issue is by restructuring the tables. Figure 4.6 provides an example of solving data redundancy through restructuring.

FIGURE 4.6 Transactional design

Project Number	Client Name
30243	ZF Friedrichshafen
37724	Johnson Controls
42523	Bosch
69937	Akrapovič
95003	Tenneco

Project Number	Employee Number	Job Class	Billable Hours
30243	39	DevOps Engineer	57
95003	39	DevOps Engineer	67
42523	68	DBA	40
95003	68	DBA	35
69937	68	DBA	35
95003	68	DevOps Engineer	28
30243	69	Developer	43
42523	69	Developer	150
95003	69	Developer	103
30243	73	Project Manager	40
95003	73	Project Manager	40
30243	80	Developer	64
37724	80	Developer	304
30243	492	Senior Developer	86
37724	492	Senior Developer	58

Employee Number	Employee First Name	Employee Last Name
39	Bruce	Logan
68	Isabel	Chanteaux
69	Roland	Clem
73	Ferdinand	Kamienski
80	Igor	Stravinsky
492	Johann	Bach

Job Class	Bill Rate
DBA	175
Developer	128
DevOps Engineer	215
Project Manager	190
Senior Developer	200

In Figure 4.6, there are tables for storing information on projects and employees. The associative table connects employees, their job class, and their role on a project. With this design, no data attribute exists redundantly.

Missing Values

Another issue that impacts data quality is the concept of missing values. *Missing values* occur when you expect an attribute to contain data but nothing is there. Missing values are also known as null values. A *null value* is the absence of a value. A null is not a space, blank, or other character. There are situations when allowing nulls makes sense. Suppose you are storing data about people and have a column for Middle Initial. Since not everyone has a middle initial, the Middle Initial column should be optional. When a column optionally contains data, it is *nullable*, meaning the column can contain null values. However, be aware that having nulls in a dataset poses calculation challenges.

Suppose a temperature sensor logs the maximum observed temperature to a table daily, as shown in Figure 4.7. An analyst expects the Temperature column to contain a value for each date. However, there was a failure on January 4, 2020, and while a record for that date exists, no temperature data is present. Since the value for Temperature for that date is absent, its value is null.

FIGURE 4.7   Missing temperature value

	A	B
1	*Date*	*Temperature*
2	1/1/2020	17
3	1/2/2020	15
4	1/3/2020	14
5	1/4/2020	
6	1/5/2020	15
7	1/6/2020	16
8	1/7/2020	17
9	1/8/2020	10
10	1/9/2020	8
11	1/10/2020	2
12	1/11/2020	-2
13	1/12/2020	6
14	1/13/2020	9
15	1/14/2020	16
16	1/15/2020	13

Null values present several challenges depending on the tools you use to analyze data. For example, if you use the AVG function in SQL to find the numeric average of the data from Figure 4.7, you will get a number because the AVG function excludes null values.

However, if you read a CSV file using the Python or R programming language, the null value for January 4th poses a problem. Trying to calculate the average, which was successful in SQL, results in an error in Python and R as the equivalent functions in those languages do not handle null values.

To handle missing values, you first have to check for their existence. SQL offers functions to check for null and functions that can replace a null with a user-specified value. There are similar functions in both Python and R.

Invalid Data

Invalid data are values outside the valid range for a given attribute. An invalid value violates a business rule instead of having an incorrect data type. As such, you have to understand the context of a system to determine whether or not a value is invalid.

For example, consider the temperature sensor that generates the data in Figure 4.7. The Date column has a date data type, and the Temperature column is numeric. Let's presume the temperature sensor measures external air temperature in Fahrenheit and that it is somewhere on Earth. With those constraints in mind, consider the data in Figure 4.8.

FIGURE 4.8   Invalid temperature value

	A	B
1	*Date*	*Temperature*
2	1/1/2020	17
3	1/2/2020	15
4	1/3/2020	14
5	1/4/2020	-99999
6	1/5/2020	15
7	1/6/2020	16
8	1/7/2020	17
9	1/8/2020	10
10	1/9/2020	8
11	1/10/2020	2
12	1/11/2020	-2
13	1/12/2020	6
14	1/13/2020	9
15	1/14/2020	16
16	1/15/2020	13

All of the values in Figure 4.8 belong to their respective data type. Historically, temperatures on Earth are between −140 and 140 degrees Fahrenheit. With this context, it becomes clear that −99,999 is an unrealistic value for temperature. The value is clearly invalid despite being numeric.

Invalid values violate business rules, not technical rules. For example, −99,999 is a valid number, but it is an invalid temperature for a location on Earth. As such, programming languages do not have native functions that definitively tell you whether or not a given value is invalid. It's up to you, as a data professional, to work with software developers to create these rules based on the unique needs of your organization. When considering data types, numeric and date data is comparatively easy to check for invalid values.

Text data is more complex. One thing that leads to invalid character data is an absence of referential integrity within a database. If two tables have a relationship but no foreign keys, the conditions for invalid character data exist. Implementing relationships appropriately reduces the likelihood of invalid character data. As you learned in Chapter 3, implementing referential integrity is an excellent way to improve data quality.

Nonparametric data

Nonparametric data is data collected from categorical variables, which you read about in Chapter 2, "Understanding Data." Sometimes the categories indicate differentiation, and sometimes they have a rank order associated with them. In this latter case, the rank order of the values is of significance, not the individual values themselves.

For example, suppose a person has abdominal pain and seeks medical attention. The doctor asks the person to rate their pain on a scale of 0 to 10. Since individuals experience pain differently, the scale in Figure 4.9 helps people put their discomfort in context.

FIGURE 4.9   Pain rating scale

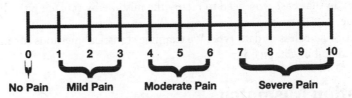

Suppose the person answers 8 in response to the "rate your pain" question. While the number 8 means nothing on its own, it equates to severe pain using the scale in Figure 4.9. With that context, the doctor checks for appendicitis and might order an X-ray or ultrasound to further inform treatment options.

On the other hand, suppose the person says their pain level is a 1. Instead of ordering additional tests, the doctor could rule out appendicitis and advise a carbonated beverage or antacid to relieve the comparatively mild distress.

We will explore nonparametric data and statistical approaches to testing it in greater detail in Chapter 5, "Data Analysis and Statistics."

Data Outliers

A *data outlier* is a value that differs significantly from other observations in a dataset. Consider the real estate sale price example in Figure 4.10. All of the properties are on the same street, city, and state. Most of the properties have a sale price between $128,000 and $153,000. However, the property at 130 Main Street has a sale price of $26,496,400. That is a dramatic difference from the rest of the sales prices.

FIGURE 4.10   Real estate sales outlier

	A	B	C	D
1	**Address**	**City**	**State**	**Sale Price**
2	123 Main St	Sampletown	Iowa	$130,000
3	124 Main St	Sampletown	Iowa	$153,000
4	125 Main St	Sampletown	Iowa	$134,000
5	126 Main St	Sampletown	Iowa	$142,000
6	127 Main St	Sampletown	Iowa	$148,000
7	128 Main St	Sampletown	Iowa	$128,000
8	129 Main St	Sampletown	Iowa	$137,000
9	130 Main St	Sampletown	Iowa	$26,496,400
10	131 Main St	Sampletown	Iowa	$144,000

With outliers, you need to understand why they exist and whether they are valid in the context of your analysis. For example, suppose you investigate why the property at 130 Main Street is more expensive than the other properties on the same street. During your investigation, you find that 130 Main Street is a commercial property, while all the other properties are residential dwellings. If your analysis is on residential real estate prices, you want to remove 130 Main Street from the dataset.

If 130 Main Street is not a commercial property, it is possible that a data entry error created the outlier. In that case, you need to rectify the mistake by replacing the bad data with the actual value.

Outliers exist regardless of data type. We examine statistical methods for identifying outliers in greater detail in Chapter 5.

Specification Mismatch

A specification describes the target value for a component. A *specification mismatch* occurs when an individual component's characteristics are beyond the range of acceptable values. For example, suppose you want to add a room to a house and you buy 15 wooden studs. Looking at the blueprint for the addition, you need wooden studs with a rectangular cross-section measuring 2 inches by 4 inches (2×4). When purchasing the studs, you want to ensure that all 15 have a consistent cross-section.

Selecting boards at the local home improvement store, you notice that one doesn't match the other 14. Getting out your tape measure, you find that its cross-section is 2 inches by 6 inches (2×6). While 2×6 is a common size for dimensional lumber, there is a specification mismatch as that specific board doesn't match your blueprint. To prevent complications while building the addition, you put the 2×6 back on the shelf and find a 2×4.

In manufacturing, a specification mismatch causes a component to fail post-production quality checks. Understanding a specification's tolerance is crucial to maintaining quality. For example, if a 2×4 is off by a 16th of an inch, it is suitable for use. However, that same measurement discrepancy isn't appropriate for an artificial heart valve.

When data is invalid, it has values that fall outside a given range. On the other hand, a specification mismatch occurs when data doesn't conform to its destination data type. For example, you might be loading data from a file into a database. If the destination column is numeric and you have text data, you'll end up with a specification mismatch. To resolve this mismatch, you must validate that the inbound data consistently map to its target data type.

Data Type Validation

Data type validation ensures that values in a dataset have a consistent data type. Consider the schema excerpt in Figure 4.11. The primary keys for both the Manufacturer and Model expect integer values, while the Manufacturer_Name and Model_Name are characters. Recall from Chapter 3 that the foreign key on Manufacturer_ID enforces referential integrity between the two tables.

FIGURE 4.11   Automotive schema excerpt

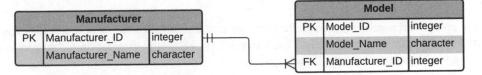

Now imagine that you need to load the data from Figure 4.12 into the schema in Figure 4.11. The first nine rows load successfully, while the 10th row fails because the identifier consists of two asterisks, which is not a valid integer.

How the load process handles the data type validation failure determines whether or not the remaining rows load successfully. Depending on the tool, a single failure may cause the load process to stop. Alternatively, the load process might write each failed record to an error file before loading the remaining records.

FIGURE 4.12   List of automotive manufacturers

	A	B
1	*Identifier*	*Manufacturer*
2	1	Lexus
3	2	Lincoln
4	3	Maserati
5	4	Mazda
6	5	Mercedes-Benz
7	6	MINI
8	7	Mitsubishi
9	8	Nissan
10	9	Pontiac
11	**	Porsche
12	11	RAM
13	12	Scion
14	13	Subaru
15	14	Toyota
16	15	Volkswagen
17	16	Volvo

Programming languages, including SQL, Python, and R, all have data type validation functions. Use these functions to validate the data type for each column in a data file before attempting a database load. It's in your best interest to detect and remediate data type issues as early as possible to ensure data is ready for analysis.

Data Manipulation Techniques

There are several potential issues to be aware of and account for when working with data. With those possibilities in mind, let's explore some of the data manipulation techniques you can use to resolve potential data quality issues.

Recoding Data

Recoding data is a technique you can use to map original values for a variable into new values to facilitate analysis. Recoding groups data into multiple categories, creating a *categorical variable*. A categorical variable is either nominal or ordinal. *Nominal* variables are any variable with two or more categories where there is no natural order of the categories, like hair color or eye color. *Ordinal* variables are categories with an inherent rank. For example, T-shirt size is an example of an ordinal variable, as sizes come in small, medium, large, and extra large. Variable values fit into a fixed number of categories, similar to how lookup tables work in Chapter 3. Recoding is helpful when you have numeric data you want to analyze by category.

For example, suppose a hospital administrator gives you the data in Figure 4.13 and asks you to determine how many people entering an emergency room report moderate pain according to the pain scale in Figure 4.9. The pain levels on the scale belong to the categories No Pain, Mild Pain, Moderate Pain, and Severe Pain. Since these groupings exist, the pain scale is categorical. The data you have is numeric, whereas the administrator is asking to understand it by category.

FIGURE 4.13   Patient pain data

	A	B
1	*Patient_ID*	*Reported_Pain*
2	1054	3
3	1055	1
4	1056	5
5	1057	3
6	1058	2
7	1059	9
8	1060	10
9	1061	4
10	1062	9
11	1063	3

To complete this analysis, you recode the numeric data and create a categorical variable. Recoding maps the numeric value to the appropriate category. You can implement recoding logic regardless of the programming language you use. Figure 4.14 illustrates the recoding process. Note that you create the Pain_Category column. With this new categorical variable, you are ready to inform the administrator that two people reported moderate pain.

FIGURE 4.14   Recoded patient pain data

Original Data	→	Recoding Logic	→	New Categorical Variable

	A	B
1	Patient_ID	Reported_Pain
2	1054	3
3	1055	1
4	1056	5
5	1057	3
6	1058	2
7	1059	9
8	1060	10
9	1061	4
10	1062	9
11	1063	3

```
# Recoding in Python
if Reported_Pain == 0:
    Pain_Category = "None"
elif 0 < Reported_Pain <= 3:
    Pain_Category = "Mild"
elif 3 < Reported_Pain <= 6:
    Pain_Category = "Moderate"
elif 6 < Reported_Pain <= 10:
    Pain_Category = "Severe"
else:
    Pain_Category = "Invalid"
```

	A	B	C
1	Patient_ID	Reported_Pain	Pain_Category
2	1054	3	Mild
3	1055	1	Mild
4	1056	5	Moderate
5	1057	3	Mild
6	1058	2	Mild
7	1059	9	Severe
8	1060	10	Severe
9	1061	4	Moderate
10	1062	9	Severe
11	1063	3	Mild

Derived Variables

A *derived variable* is a new variable resulting from a calculation on an existing variable. In the case of the recoded data in Figure 4.14, the *Pain_Category* categorical variable is an example of a derived variable. However, derived variables don't have to be categorical. Consider the patient data in Figure 4.15 consisting of a unique identifier, first and last name, and date of birth.

FIGURE 4.15   Patient data

	A	B	C	D
1	Patient_ID	First_Name	Last_Name	Date_of_Birth
2	1054	Maurene	Easton	1/29/1994
3	1055	Stewart	Atterberry	4/10/2001
4	1056	Vince	Clifford	8/12/1978
5	1057	Diana	Ivers	10/30/1990
6	1058	Bruce	Hutson	9/13/2015
7	1059	Wilda	Duke	3/8/1970
8	1060	Darnell	Styles	11/25/1989
9	1061	Vance	Whitehead	12/2/2011
10	1062	Houston	Koop	1/17/1987
11	1063	Sarah	Babcock	7/26/1996

A person's date of birth doesn't change over time. However, the person's age is a function of the current date. Suppose you need to conduct age-related analysis on patients as of January 1, 2022. Figure 4.16 illustrates deriving an Age variable using Date_of_Birth. Storing age as a derived column is a bad practice, as it would need constant updates over time. Instead of keeping age as a derived variable, you should embed the formula to derive age in code. That way, you derive the value of Age exactly when you need it, and you avoid potential age-related data errors.

FIGURE 4.16   Deriving age

Original Data $\longrightarrow$ Derivation Logic $\longrightarrow$ New Derived Variable

Patient_ID	First_Name	Last_Name	Date_of_Birth
1054	Maurene	Easton	1/29/1994
1055	Stewart	Atterberry	4/10/2001
1056	Vince	Clifford	8/12/1978
1057	Diana	Ivers	10/30/1990
1058	Bruce	Hutson	9/13/2015
1059	Wilda	Duke	3/8/1970
1060	Darnell	Styles	11/25/1989
1061	Vance	Whitehead	12/2/2011
1062	Houston	Koop	1/17/1987
1063	Sarah	Babcock	7/26/1996

Age = 1/1/2022 - Date_of_Birth

Patient_ID	First_Name	Last_Name	Date_of_Birth	Age
1054	Maurene	Easton	1/29/1994	28
1055	Stewart	Atterberry	4/10/2001	21
1056	Vince	Clifford	8/12/1978	44
1057	Diana	Ivers	10/30/1990	32
1058	Bruce	Hutson	9/13/2015	7
1059	Wilda	Duke	3/8/1970	52
1060	Darnell	Styles	11/25/1989	33
1061	Vance	Whitehead	12/2/2011	11
1062	Houston	Koop	1/17/1987	35
1063	Sarah	Babcock	7/26/1996	26

Data Merge

A *data merge* uses a common variable to combine multiple datasets with different structures into a single dataset. Merging data improves data quality by adding new variables to your existing data. Additional variables make for a richer dataset, which positively impacts the quality of your analysis. ETL processes commonly append data while transforming data for use in analytical environments.

Since a data merge adds columns to a dataset, merging gives you additional data about a specific observation. Imagine you want to get an overall picture of a person's health. To get the data, you obtain records from the person's primary care physician and other medical specialists. You also get self-reported dietary and exercise habits. Figure 4.17 illustrates merging these sources of data. You can imagine the resulting table as having additional columns, as you are augmenting the amount of data about each person in the population.

FIGURE 4.17   Merging disparate data

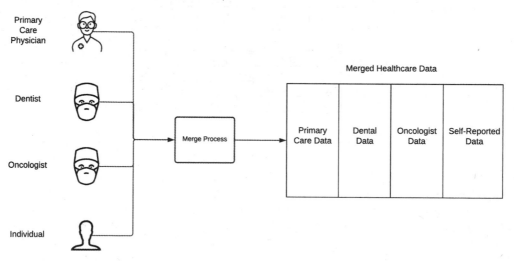

Consider the systems that support a university. When a person applies, the university stores data, including admissions essays, high school transcripts, letters of recommendation, and standardized test scores. Upon becoming a student, a person generates academic data, including course enrollment and grades. Some students have work-study jobs, which create payroll data, including hours worked and hourly rate.

Suppose you want to examine factors that contribute to academic success. In the interest of improving data quality, you decide to include applicant and admission data in addition to student data. You want all of this data in a single table to facilitate advanced analytical techniques, so you perform a data append as part of the ETL process in Figure 4.18.

FIGURE 4.18   ETL and the data merge approach

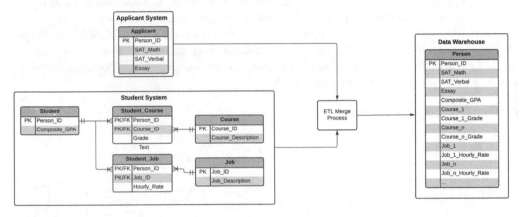

Data Blending

Data blending combines multiple sources of data into a single dataset at the reporting layer. While data blending is conceptually similar to the extract, transform, and load process in Chapter 3, there is a crucial difference. Recall that ETL processes operate on a schedule, copying data from source systems into analytics environments. Business requirements drive the scheduling, such as near real-time, hourly, daily, weekly, monthly, or annually. Typically, an organization's IT department designs, builds, operates, and maintains ETL processes.

Data blending differs from ETL in that it allows an analyst to combine datasets in an ad hoc manner without saving the blended dataset in a relational database. Instead of the blended dataset persisting over time, it exists only at the reporting layer, not in the source databases.

For example, data visualization tools such as Tableau allow analysts to connect to different source systems and blend the data using a shared attribute. Data blending can reduce the burden on IT as it gives analysts the ability to merge data.

One important consideration is the level of knowledge the analyst has to have to be productive. Consider the illustration in Figure 4.19. With the traditional ETL workflow, the analyst needs to understand the data warehouse's structure to create a visualization. For routine analysis, such as weekly profitability, the ETL approach works well.

FIGURE 4.19 Extract, transform, and load process

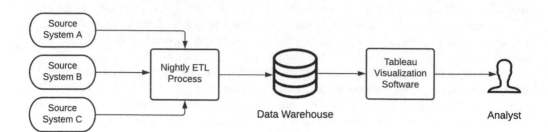

Now suppose the analyst sees a dramatic shift in profitability, and leadership wants to understand the cause. The analyst can blend data from additional sources with the data warehouse to shed light on the profitability change, as shown in Figure 4.20. While this type of analysis does not modify ETL processes, the analyst must understand how data maps across systems. Where data warehouses enforce referential integrity, the accuracy of blended data depends on the analyst's domain knowledge.

FIGURE 4.20 Data blending

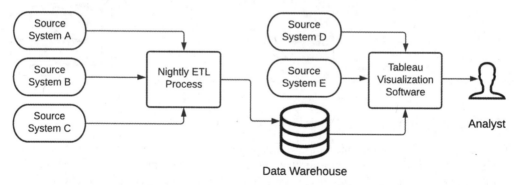

Exam Tip

As you prepare for the Data+ exam, remember that ETL/ELT processes are programmatic and operate on a schedule, resulting in a merged dataset that persists at the data layer. After creation, ETL/ELT processes perform the same action on a routine basis. While conceptually similar, data blending combines data at the visualization layer and allows an analyst to integrate additional data sources in an ad hoc, exploratory manner. ETL/ELT connects data at the database layer whereas data blending connects data at the visualization layer.

Concatenation

Concatenation is the merging of separate variables into a single variable. Concatenation is a highly effective technique when dealing with a source system that stores components of a single variable in multiple columns. The need for concatenation frequently occurs when dealing with date and time data. Concatenation is also useful when generating address information. For example, suppose you want to send an email campaign using first and last names from independent columns. You can concatenate the first and last names together for use in the campaign.

FIGURE 4.21   Creating a date variable with concatenation

	Source Data						Concatenation		Concatenated Data		
Reporting_Station	**Temperature**	**Day**	**Month**	**Year**					**Reporting_Station**	**Temperature**	**Date**
RINK_01	28	1	1	2022					RINK_01	28	1/1/2022
RINK_01	29	2	1	2022					RINK_01	29	1/2/2022
RINK_01	26	3	1	2022			Concatenate		RINK_01	26	1/3/2022
RINK_01	27	4	1	2022			Day, Month,		RINK_01	27	1/4/2022
RINK_01	24	5	1	2022			Year		RINK_01	24	1/5/2022
RINK_01	24	6	1	2022					RINK_01	24	1/6/2022
RINK_01	29	7	1	2022					RINK_01	29	1/7/2022
RINK_01	22	8	1	2022					RINK_01	22	1/8/2022
RINK_01	21	9	1	2022					RINK_01	21	1/9/2022
RINK_01	20	10	1	2022					RINK_01	20	1/10/2022

Suppose you are working on aggregating temperature sensor data for the National Weather Service. On the left side of Figure 4.21 is a data sample from a weather station in North Kingston, Rhode Island. Note that the sensor stores the day, month, and year as individual numeric variables. To make it easier to use date functions in your analysis tools, you want to merge the day, month, and year into a single date variable. Combining this data is a straightforward activity, as programming languages, including SQL, Python, and R, have functions that make concatenation easy.

Data Append

A *data append* combines multiple data sources with the same structure, resulting in a new dataset containing all the rows from the original datasets. When appending data, you save the result as a new dataset for ongoing analysis.

Imagine you are a meteorologist working on a weather report for the evening national news. To improve the accuracy of your forecast, you want current data from as many locations across the country area as possible and rely on the National Weather Service (NWS) to provide this data.

In turn, the NWS appends data from multiple individual weather stations before making it available. A particular weather station collects weather data and then transmits it via an API to an NWS server. The server appends the data, giving you a reliable source on which to base your forecast. Figure 4.22 illustrates this append scenario.

FIGURE 4.22   Appending weather data

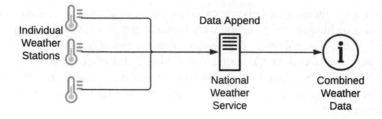

Consider the needs of a franchisor with multiple franchisee locations. Although each franchise operates independently, they use the same point of sales system. When the franchisor conducts aggregate sales analysis, it appends data from each franchisee's point of sales system into a single, unified table for ongoing analysis.

Imputation

Imputation is a technique for dealing with missing values by replacing them with substitutes. When merging multiple data sources, you may end up with a dataset with many nulls in a given column. If you are collecting sensor data, it is possible to have missing values due to collection or transmission issues.

For example, Figure 4.23 is a log of someone who tracks their weight daily. Looking at the data, we see four days where there is no recorded weight.

FIGURE 4.23   Weight log with missing values

	A	B	C
1	**Day**	**Date**	**Weight**
2	Fri	2/12/2021	189.4
3	Sat	2/13/2021	
4	Sun	2/14/2021	
5	Mon	2/15/2021	190.0
6	Tue	2/16/2021	187.4
7	Wed	2/17/2021	188.6
8	Thu	2/18/2021	187.4
9	Fri	2/19/2021	
10	Sat	2/20/2021	
11	Sun	2/21/2021	190.0
12	Mon	2/22/2021	189.0
13	Tue	2/23/2021	189.4
14	Wed	2/24/2021	190.6
15	Thu	2/25/2021	189.6

There are many potential reasons why the data is missing. Perhaps the person is using a smart scale, and the scale lost its network connection. It could be that the person is using a manual scale and forgot to record the value. Another possibility is that the person didn't get on the scale on those four days. Regardless of the reason, the analyst has to decide how to handle the missing data. Here are a few approaches an analyst can use for imputing values:

- **Remove Missing Data:** With this approach, you can remove rows with missing values without impacting the quality of your overall analysis.

- **Replace with Zero:** With this approach, you replace missing values with a zero. Whether or not it is appropriate to replace missing data with a zero is contextual. In this case, zero isn't an appropriate value, as a person's weight should be a positive number. In addition, replacing a zero in this case has an extraordinary impact on the overall average weight.

- **Replace with Overall Average:** Instead of using a zero, you can compute the average Weight value for all rows that have data and then replace the missing Weight values with that calculated average.

- **Replace with Most Frequent (Mode):** Alternatively, you can take the most frequently occurring value, called the *mode*, and use that as the constant.

- **Closest Value Average:** With this approach, you use the values from the rows before and after the missing values. For example, to replace the missing measurements for 2/13/2021 and 2/14/2021, take the values from 2/12/2021 and 2/15/2021 to compute the average.

Figure 4.24 illustrates the impact of four of these approaches to imputation on the overall average for this dataset. Chapter 5 explores this in greater detail.

FIGURE 4.24   Various imputation techniques

Day	Date	Weight	Zero	Overall_Average	Most_Often (Mode)	Closest_Value_Average
Fri	2/12/2021	189.4	189.4	189.4	189.4	189.4
Sat	2/13/2021		0.0	189.1	187.4	189.7
Sun	2/14/2021		0.0	189.1	187.4	189.7
Mon	2/15/2021	190.0	190.0	190.0	190.0	190.0
Tue	2/16/2021	187.4	187.4	187.4	187.4	187.4
Wed	2/17/2021	188.6	188.6	188.6	188.6	188.6
Thu	2/18/2021	187.4	187.4	187.4	187.4	187.4
Fri	2/19/2021		0.0	189.1	187.4	188.7
Sat	2/20/2021		0.0	189.1	188.7	188.7
Sun	2/21/2021	190.0	190.0	190.0	190.0	190.0
Mon	2/22/2021	189.0	189.0	189.0	189.0	189.0
Tue	2/23/2021	189.4	189.4	189.4	189.4	189.4
Wed	2/24/2021	190.6	190.6	190.6	190.6	190.6
Thu	2/25/2021	189.6	189.6	189.6	189.6	189.6
	Overall Average	**189.1**	**135.1**	**189.1**	**188.7**	**189.2**

Reduction

When dealing with big data, it is frequently unfeasible and inefficient to manipulate the entire dataset during analysis. *Reduction* is the process of shrinking an extensive dataset without negatively impacting its analytical value. There are a variety of reduction techniques from which you can choose. Selecting a method depends on the type of data you have and what you are trying to analyze. Dimensionality reduction and numerosity reduction are two techniques for data reduction.

Dimensionality Reduction

One reduction technique is *dimensionality reduction*, which removes attributes from a dataset. Removing attributes reduces the dataset's overall size. For instance, suppose you want to explore a person's weight as a function of time using the Weight Log data in Figure 4.25. Although the Weight Log has 12 attributes, you only need Date and Weight for your purposes. If you end up needing the day of the week for future analysis, you can derive it from the values in the Date column.

FIGURE 4.25 Dimensionality reduction example

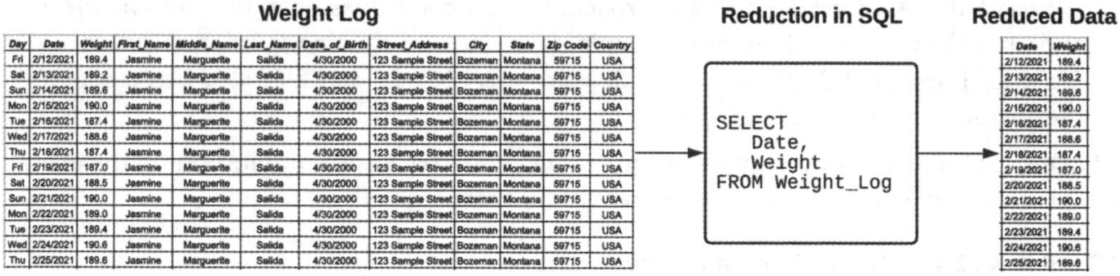

Weight Log

Day	Date	Weight	First_Name	Middle_Name	Last_Name	Date_of_Birth	Street_Address	City	State	Zip Code	Country
Fri	2/12/2021	189.4	Jasmine	Marguerite	Salida	4/30/2000	123 Sample Street	Bozeman	Montana	59715	USA
Sat	2/13/2021	189.2	Jasmine	Marguerite	Salida	4/30/2000	123 Sample Street	Bozeman	Montana	59715	USA
Sun	2/14/2021	189.6	Jasmine	Marguerite	Salida	4/30/2000	123 Sample Street	Bozeman	Montana	59715	USA
Mon	2/15/2021	190.0	Jasmine	Marguerite	Salida	4/30/2000	123 Sample Street	Bozeman	Montana	59715	USA
Tue	2/16/2021	187.4	Jasmine	Marguerite	Salida	4/30/2000	123 Sample Street	Bozeman	Montana	59715	USA
Wed	2/17/2021	188.6	Jasmine	Marguerite	Salida	4/30/2000	123 Sample Street	Bozeman	Montana	59715	USA
Thu	2/18/2021	187.4	Jasmine	Marguerite	Salida	4/30/2000	123 Sample Street	Bozeman	Montana	59715	USA
Fri	2/19/2021	187.0	Jasmine	Marguerite	Salida	4/30/2000	123 Sample Street	Bozeman	Montana	59715	USA
Sat	2/20/2021	188.5	Jasmine	Marguerite	Salida	4/30/2000	123 Sample Street	Bozeman	Montana	59715	USA
Sun	2/21/2021	190.0	Jasmine	Marguerite	Salida	4/30/2000	123 Sample Street	Bozeman	Montana	59715	USA
Mon	2/22/2021	189.0	Jasmine	Marguerite	Salida	4/30/2000	123 Sample Street	Bozeman	Montana	59715	USA
Tue	2/23/2021	189.4	Jasmine	Marguerite	Salida	4/30/2000	123 Sample Street	Bozeman	Montana	59715	USA
Wed	2/24/2021	190.6	Jasmine	Marguerite	Salida	4/30/2000	123 Sample Street	Bozeman	Montana	59715	USA
Thu	2/25/2021	189.6	Jasmine	Marguerite	Salida	4/30/2000	123 Sample Street	Bozeman	Montana	59715	USA

Reduced Data

Date	Weight
2/12/2021	189.4
2/13/2021	189.2
2/14/2021	189.6
2/15/2021	190.0
2/16/2021	187.4
2/17/2021	188.6
2/18/2021	187.4
2/19/2021	187.0
2/20/2021	188.5
2/21/2021	190.0
2/22/2021	189.0
2/23/2021	189.4
2/24/2021	190.6
2/25/2021	189.6

Note that Figure 4.25 illustrates dimensionality reduction using SQL. However, you can use any programming language, including Python or R, to remove dimensions.

Numerosity Reduction

Another technique is *numerosity reduction*, which reduces the overall volume of data. Suppose you are working with a decade's worth of Weight Log data from Figure 4.25, and you want to identify the most frequently occurring weight. With 365 observations per year, a decade represents 3,650 individual data points per person. If you are studying 10,000 people, the total number of data points jumps to 36.5 million. Your laptop or desktop may lack the computing power to manipulate 36.5 million records. As data volumes grow, numerosity reduction can improve the efficiency of your analysis.

One way to reduce the volume of quantitative data is by creating a *histogram*. You can create a histogram in Python, R, and many visualization-specific tools. A histogram is a diagram made up of rectangles, or bars, that show how frequently a specific value occurs. When creating a histogram, you can configure the width of a rectangle to represent a range of values.

Consider the two histograms in Figure 4.26. Both diagrams represent 10 years of Weight Log data. However, the histogram on the left is for a single person's data, whereas the one on the right uses the data for 10,000 people. Note the difference in the y-axis. When dealing with a single person, the number of observations of 190 pounds is between 600 and 700. With 10,000 people, the number swells to more than 4 million. Regardless of the number of data points, both histograms convey the number of times each weight occurs in the data.

FIGURE 4.26   Numerosity reduction with histograms

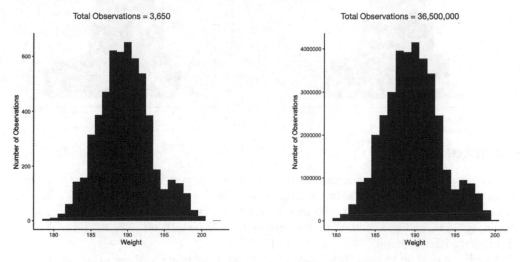

Whether you're dealing with one person or 10,000 people's data, histograms are great at reducing the number of data points you have to consider. Glancing at a histogram is a much more efficient way of analyzing data, especially when an alternative is combing through millions of rows of data.

Another approach to reducing the data is through *sampling*. Sampling is a technique that selects a subset of individual records from the initial dataset. There are many sampling approaches to take depending on dataset characteristics. The most straightforward technique is a random sample and applies in many cases. Consider the pair of histograms in Figure 4.27. The diagram on the left uses the complete data for 10,000 people, whereas the one on the right uses a random sample from the original dataset. The histograms are roughly the same shape. The big difference is in the time to produce these diagrams. A standard laptop can process the entire dataset in about 45 seconds, while creating the sample-based histogram needs only 0.2 seconds. As data volumes increase, sampling is a common approach for improving an analyst's efficiency.

FIGURE 4.27   Sampling and histograms

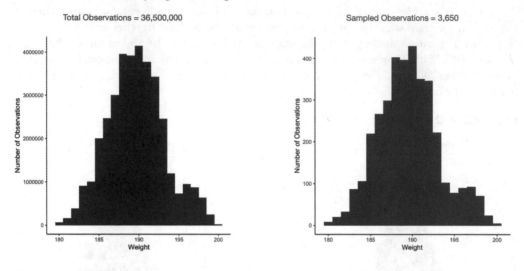

Aggregation

Data aggregation is the summarization of raw data for analysis. When you are dealing with billions of individual records, a data summary can help you make sense of it all. Recall that a daily log of activity for 10,000 people over 10 years produces 36.5 million records. You might want to know facts about the data that would be difficult to figure out looking through the data by hand.

Suppose you want to know the lowest and highest weights in the Weight Log data from Figure 4.25. Instead of searching through the data, you can use calculations that operate on the data, giving you what you need. Figure 4.28 shows some summary statistics for the complete Weight Log dataset. For example, this summary shows that the minimum weight in the dataset is 180 pounds, while the maximum is 199.8.

FIGURE 4.28   Summary statistics

```
      Weight
Min.    :180.0
1st Qu.:187.5
Median :189.6
Mean   :189.8
3rd Qu.:192.0
Max.   :199.8
```

Aggregating data provides answers that help make decisions. Imagine you are on a road trip. While traveling, running out of fuel is the last thing you want to do. Onboard computers summarize your control inputs and give you a meaningful metric: distance to empty. With an understanding of how far you can travel with the fuel remaining, you have the data you need so you can stop, refuel, and avoid being stranded.

Aggregation is also a means of controlling privacy. Suppose you have payroll information for an organization with 100,000 employees and only one chief executive officer (CEO). If you look at salary information by job role, it will expose the CEO's salary. However, if you aggregate the data and examine average compensation, the CEO's privacy is intact.

Transposition

Transposing data is when you want to turn rows into columns or columns into rows to facilitate analysis. Suppose you have sales data with details for each salesperson and their sales territory. Figure 4.29 shows a sample of this sales data. Corporate leadership likely wants to track total sales per salesperson by fiscal year. The first step is to transpose the data.

FIGURE 4.29   Sales data

SalesPersonID	280	280	280	280
FirstName	Pamela	Pamela	Pamela	Pamela
LastName	Ansman-Wolfe	Ansman-Wolfe	Ansman-Wolfe	Ansman-Wolfe
SalesTerritory	Northwest	Northwest	Northwest	Northwest
Sales	$24,432.61	$10,993.39	$4,076.39	$32,673.04
FiscalYear	2011	2012	2012	2012

When transposing, each value from a column becomes a new column. Transposing the data from Figure 4.29, you wind up with Figure 4.30. In this case, the transposed data could be more helpful, especially if you imagine thousands of rows of sales data.

FIGURE 4.30   Transposed sales data

SalesPersonID	FirstName	LastName	SalesTerritory	Sales	FiscalYear
280	Pamela	Ansman-Wolfe	Northwest	$24,432.61	2011
280	Pamela	Ansman-Wolfe	Northwest	$10,993.39	2012
280	Pamela	Ansman-Wolfe	Northwest	$4,076.39	2012
280	Pamela	Ansman-Wolfe	Northwest	$32,673.04	2012
280	Pamela	Ansman-Wolfe	Northwest	$20,628.57	2012
280	Pamela	Ansman-Wolfe	Northwest	$32,492.60	2012

To organize the data to be beneficial to leadership, you can combine transposition of the FiscalYear column with aggregation of Sales data to generate the table in Figure 4.31. Combining aggregation with transposition is a powerful data manipulation technique. With this approach to organizing the data, you get a column for each fiscal year and total sales for each salesperson by territory. This data representation makes it easy to view performance across fiscal years at a glance. This format also makes it easier to visualize data, which we will explore in detail in Chapter 7, "Data Visualization with Reports and Dashboards."

FIGURE 4.31   Combining transposition with aggregation

SalesPersonID	FirstName	LastName	SalesTerritory	FY2011	FY2012	FY2013	FY2014
286	Lynn	Tsoflias	Australia	$0.00	$0.00	$184,105.70	$1,237,705.23
282	José	Saraiva	Canada	$106,251.73	$2,171,995.26	$1,388,793.28	$2,259,378.09
278	Garrett	Vargas	Canada	$9,109.17	$1,254,087.33	$1,179,530.57	$1,166,720.15
277	Jillian	Carson	Central	$46,695.56	$3,496,243.82	$3,940,665.19	$2,582,198.97
290	Ranjit	Varkey Chudukatil	France	$0.00	$360,245.82	$1,770,366.53	$2,379,276.58
288	Rachel	Valdez	Germany	$0.00	$0.00	$371,973.20	$1,455,093.52
275	Michael	Blythe	Northeast	$63,762.92	$2,399,593.15	$3,765,459.20	$3,065,087.73
280	Pamela	Ansman-Wolfe	Northwest	$24,432.61	$1,533,075.67	$587,779.21	$1,179,815.11
283	David	Campbell	Northwest	$69,473.00	$1,291,904.81	$1,151,080.99	$1,217,486.55
284	Tete	Mensa-Annan	Northwest	$0.00	$0.00	$958,999.53	$1,353,546.16
279	Tsvi	Reiter	Southeast	$104,419.33	$3,037,174.76	$2,159,685.19	$1,869,733.48
281	Shu	Ito	Southwest	$59,708.32	$1,953,000.66	$2,439,216.08	$1,975,080.50
276	Linda	Mitchell	Southwest	$5,475.95	$3,013,884.39	$4,064,078.24	$3,283,568.85
289	Jae	Pak	United Kingdom	$0.00	$963,345.11	$4,188,307.00	$3,351,686.53

Normalization

In the context of data manipulation, normalizing data differs from our discussion of database normalization in Chapter 3. In this context, *normalizing data* converts data from different scales to the same scale. If you want to compare columns whose measurements use different units, you want to normalize the data. After normalization is complete, the dataset is ready for statistical analysis.

FIGURE 4.32   Raw athlete data

AthleteID	Weight (pounds)	Height (inches)	MileTime (seconds)
1	190.5	71	315
2	190	69	338
3	190.5	68	377
4	190	68	319
5	190	75	334
6	190	71	343
7	190	69	341
8	190	73	365
9	187.5	70	361
10	189.5	74	377
11	188.5	75	340
12	189	74	356
13	188	76	353
14	190	70	336
15	190	75	330
16	190	74	341
17	190	69	367
18	190	68	321
19	190	73	367
20	190	76	327

For example, suppose you want to compare the height and weight of a group of athletes. As Figure 4.32 shows, height is in inches, and weight uses pounds. Since inches and pounds describe different attributes, it doesn't make sense to compare the numerical values of the height and weight columns. With the data from Figure 4.32, the weight column will take on greater importance than height simply because its values are greater.

FIGURE 4.33   Scaled athlete data

AthleteID	Scaled Weight	Scaled Height	MileTime (seconds)
1	1.000	0.375	315
2	0.833	0.125	338
3	1.000	0.000	377
4	0.833	0.000	319
5	0.833	0.875	334
6	0.833	0.375	343
7	0.833	0.125	341
8	0.833	0.625	365
9	0.000	0.250	361
10	0.667	0.750	377
11	0.333	0.875	340
12	0.500	0.750	356
13	0.167	1.000	353
14	0.833	0.250	336
15	0.833	0.875	330
16	0.833	0.750	341
17	0.833	0.125	367
18	0.833	0.000	321
19	0.833	0.625	367
20	0.833	1.000	327

To compare height and weight, you need to scale the data. Figure 4.33 shows the data after using the min-max normalization technique that sets 0 and 1 as the lower and upper limits for numeric column values. Normalizing the data in this way lets you compare weight and height.

Min-Max Normalization

If you're curious about how the min-max normalization, consider its mathematical definition:

$$x' = \frac{x - min(x)}{max(x) - min(x)}$$

Let's walk through it using the Height data for AthleteID 1 in Figure 4.32. The first thing you need to do is find the minimum value of the Height column, which is 68. Then, find the maximum value of the Height column, which is 76. For AthleteID 1, the value you want to convert is 71. Once you have these values, you can plug them into the formula as follows:

$$0.375 = \frac{71 - 68}{76 - 68}$$

Min-max normalization is one of the most straightforward approaches to normalizing data. We will explore other approaches, including mean normalization and Z-score normalization, in detail in Chapter 5.

Parsing/String Manipulation

Raw data can contain columns with composite or distributed structural issues. A composite issue is when a raw data source has multiple, distinct values combined within a single character column. When this happens, each value in a composite column has data that represents more than one attribute. Composite columns need to be split into their component parts to aid analysis.

FIGURE 4.34   Splitting a composite column

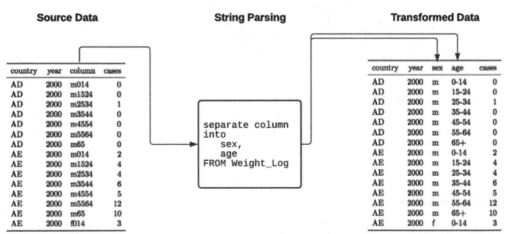

Consider the string parsing process in Figure 4.34. In the source data, one of the columns contains values representing both sex and age range. You can use string manipulation functions in your programming language of choice to convert the original column into two new columns.

Similarly, it is possible to have a distributed structural issue when data in a single column spreads across multiple columns. When that happens, you need to combine the individual columns. Whenever you have composite or distributed structural data issues, you need to manipulate the strings before starting your analysis.

FIGURE 4.35   Combining multiple columns

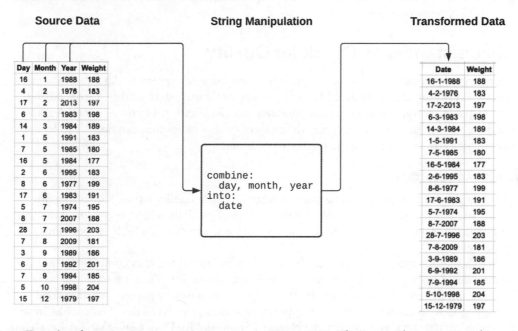

Examine the string concatenation process in Figure 4.35. The source data contains date elements in individual columns. In order to analyze the data by date, the string manipulation process combines the values from the Day, Month, and Year columns into a new Date column. Once you have a Date column, you can use programming functions to extract the day, month, and year if you need them.

You also may need to manipulate string data to improve data quality. For example, suppose you have a data source containing address information. Due to a lack of upstream data quality controls, the data you receive is inconsistent. Figure 4.36 illustrates a string transformation that brings consistency to the State data.

FIGURE 4.36   Improving data quality with string manipulation

Source Data

Street	City	State
1232 Main St	Davenport	ioWa
2922 Oak St	Pensacola	florida
38 Ash St	Grand Haven	Michigan
2716 Walnut St	Dayton	Ohio
2782 Hillcrest Lr	Moreno Valley	california

String Manipulation

```
Modify the State
column so the
first letter is
capitalized
```

Transformed Data

Street	City	State
1232 Main St	Davenport	Iowa
2922 Oak St	Pensacola	Florida
38 Ash St	Grand Haven	Michigan
2716 Walnut St	Dayton	Ohio
2782 Hillcrest Lr	Moreno Valley	California

Managing Data Quality

There are many techniques you can use to improve data quality. To be a successful analyst, you must recognize scenarios that create the conditions for data quality issues. To help you develop a mental data quality checklist, let's explore various situations and see how different data quality controls apply.

Circumstances to Check for Quality

There are numerous circumstances where it is appropriate to implement data quality control checks. Every stop along the data life-cycle journey can impact data quality. Errors during data acquisition, transformation, manipulation, and visualization all contribute to degrading data quality. You should recognize the types of quality issues that can occur and have an overarching strategy to ensure the quality of your data.

Data Acquisition

The data acquisition process is one place to introduce data quality issues. Source systems inconsistencies can result in missing or invalid values. Especially when you are working with multiple data sources, you need to understand when to double-check for potential quality gaps.

For example, suppose you work with a major international logistics company to inform routing decisions. One of the impediments to shipping is sea ice. Since it would cost too much to implement your own network of satellites to monitor the planet's weather conditions, you look to see what federal and private data sources are available. Since it has "near-real-time" in its name, you identify the National Snow and Ice Data Center's Near-Real-Time Daily Global Ice Concentration and Snow Extent data as a potential source.

However, as Figure 4.37 illustrates, the metadata for this data clearly states that it is not for real-time navigation decisions. This limitation informs whether or not this data source will work for you. Although the data is valuable and provides insight into what is currently happening with sea ice, it's not appropriate for making real-time decisions about whether a specific part of the ocean is navigable. Understanding the limitations of source data is one way to ensure data quality.

You also have to consider your data source when evaluating data quality. For example, suppose you use a website to sell automotive parts. You typically require the year, make, and model to match the right parts with customer vehicles. An optimal way to ensure data quality is to present drop-down lists for the year, make, and model. If you allow the customer to type in values for these attributes, you will have data inconsistencies. In addition to "Chevrolet," you will end up abbreviations like "Chevy" or misspellings like "Chevorlet." Positively influencing data quality as early as possible in the acquisition process will reduce your data cleaning efforts.

FIGURE 4.37 Data source description

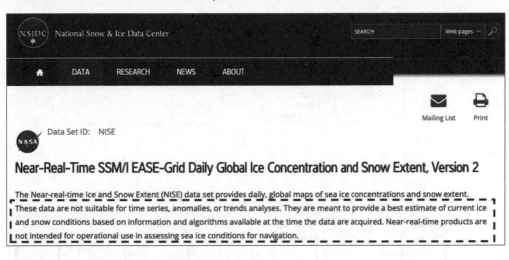

Data Transformation and Conversion

Another circumstance where quality issues can arise is during transformation. For each data source, you need to understand how many times data gets transformed before reaching the analytics environment. Figure 4.38 illustrates how customer order data flows through three different systems and ETL processes before reaching its destination. Each ETL is an intrahop within the organization and presents an opportunity to transform data incorrectly.

FIGURE 4.38 Three opportunities to impact data quality

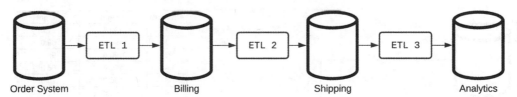

The U.S. Postal Service partners with the mailing industry to create a standardized format for address information. This standard address format aids the efficient processing and delivery of mail. Online retailers need a valid shipping address when processing customer orders. Validating the shipping address as early as possible is the best way to ensure high-quality address data.

Suppose a customer submits their address information into the ordering system. Figure 4.39 shows the difference between a customer submission and the postal standard. Specifically, the customer submission is missing the designation for avenue, and the zip code is absent. The address standardization process compares customer input with postal standards and generates a validated address. After the customer confirms the validated address, it makes its way into the order system. From that point on, the ETL processes serve as a passthrough, sending the data along without examining data values.

FIGURE 4.39 Address standardization

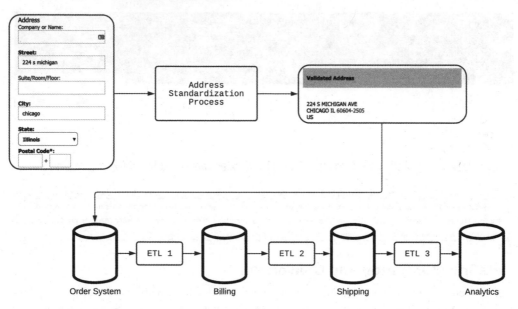

Data conversion is another possible source of data quality issues. Specifically, attribute values need to use consistent units of measure. In Figure 4.40, the values for the Weight and Height columns abruptly change starting with AthleteID 10.

FIGURE 4.40 Data conversion issue

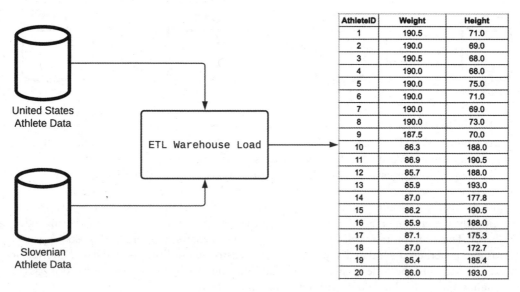

AthleteID	Weight	Height
1	190.5	71.0
2	190.0	69.0
3	190.5	68.0
4	190.0	68.0
5	190.0	75.0
6	190.0	71.0
7	190.0	69.0
8	190.0	73.0
9	187.5	70.0
10	86.3	188.0
11	86.9	190.5
12	85.7	188.0
13	85.9	193.0
14	87.0	177.8
15	86.2	190.5
16	85.9	188.0
17	87.1	175.3
18	87.0	172.7
19	85.4	185.4
20	86.0	193.0

One possible reason for this change is that the ETL process somehow transposed the values for Weight and Height. However, the source of this inconsistency is a conversion issue. AthleteIDs 1 through 10 are coming from the U.S. Athlete Data source, which has Weight in pounds and Height in inches. Starting with AthleteID 10, the remaining records are from the Slovenian Athlete Data source, which uses the metric system. As such, Weight is in kilograms and Height is in centimeters. To fix this conversion issue, you need to modify the ETL Warehouse Load process to be aware of the source data differences and convert the data appropriately.

Data Manipulation

Recall that a data manipulation language defines table structures within a relational database. Data manipulation occurs when data is reshaped as part of an ETL process. Suppose that in Figure 4.39, the Analytics database has a snowflake schema while the Order, Billing, and Shipping databases are in third normal form. The ETL 3 process has to denormalize the transactional data in preparation for the analytics environment. As part of this manipulation, it is possible to introduce errors.

Figure 4.41 illustrates two different ETL scenarios that focus exclusively on manipulating the zip code. In reality, zip code is just one of many attributes that are manipulated when moving from a normalized to denormalized schema. In the Bad ETL scenario, the last four digits of the zip code get dropped. Losing the last four digits could be due to various factors, including an error in the ETL code or a field-length limitation in the data warehouse.

FIGURE 4.41   Data manipulation issue

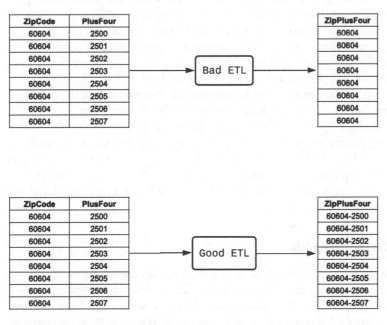

The process in Figure 4.39 ensures quality early in the process. However, as Figure 4.41 shows, a manipulation error can cause downstream data quality issues, even though the ETL does not have to verify the address data quality. Identifying when data is acquired and how it gets transformed and manipulated is an example of why it is crucial to consider acquisition and transformation when thinking about approaches to ensuring high-quality data.

Final Product Preparation

Data eventually gets packaged into reports and dashboards to help people make data-informed decisions. As part of the final data production process, it is possible to introduce data quality issues. For example, suppose you want to create a dashboard using a piece of data visualization software like Tableau. While designing the dashboard, it is possible to use Tableau to link multiple data sources together. If you don't have a good understanding of the source data, you may use the wrong join condition when linking data across systems. You will learn more about data visualization in Chapter 7, "Data Visualization with Reports and Dashboards."

Automated Validation

Many data sources feed analytics environments. While some of these data sources are other computer systems, others depend directly on people. Whenever people interact with systems, it's possible to introduce data-related errors. Whether source data is machine- or human-generated, one way to prevent data entry mistakes from adversely impacting data quality is to automate data validation checks.

Before automatically validating input data, you need to understand how source data fields map to their corresponding database columns. When mapping input data, pay close attention to the data types in the database. For example, suppose you have a web form where customers supply phone numbers, and the destination database uses a numeric data type to store phone data. If the input form allows for free text entry, someone may enter *(312) 555-1212*. Attempting to insert the parentheses and hyphen into a numeric column results in a database error due to a data type mismatch. Automating the data type validation before passing the data to the database prevents this from happening.

Another example of automation is verifying the number of data points. For example, suppose you are collecting hourly temperature data from a collection of sensors. For each sensor, you would expect to have 24 data points per day. If a sensor fails, it no longer reports data. Automating the verification of the number of data points instead of their values can help you identify a sensor failure. Early identification of sensor failure prevents missing data from flowing into your analytics environment.

Data Quality Dimensions

It is essential to consider multiple attributes about data when considering its quality. Six dimensions to take into account when assessing data quality are accuracy, completeness, consistency, timeliness, uniqueness, and validity. Understanding these dimensions and how they are related will help you improve data quality. Let's take a closer look at each of these dimensions.

Data Accuracy

Data accuracy denotes how closely a given attribute matches its intended use. For example, when collecting address data in the United States, you need to determine whether the five-digit zip code meets your needs or if you need the complete nine-digit zip code. The answer depends on the context of what you are trying to do. If you are analyzing income by geography, the five-digit zip code is sufficient. If you are looking to reduce postage costs, you need the nine-digit zip code's improved accuracy.

Data Completeness

Data completeness is the minimum amount of information you need to fulfill a business objective. For example, suppose you are collecting customer profile data. Your database design can accommodate storing a person's title, first name, middle name, last name, and suffix. You don't need all of those attributes to communicate successfully with a customer, since first and last name is sufficient to generate an email or personalize a web page. When considering completeness, think about database columns that can't have a null value. If a column is required, then it's something you need for minimum viable data completeness.

Data Consistency

Data consistency describes the reliability of an attribute. Data consistency typically comes into play in large organizations that store the same data in multiple systems. For example, a hotel may have separate systems to handle reservation and loyalty activity. Both of these systems need to share customers' names and addresses. Ideally, both the reservation and loyalty systems have access to a single source of customer data. If that isn't the case, the name information exists in both systems.

The challenge is to keep the data consistent. Figure 4.42 illustrates a customer making a change in the Reservation system. The Address Synchronization Process has to propagate the updated address information to the Loyalty system to ensure consistency.

Considering data consistency is especially important when designing a data warehouse as it sources data from multiple systems. If a customer's address is different in the source systems, data quality in the warehouse suffers. Ensuring consistency as early as possible resolves potential data quality problems before they occur in a data warehouse.

Data Timeliness

Data timeliness measures whether or not the data you need is available at the right time. For example, suppose you are running a marketing campaign and encouraging existing customers to buy additional products from your company. The success of that campaign

FIGURE 4.42   Ensuring consistency

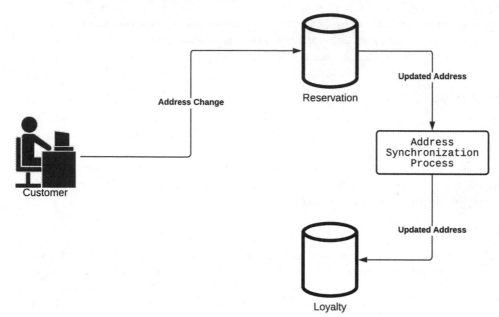

depends on timely access to which of your products the customer already owns. Trying to sell a product to an existing customer who already owns it gives your company an uninformed appearance. With the abundance of data available in the world today, timeliness is essential to informing strategic decisions.

Data Uniqueness

Data uniqueness describes whether or not a data attribute exists in multiple places within your organization. Closely related to data consistency, the more unique your data is, the less you have to worry about replication and consistency. While you may aspire to have each attribute stored in its own location, the system complexities of modern organizations make that difficult to achieve.

Recall the challenge of a hotel having customer names and addresses in both the reservation and loyalty system in Figure 4.42. Unless the Address Synchronization Process synchronizes changes as they occur, a loyalty statement can end up at the customer's old address. Figure 4.43 illustrates how improving the uniqueness of where name and address information is stored removes the need to make it consistent. In this figure, name and address data exist only in the Customer Profile database. Improving the uniqueness of those attributes ensures consistent delivery of reservation and loyalty information.

FIGURE 4.43   Using uniqueness to improve consistency

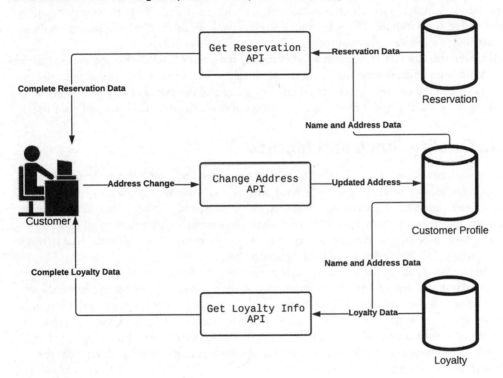

Data Validity

Data validity, also known as data integrity, indicates whether or not an attribute's value is within an expected range. One way to ensure data validity is to enforce referential integrity in the database. Consider Figure 4.44, which shows a customer trying to enter an address with an invalid value for the state.

FIGURE 4.44   Referential integrity and data validity

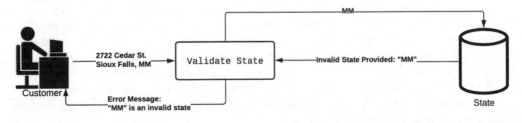

Within the database, the state column has a character data type. Since "MM" is a character value, a data type check is successful. Without a validity check, this invalid value gets stored in the database. This situation illustrates the limitation of relying purely on data type attributes for data quality purposes.

However, the Validate State process takes the input value of "MM" and compares it to the list of valid state abbreviations in the database. Since "MM" is not a valid state, the validity check fails, and the customer receives an error message and the option to fix the error. Checking data validity at the moment of creation improves the overall quality of your data.

Data Quality Rules and Metrics

With an understanding of data quality dimensions, you need to consider how to measure each of them in your quest to improve overall quality. Let's consider data conformity, which encompasses elements of accuracy, consistency, uniqueness, and validity. When consolidating data from multiple source systems into an analytics environment, one factor you want to assess is the conformity or nonconformity of data. If source data does not match the destination data type size and format, you have nonconformity.

For example, consider the source systems in Figure 4.45. Since the Ordering, Billing, and Shipping databases are all distinct, customer information exists independently within these systems. The Warehouse Load ETL needs to ensure consistency as it propagates data from these source systems into the Data Warehouse to ensure data quality. As the source systems are from different vendors, they use different data types for similar attributes. For instance, the Ordering system has a 15-character field for storing a person's last name, whereas the Billing system only supports 10 characters.

This nonconformity presents an ETL challenge. Suppose a customer with an 11-character last name places an order, and the ETL propagates that order information into the Data Warehouse. After fulfilling an order, a bill is generated. However, the Billing system only supports a 10-character last name. Therefore, the ETL job needs to copy the bill details but not the last name field when loading the Data Warehouse. If the ETL overwrites an 11-character last name from the Ordering system with the 10-character last name from the Billing system, it creates a data quality issue in the Data Warehouse.

One way to validate data conformity issues is to confirm how many rows pass successfully to the target environment and how many fail. Suppose you have 1 million billing records to migrate into the Data Warehouse. Figure 4.46 shows what happens when only 900,000 rows are successful. Instead of aborting the entire data load, the Warehouse Load ETL job sends the 100,000 nonconforming rows to a Bad Data staging area. A data engineer then resolves the root cause of the data quality issue before sending the remediated data into the Data Warehouse. With this design, the nonconformity of a single row does not cause the entire load process to fail. By only reprocessing failed rows, this approach makes efficient use of resources as well as improving quality.

FIGURE 4.45   Multiple source systems and the potential for nonconformity

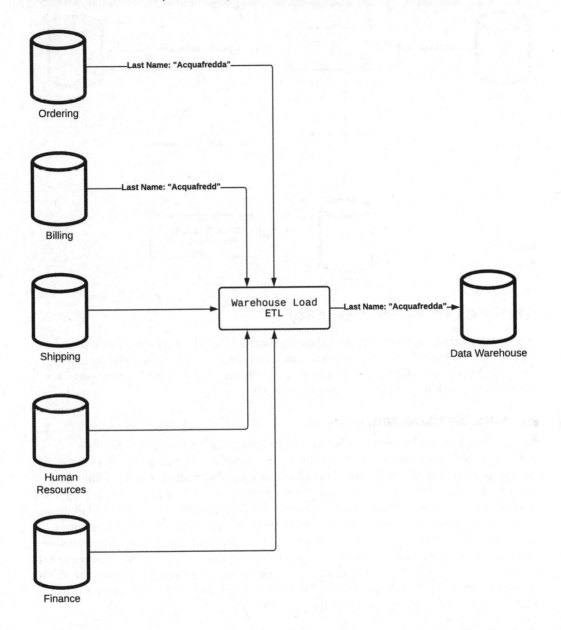

FIGURE 4.46   Reprocessing of bad data

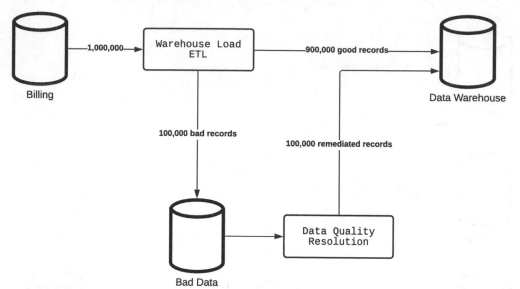

Methods to Validate Quality

Numerous methods are available for validating data quality. These methods range from whether or not your data passes reasonable expectations to statistical methods that look for irregular patterns within your data. A sound approach to ensuring and improving data quality is by combining these methods appropriately.

Reasonable Expectations

One approach is to determine whether or not the data in your analytics environment meets your reasonable expectations. For example, if your transactional systems process 10 million records per day, it is reasonable to expect an incremental 300 million records in your analytics environment at the end of 30 days. If after 30 days you only see an additional 20 million records, it is reasonable for you to presume that the data propagation ETL is failing.

It is worth spending time reflecting on what measures are reasonable for your environment. After defining how you want to measure your expectations, automate the reasonable expectation check by creating exception reports as part of your ETL processes. For example, if the number of successful rows is less than a large percentage of attempted rows, your internal alarm bells should start ringing. The root cause of the ETL load failure needs remediation to prevent ongoing issues with data quality.

Data Profiling

Another approach to improving quality is to profile your data. *Data profiling* uses statistical measures to check for data discrepancies, including values that are missing, that occur either infrequently or too frequently, or that should be eliminated. Profiling can also identify irregular patterns within your data.

For example, suppose you are trying to analyze customer engagement by examining the frequency with which customers log into your website. On average, you see that customers log in once per day from one of four devices. However, profiling your data shows that a specific customer is logging in three hundred times per day from three hundred unique devices. Further analysis shows that these logins originate from multiple different places around the globe.

The results of your data profiling activity fail the reasonable expectation test, as customers typically log in less frequently and from fewer devices. Instead of trusting this data, you proceed to investigate whether or not this activity is fraudulent.

Data Audits

Another method to keep in mind is auditing your data. *Data audits* look at your data and help you understand whether or not you have the data you need to operate your business. Data audits use data profiling techniques and can help identify data integrity and security issues.

For example, suppose you work with a large company that has relationships with numerous suppliers. To understand what is reasonable, you create a report to show the average payment amount by supplier. One day, you notice an unusually large supplier payment. Looking into the disbursement, you also discover that the payment was sent to a new financial institution.

As you continue your investigation, you learn that one of your employees fell victim to a social engineering scheme that commits financial fraud. As a result of your data audit, you work with the Federal Bureau of Investigation and your financial institution to investigate the fraud. You also develop a security awareness program to help your employees recognize fraudulent transfer requests.

Sampling

Another method for validating data quality is by examining a sample of your data. *Sampling* is a statistical technique in which you use a subset of your data to inform conclusions about your overall data. For example, suppose you are an automotive manufacturer and want to ensure the quality of fasteners from one of your suppliers. Suppose you have a daily production volume of 10,000 at one of your assembly plants. If each vehicle requires 3,500 fasteners, you need 35 million per day. Fastener failures can lead to quality issues, safety issues, and recalls. All of these quality issues are expensive to address and generate bad press.

Since each fastener is a low-cost component and you use over 1 billion per month, it is not cost-effective to assess the quality of each one individually. Instead, you take a sample from each shipment of fasteners and evaluate it against the specifications for that fastener. There are a variety of sampling approaches available. Selecting one depends on the context and is best done in partnership with a statistician.

Now imagine that you are responsible for data quality at a streaming media company. With millions of subscribers, it would be costly to store, process, and assess the quality of each movie being streamed. Taking a sample of the data transmitted across a network connection lets you assess quality while controlling cost.

Cross-Validation

Analysts frequently use existing data to generate predictive models using a variety of statistical methods. *Cross-validation* is a statistical technique that evaluates how well predictive models perform. Cross-validation works by dividing data into two subsets. The first subset is the training set, and the second is the testing, or validation, set.

You use data from the training set to build a predictive model. You then cross-validate the model using the testing subset to determine how accurate the prediction is. Cross-validation is also helpful in identifying data sampling issues.

For example, suppose you want to predict overall automotive fastener quality using data from a sample. To generate the most accurate predictions, you want a random sample representing all of the fasteners in a shipment. However, instead of being random, you only test fasteners from one box in a shipment of 1,000. Using a single box is an example of sampling bias, where there is a systematic error in how you obtain a sample. Cross-validation can help identify sampling bias since predictions using biased data are inaccurate.

Summary

Having high-quality data is the foundation for all things analytical. A good analyst needs a firm understanding of why data needs to be clean, techniques for cleaning, and ways to verify data quality.

When assessing data quality, keep in mind that organizations with complex systems frequently encounter data duplication challenges. When an organization integrates multiple systems, you need to be on the lookout for redundant data. Apart from duplication and redundancy, you need to check data values for inconsistencies. Inconsistencies can include data that is missing, that falls outside an expected range of values, or that doesn't match the target data type. Keep in mind that outliers have an outsized effect on statistical analysis. When initially exploring your data, it is imperative to identify, understand, and address any outliers in your data.

When preparing data for analysis, there are numerous manipulation techniques you can use. Analysts need a deep understanding of how your data sources will work together. You may have to merge or blend sources, or concatenate or split columns within an individual source. Depending on your statistical technique of choice, you may end up recoding a categorical variable as numeric. In today's world, there is an overabundance of data. You may need to reduce the number of rows or columns to facilitate your analysis.

Invariably, you will want to compare the effects of different attributes. Recall that when you have multiple columns using disparate measurements, you need to normalize the data values. Normalizing avoids exaggerating the impact of a column based on the numeric values it contains.

Recognizing opportunities where data quality errors can occur is essential for the modern data analyst. Data acquisition, transformation, conversion, manipulation, and visualization are steps in the analytical process where quality issues arise. Beyond recognizing when quality errors happen, an analyst needs to consider automatically injecting quality improvements into data collection and preparation processes.

When thinking about how to assess quality, keep in mind the dimensions of data quality. It is essential to define your business objectives through the lenses of data accuracy, completeness, consistency, uniqueness, and validity. Having the right data at the right time improves your ability to make data-informed decisions.

Once you understand where your data comes from and how you are going to use it, be sure to define ways in which you will continuously assess its quality. Quality assessment methods include everything from reasonable expectations and audits to advanced statistical techniques.

Exam Essentials

Describe the unique challenge of missing data values. A missing value is the absence of a value. Regardless of the programming language you use to manipulate data, you need additional checks to account for the lack of a value. You cannot compare values to the absence of a value. Instead, you first have to determine whether or not a value exists before doing the comparison.

Describe why it is crucial to account for data outliers. An outlier is an observation whose value differs significantly from other observations of the same type. Leaving outliers in your data can negatively impact the quality of your analysis.

Describe the difference between data merging and data blending. Both data merging and data blending combine data sources. However, data merging combines sources programmatically, typically through an ETL operation. Data blending is when an analyst merges data temporarily while exploring or visualizing data.

Differentiate between dimensionality and numerosity reduction. Dimensionality reduction is a technique for removing attributes that are not relevanDt for the analysis at hand. Numerosity reduction is a technique for reducing the overall size of a dataset to facilitate processing efficiency.

Describe how you can enforce data validity. Data validity is the data quality dimension that identifies whether a given value falls within an expected range. Combining referential integrity in the database with data type validation is a layered approach to ensuring only valid data gets into a system.

Review Questions

1. Jackie is designing an ETL process that pulls data from four different source systems. Examining the source data, she sees that data about people exists in three of the four systems. What does she have to ensure that her ETL accounts for? Choose the best answer.

    A. Duplicate data

    B. Redundant data

    C. Invalid data

    D. Missing data

2. Diego is exploring daily rainfall data from weather stations in South America. Looking at the data, he sees one station is consistently reporting values of –10 over time. What is this an example of?

    A. Duplicate data

    B. Redundant data

    C. Invalid data

    D. Missing data

3. Tony is looking at a dataset about movies. One of the attributes is the genre a movie belongs to. For a specific science fiction movie, the genre is listed as "star." What is this an example of?

    A. Duplicate data

    B. Redundant data

    C. Invalid data

    D. Missing data

4. Josephine is exploring emergency room data from a set of regional hospitals. Using a Python script, she encounters an error when trying to get the average patient temperature at time of admittance. What is this a symptom of? Choose the best answer.

    A. Duplicate data

    B. Redundant data

    C. Invalid data

    D. Missing data

5. Larry is evaluating the price of concrete in the European Union (EU). When exploring the data, he sees that prices in Spain are 10 times greater than the other countries in the EU. What is the price of concrete in Spain an example of?

    A. Nonparametric data

    B. Specification mismatch

    C. Duplicate data

    D. Data outlier

6. Melinda is analyzing a movie dataset, where individual films have a star rating between 1 and 5. What type of data is this?

   A. Nonparametric data

   B. Redundant data

   C. Duplicate data

   D. Data outlier

7. Raphael is designing the ETL process to load a data warehouse. He notices that all the data is coming from a single, well-designed transactional system. To ensure a high success rate for the load process, what is the most important thing Raphael needs to account for?

   A. Data type validation

   B. Redundant data

   C. Duplicate data

   D. Data outlier

8. Jorge's company just acquired a competitor, and he is responsible for integrating the Human Resources systems. One of the things he needs to account for are employees who work at his current company who used to work at the acquired company, and vice versa. What is this an example of?

   A. Data type validation

   B. Redundant data

   C. Duplicate data

   D. Data outlier

9. Lars is analyzing storm wind speed data to understand the number of worldwide Category 5 hurricanes over a 10-year period. A storm reaches Category 5 when wind speed exceeds 157 miles per hour. What does Lars need to do to the wind speed data to proceed with his analysis?

   A. Merge the wind speed data with the Category data

   B. Recode the numeric wind speed data

   C. Impute the category based on wind speed data

   D. Parse the category from the wind speed data

10. Mauro is an oceanographer who wants to analyze the temperature trends in the Mediterranean and Aegean Seas. Mauro has access to data from 18,392 temperature sensors across these bodies of water. How should he manipulate this data to prepare for analysis?

    A. Convert the temperature data from Fahrenheit to Celsius

    B. Transpose water temperature and pressure data

    C. Derive a new variable to indicate whether the water is "hot" or "cold"

    D. Merge the data from these 18,392 sources together

11. Ashley works as a data analyst for a major retailer. While reviewing monthly website impressions, she notices that the current month has double the number of expected impressions. To help her understand why, Ashley brings in some additional data from the marketing system using a data visualization tool. What is this an example of? Choose the best answer.

   A. Modifying an ETL process

   B. Blending data

   C. Recoding data

   D. Concatenating data

12. Alex's company is about to launch a new product, and Alex is trying to identify customers who will want to and have the ability to purchase it. He needs data to join data from four systems together for his analysis. What has to happen during the ETL process? Choose the best answer.

   A. Data needs to be recoded as numeric.

   B. Data from the four systems needs to be appended into a wide table.

   C. Product IDs from past purchases need to be concatenated.

   D. Price needs to be numeric.

13. Maggie is working on pricing a new product. As part of her analysis, she is looking at the average sales price and volume for competitive products. Noticing that the average price and volume are significantly smaller for a region, Maggie suspects a data quality problem. What should she start looking to see if her hunch is correct?

   A. Check for null values in the source data for the affected region

   B. Verify that the average function is working correctly

   C. Search online for the correct price

   D. Escalate the issue to IT support

14. Sebastien is performing a geospatial analysis to understand household income across a geographic region. He wants to be able to zoom in to the street level and see income on a household-by-household basis. In addition to income, his source data contains demographic and psychographic data. To make his analysis more efficient, what should Sebastien do?

   A. Perform a numerosity reduction technique

   B. Perform an aggregation technique

   C. Perform a dimensionality reduction technique

   D. Normalize the income data

15. Kathy wants to look at sales volume across three product categories. Her source dataset consists of 3 million rows, with columns including product, sales price, region, and product category. How should she manipulate the data to facilitate her analysis? Choose the best answer.

   A. Transpose by sales price and summarize

   B. Transpose by region

   C. Remove all rows with null values for product category

   D. Transpose by product category and summarize

16. Randall is designing an ETL process to map source data into a data warehouse. When reviewing the metadata for the source data, he sees that one of the columns consists of Full Name, e.g., "Robert L Cormier." What should he consider designing into his ETL? Choose the best answer.

    A. Drop all data with a missing Full Name

    B. Separate Full Name into First Name, Middle Name, and Last Name

    C. Aggregate the data based on Full Name

    D. Transpose the data based on Full Name

17. Edgar is developing a model to predict which new product feature will appeal to his existing customers. What can he do to validate the accuracy of his model? Choose the best answer.

    A. Cross-validate using a subset of data

    B. Aggregate the number of customers

    C. Trust his instincts and what he feels is a reasonable expectation

    D. Normalize any attributes that use different units of measure

18. Jane wants to conduct a marketing campaign. To be minimally successful, she needs the first name and a valid email address for each intended recipient. What quality dimension is most crucial for Jane to consider? Choose the best answer.

    A. Accuracy

    B. Completeness

    C. Consistency

    D. Validity

19. Ron's company is acquiring a competitor. Ron's original company and the one being acquired sell to the same clients. When integrating transactional data from both companies into a data warehouse, what dimension of quality should Ron be most concerned with? Choose the best answer.

    A. Accuracy

    B. Completeness

    C. Consistency

    D. Validity

20. Shelton works with the International Olympic Committee on analyzing the effect of javelin weight on athlete performance over the past 10 Olympiads. Looking in the data warehouse, Shelton sees that javelin weight is recorded in kilograms and determines the data available to him is of insufficient quality to complete the analysis. On what dimension of quality is he basing his conclusion? Choose the best answer.

    A. Accuracy

    B. Completeness

    C. Consistency

    D. Validity

Chapter

5

Data Analysis and Statistics

THE COMPTIA DATA+ EXAM TOPICS COVERED IN THIS CHAPTER INCLUDE:

✓ Domain 3.0: Data Analysis

✓ 3.1. Given a scenario, apply the appropriate descriptive statistical methods

✓ 3.2. Explain the purpose of inferential statistical methods

✓ 3.3. Summarize types of analysis and key analysis techniques

In Chapter 4, "Data Quality," you learned where data comes from, when quality issues crop up and how to mitigate them, and techniques to prepare data for analysis. Once you have good, clean data, you are ready to develop insights. An *insight* is a new piece of information you create from data that then influences a decision.

While it's possible to make decisions using intuition, it is preferable to be analytical and use data. An analytical approach applies statistical techniques to analyze data on your journey to create insights.

This chapter will explore foundational statistical techniques that describe data and show why they are essential. You will also develop an understanding of how to generate and test hypotheses using statistics and whether or not you can make generalizations using your analysis. We will wrap up the chapter by exploring situations where statistical techniques are particularly helpful in developing context and influencing decisions.

Fundamentals of Statistics

Knowledge of statistics is foundational for the modern data analyst. Before we explore the different branches of statistics, it is essential to understand some core statistical concepts.

One key concept is the definition of a population. A *population* represents all the data subjects you want to analyze. For example, suppose you are an analyst at the National Highway Traffic Safety Administration (NHTSA) and start to receive reports about a potential defect in Ford F-Series trucks. In this case, the population is all Ford F-Series trucks. If you want to examine all Ford F-Series vehicles, you'd have to conduct a census. A *census* is when you obtain data for every element of your population. Conducting a census is typically infeasible due to the effort involved and the scarcity of resources.

Collecting a sample is a cost-effective and time-effective alternative to gathering census data. A *sample* is a subset of the population. Suppose that further investigation into the potential defect identifies a batch of faulty third-party windshield wiper switches. Tracing the distribution of the defective component identifies F-Series vehicles made in Chicago between February 14, 2000, and August 4, 2000, as being potentially impacted. In this case, F-Series vehicles made in Chicago between February 14 and August 4, 2000, represent a sample. For this chapter, presume that you are working with sample data.

A *variable* is a unique attribute about a data subject. Recalling the definition of tabular data from Chapter 2, "Understanding Data," a variable corresponds to a column in a table. In this example, the serial number that uniquely identifies a wiper switch is a variable. *Univariate analysis* is when you explore the characteristics of a single variable, independent of the rest of the dataset.

An *observation* is an individual record in a dataset corresponding to a tabular data row. Continuing the example, whereas the serial number for a wiper switch is a variable, the serial number's unique value for a specific switch is an observation of the wiper switch variable.

When working with statistics, one thing to be mindful of is the sample size. Since it is unusual to have a full census for the population you are studying, you typically analyze data for a sample taken from the population. For example, suppose you want to discern the average height for females in the United States. Collecting that information about every female is infeasible. Instead, you would gather that data from a representative sample of females in the United States. The *sample size* is the number of observations you select from the population. For example, instead of measuring every female, you may identify 1,000 females and obtain their heights. An *n* represents sample size in statistical formulas. The larger the sample size, the more confident you can be that the results of your analysis accurately describe the population.

You analyze samples in terms of statistics. A *statistic* is a numeric representation of a property of a sample. Considering the aforementioned sample of females, the average height is a statistic. You use statistics to infer estimates about the population as a whole.

You also use a sample statistic to estimate a population parameter. A *parameter* is a numeric representation of a property for the population. Continuing the example, you can use the average height of females from your sample to estimate the average height of all females. Just as statistics summarize sample information, parameters summarize the entire population.

When working with statistics, keep in mind that they depend entirely on the sample taken from the population. Every calculation you perform is specific to that sample. If you were to take a different sample from the same population, you'd have to recalculate all your statistics.

Common Symbols in Statistics

Statistics is all about exploring numbers and performing calculations. People use emojis when texting to symbolize emotions. Similarly, statisticians use symbols to convey meaning. To help provide context into some of the formulas in this chapter, please use Table 5.1 as a guide.

TABLE 5.1   Common symbols in statistics

Symbol	Meaning
x	A variable
$\lvert x \rvert$	Absolute value of a variable The absolute value of a number is always positive, so $\lvert -5 \rvert = 5$.
Σ	Summation For example, Σx_i denotes adding all observations of a variable together.
N	Population size
μ	Population mean
σ^2	Population variance
σ	Population standard deviation
n	Sample size
$\bar{x}$	Sample mean
$\tilde{x}$	Sample median
s^2	Sample variance
s	Sample standard deviation
C	Confidence level value
Z	Standardized score
α	Significance level
$Z_{\alpha/2}$	Critical value for a confidence interval level
r	Pearson correlation coefficient

Descriptive Statistics

Descriptive statistics is a branch of statistics that summarizes and describes data. As you explore a new dataset for the first time, you want to develop an initial understanding of the size and shape of the data. You use descriptive statistics as measures to help you understand the characteristics of your dataset.

When initially exploring a dataset, you may perform univariate analysis to answer questions about a variable's values. You also use descriptive measures to develop summary information about all of a variable's observations. This context helps orient you and informs the analytical techniques you use to continue your analysis.

Measures of Frequency

Measures of frequency help you understand how often something happens. When encountering a dataset for the first time, you want to determine how much data you are working with to help guide your analysis. For example, suppose you are working with human performance data. One of the first things to understand is the size of the dataset. One way to accomplish this quickly is to count the number of observations.

Consider Figure 5.1, which has four variables. The first variable uniquely identifies an individual, the second is a date, the third is the person's sex, and the fourth is the person's weight on that date. Looking at this excerpt, you have no idea how many total observations exist. Understanding the total number helps influence the tools you use to explore the data. If there are 2 million observations, you can analyze the data on a laptop computer. If there are 2 billion observations, you will need more computing power than a laptop provides.

FIGURE 5.1 Weight log

ID	Date	Sex	Weight
993487	3/2/2003	Male	191
993488	3/2/2003	Male	233
993489	3/2/2003	Male	211
993490	3/2/2003	Male	232
993491	3/2/2003	Male	181
993492	3/2/2003	Male	248
993493	3/2/2003	Male	232
993494	3/2/2003	Male	225
993495	3/2/2003	Male	204
993496	3/2/2003	Male	199
993497	3/2/2003	Male	188
993498	3/2/2003	Male	250
993499	3/2/2003	Male	170
993500	3/2/2003	Male	218
993501	3/2/2003	Male	233
993502	3/2/2003	Male	244
993503	3/2/2003	Male	239
993504	3/2/2003	Male	176
993505	3/2/2003	Male	217

Count

The most straightforward way to understand how much data you're working with is to *count* the number of observations. Understanding the total number of observations is a frequently performed task. As such, there is a count function in everything from spreadsheets to programming languages. As Table 5.2 shows, you have to decide how to account for null values and then make sure you're using the appropriate function.

TABLE 5.2   Selected implementations of count

Technology	Count implementation	Description
Google Sheet	`counta(cell range)`	Counts the number of values in a dataset, excluding null values
Google Sheet	`count(cell range)`	Counts the number of numeric values in a dataset
Microsoft Excel	`counta(cell range)`	Counts the number of values in a dataset, excluding null values
Microsoft Excel	`count(cell range)`	Counts the number of numeric values in a dataset
SQL	`count(*)`	Counts the number of rows in a table
SQL	`count(column)`	Counts the number of rows in the specified column, excluding null values
R	`nrow(data frame)`	Counts the number of rows in a data frame
R	`nrow(na.omit(data frame))`	Counts the number of rows in a data frame, excluding null values
Python	`len(data frame)`	Counts the number of rows in a data frame
Python	`len(data frame.dropna())`	Counts the number of rows in a data frame, excluding null values

Percentage

The *percentage* is a frequency measure that identifies the proportion of a given value for a variable with respect to the total number of rows in the dataset. To calculate a percentage, you need the total number of observations and the total number of observations for a specific value of a variable.

Table 5.3 illustrates the count of males and females for the sex variable in a dataset. Note that the total number of males and females together equals 200. You would use the following formula to calculate the percentage of females in the data:

$$Percentage\ Female = \frac{102}{200} = 0.51 * 100 = 51\%$$

TABLE 5.3   Sample data

Count of Males	Count of Females
98	102

Knowing that 51 percent of the sample is female helps you understand that the balance between males and females is pretty even.

Understanding proportions across a dataset aids in determining how you proceed with your analysis. For example, suppose you are an analyst for the National Weather Service and receive a new dataset from a citizen-provided weather station. Using a count function, you determine it has 1 million observations. Upon further exploration, you observe that 95 percent of the observations for the temperature variable are null. With such a large percentage of the data not containing meaningful values, you would want to discuss this initial finding with the data provider to ensure something isn't wrong with the data extraction process.

Exploring percentages also gives you a better understanding of the composition of your data and can help identify any biases in your dataset. When data has a *bias*, your sample data isn't representative of the overall population you are studying. Suppose you are working with the complete dataset of which Figure 5.1 is an excerpt. Examining the Sex column, it takes you by surprise that all observations in the dataset are male, as Table 5.4 illustrates. To determine whether or not this is appropriate, you need to put it in context regarding the objective of your analysis.

TABLE 5.4   Exploring percentages

Male	Female
100%	0%

For instance, if you are analyzing a men's collegiate athletic team, having 100 percent males in your data makes sense. However, suppose you are studying weight across all students at a coeducational university and the university's enrollment is evenly split between males and females. With this context, you would expect 50 percent of your data to be for males, with females representing the other 50 percent. An absence of data about females indicates a bias in the data and that your sample data doesn't accurately represent the population. To remediate the bias, you would want to understand the data collection methods to ensure equal male and female participation. After ensuring there is no collection bias, you would expect the proportion of males and females in your sample to align more appropriately with your knowledge about the population.

Apart from examining the static percentage for a variable in a dataset, looking at *percent change* gives you an understanding of how a measure changes over time. You can calculate the relative change by subtracting the initial value from the final value and then dividing by the absolute value of the initial value:

$$Percent\ Change = \frac{x_2 - x_1}{|x_1|} \times 100$$

For example, if a stock's price at the beginning of a trading day is 100 and its price at the end of the day is 90, there was a 10 percent decrease in its value.

Percent values are also applicable when comparing observations for a variable. The *percent difference* compares two values for a variable. You calculate the percent difference by subtracting the initial value from the final value and then dividing by the average of the two values:

$$Percent\ Difference = \frac{x_1 - x_2}{\dfrac{x_1 + x_2}{2}} \times 100$$

For example, suppose you receive two datasets. Each dataset is from a factory that creates automotive switches. Upon initial exploration, you find the first dataset has 4,000 observations while the second dataset has 6,000 observations, for a difference of 40 percent. You would want to understand why there is a discrepancy in the number of observations. If the factories are supposed to generate the same output, you are missing data, which will impact your ongoing analysis.

Frequency

Frequency describes how often a specific value for a variable occurs in a dataset. You typically explore frequency when conducting univariate analysis. The histogram, which you first saw in Chapter 4, is an optimal way to visualize frequency for continuous data. In Chapter 7, "Data Visualization with Reports and Dashboards," you will meet the bar chart. Bar charts are the visualization of choice for categorical data as there is no continuity to the values.

In the United States, the Scholastic Aptitude Test (SAT) is an admissions test that some colleges and universities use to assess applicants. Figure 5.2 illustrates the average SAT score for admitted students at colleges and universities across the United States.

FIGURE 5.2   Histogram of average SAT score for U.S. institutions of higher education

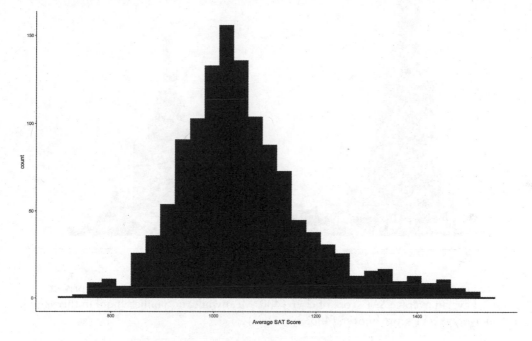

It is often helpful to compare frequency across values for an observation. For example, consider the histograms in Figure 5.3, which show the count of average SAT scores for private and public institutions. Since the histogram for private schools looks larger than the one for public schools, you might think that there are more private schools than public schools. To validate this conclusion, you can analyze the percentage of public and private schools, as shown in Table 5.5.

TABLE 5.5   Institutional control percentage

Private	Public
60%	40%

FIGURE 5.3   Histograms of SAT averages and institutional control

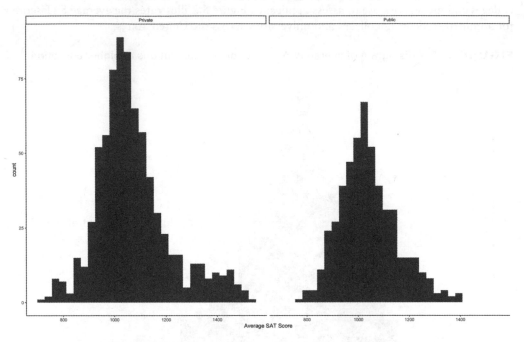

Returning your attention to the x-axis of Figure 5.3, you conclude that some private schools have an average SAT score of over 1400. Meanwhile, no public school in this sample has an average SAT score of over 1400.

Measures of Central Tendency

To help establish an overall perspective on a given dataset, an analyst explores various measures of central tendency. You use *measures of central tendency* to identify the central, or most typical, value in a dataset. There are numerous ways to measure central tendency, and you end up using them in conjunction with each other to understand the shape of your data. We will explore the different shape types when we discuss distributions later in this chapter.

Mean

The *mean*, or *average*, is a measurement of central tendency that computes the arithmetic average for a given set of numeric values. To calculate the mean, you take the sum of all values for an observation and divide by the number of observations. In the comparatively unlikely event that you have a complete census for your population, the following formula is the mathematical definition for calculating the mean of a population:

$$\mu = \frac{1}{N}\sum x_i$$

Although the formula for calculating the sample mean looks slightly different, the process is the same. You sum all sample observations for a variable and then divide by the number of observations:

$$\bar{x} = \frac{1}{n}\sum x_i$$

Data analysis tools, including spreadsheets, programming languages, and visualization tools, all have functions that calculate the mean.

While the mean is one of the most common measurements of central tendency, remember that you can only calculate a mean for quantitative data. You should also be mindful of the effect outliers have on the mean's value. An *outlier* is a value that differs significantly from the other values of the same observation. In Figure 5.4A, the mean salary for the 10 individuals is $90,600. In Figure 5.4B, ID 993496 has a salary of $1,080,000 instead of $80,000 in Figure 5.4A. The salary value for 993496 in Figure 5.4B is an outlier. The effect of the outlier on the mean is dramatic, increasing it by $100,000 to $190,600.

FIGURE 5.4A   Mean salary data

	ID	Salary
	993487	$72,000
	993488	$117,000
	993489	$138,999
	993490	$75,000
	993491	$124,000
	993492	$82,000
	993493	$81,000
	993494	$44,000
	993495	$92,000
	993496	$80,000
Average Salary		$90,600

FIGURE 5.4B   Effect of an outlier on the mean

	ID	Salary
	993487	$72,000
	993488	$117,000
	993489	$138,999
	993490	$75,000
	993491	$124,000
	993492	$82,000
	993493	$81,000
	993494	$44,000
	993495	$92,000
	993496	$1,080,000
Average Salary		$190,600

Median

Another measurement of central tendency is the *median*, which identifies the midpoint value for all observations of a variable. The first step to calculating the median is sorting your data numerically. Once you have an ordered list of values, the next step depends on whether you have an even or an odd number of observations for a variable.

Identifying the median for an odd number of observations is straightforward—you just select the number in the middle of the ordered list of values. Mathematically, you add one to the total number of values, divide by 2, and retrieve the value for that observation. The formula for calculating the median for an odd number of values is as follows:

$$\tilde{x} = \left(\frac{n+1}{2} \right)$$

Suppose you have the following numbers: {1,3,5,7,9}. To find the median, you take the total number of values, add 1, divide by 2, and retrieve the corresponding value. In this case, there are five numbers in the dataset, so you retrieve the value for the third number in the ordered list, which is 5.

For datasets with an even number of observations, you need to take the average of the two observations closest to the midpoint of the ordered list. The following formula describes how to calculate the median:

$$\tilde{x} = \left(\frac{\left(\frac{n}{2} \right) + \left(\frac{n}{2} + 1 \right)}{2} \right)$$

Suppose you have the following numbers: {1,3,5,7,9,11}. Since there are six observations, the median is the mean of the values that surround the midpoint. In this case, you find the mean of 5 and 7, which is 6.

Outliers don't impact the median as dramatically as the mean. Consider the calculation for mean in Figure 5.5A, which uses the same data as for Figure 5.4A. For this small dataset with 10 data points, the difference between the mean and median is 9,100.

FIGURE 5.5A   Calculating median salary data

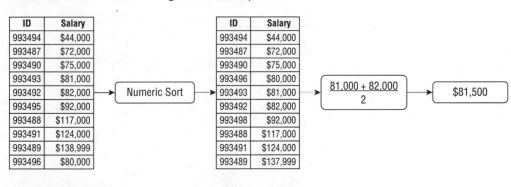

FIGURE 5.5B   Effect of an outlier on the median

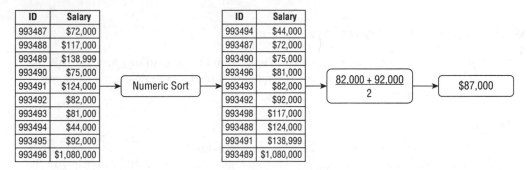

Now consider Figure 5.5B, which calculates the median using the same data from Figure 5.4B. The difference between the mean and the median is 103,600. This gap is much more significant than when there are no outliers present. Because of this effect, you should explore both the mean and median values when analyzing a dataset.

Mode

The *mode* is a variable's most frequently occurring observation. Depending on your data, you may not have a mode. For example, consider the salary data from Figure 5.4A. With only 10 values and no repeating value, there is no mode for this dataset. Depending on the level of precision and amount of data, the mode may not facilitate insight when working with numeric data.

However, the mode is more applicable when working with categorical data. For example, suppose you are collecting data about eye color from a group of people and use the survey question in Figure 5.6. Determining the mode of responses will identify the most commonly reported eye color.

FIGURE 5.6   Categorical question

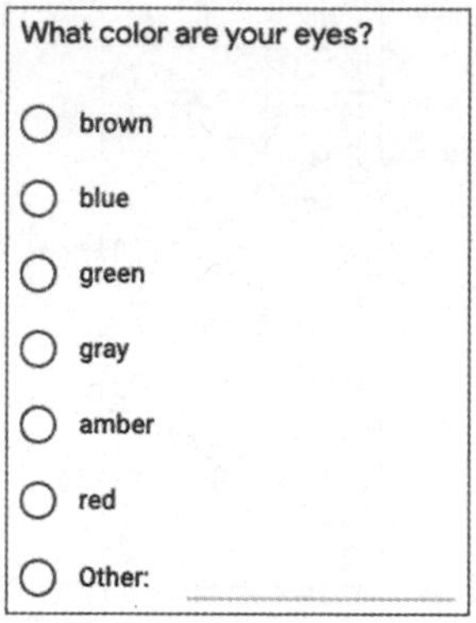

Measures of Dispersion

In addition to central tendency, it is crucial to understand the spread of your data. You use *measures of dispersion* to create context around data spread. Let's explore five common measures of dispersion.

Range

The *range* of a variable is the difference between its maximum and minimum values. Understanding the range helps put the data you are looking at into context and can help you determine what to do with outlier values. It can also identify invalid values in your data. Spreadsheets and programming languages have functions available to identify minimum and maximum values.

For example, suppose you are examining a group of people and their age in years. If the minimum value is a negative number, it indicates an invalid value as it isn't possible to have a negative age. A maximum value of 140 is similarly invalid, as the maximum recorded lifespan of a human is less than 140 years.

If you are working with temperature data, it's reasonable to expect both positive and negative values. To identify invalid temperature values, you need to establish additional context, such as location and time of year.

Distribution

In statistics, a *probability distribution*, or *distribution*, is a function that illustrates probable values for a variable, and the frequency with which they occur. Histograms are an effective tool to visualize a distribution, because the shape provides additional insight into your data and how to proceed with analysis. Distributions have many shapes possible shapes, including normal, skewed, and bimodal.

Normal Distribution

The *normal distribution* is symmetrically dispersed around its mean, which gives it a distinctive bell-like shape. Due to its shape, the normal distribution is also known as a "bell curve." Figure 5.7 is a good example of normally distributed data, with a high central peak and a high degree of symmetry.

FIGURE 5.7 Normal distribution

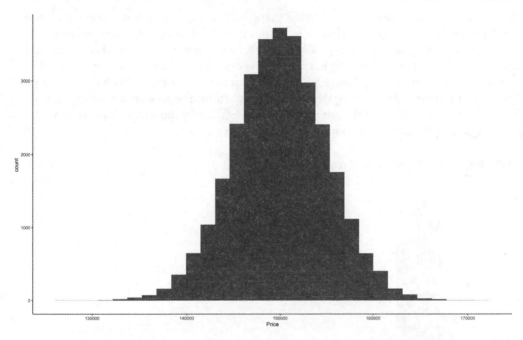

The normal distribution is applicable across a number of disciplines due to the *central limit theorem (CLT)*, a foundational theorem for statistical analysis. Recognizing that many different samples of a given sample size might be chosen for your data, the CLT tries to make sense of all the possible results you might obtain. According to the CLT, as sample size increases, it becomes increasingly likely that the sampling distribution of all those means will be normally distributed.

The sampling distribution of the mean will be normal regardless of sample size if the parent population is normal. However, if you have a skewed parent population, then having a "sufficiently large" sample size may be needed to get a normally distributed sampling distribution. Most people define sufficiently large as 30 or more observations in your sample. Because of the CLT, the normal distribution applies across a wide variety of attributes.

For example, suppose you are working with quantitative data about people. According to the CLT, you can expect the normal distribution to describe the people's height, weight, and shoe size. You can test out the CLT at home by rolling a pair of dice at least 30 times to get a sufficiently large sample and then plotting the value and frequency of your rolls.

One way to use measures of central tendency to verify the normal distribution is to examine the proximity of the mean and median. When the mean and median are relatively close together, the distribution will be symmetrical. If the mean and median are far apart, the data is *skewed*, or asymmetrical.

Skewed Distribution

A *skewed distribution* has an asymmetrical shape, with a single peak and a long tail on one side. Skewed distributions have either a right (positive) or left (negative) skew. When the skew is to the right, the mean is typically greater than the median. On the other hand, a distribution with a left skew typically has a mean less than the median.

Consider the histogram in Figure 5.8, which illustrates a distribution with a right skew. The long tail to the right of the peak shows that while most people have a salary of under $100,000, a large portion of the population earns significantly more. It is reasonable to expect that a right skew for income.

FIGURE 5.8   Right skewed distribution

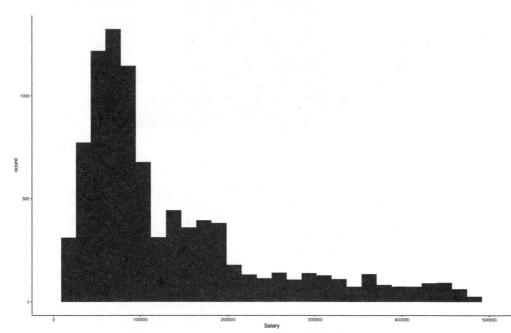

There are times when you would expect to see a left skew in the data. For example, imagine grades on a 100-point exam for students in a graduate statistics class. You would expect these students to have high intrinsic motivation and an innate desire to learn. While it is inevitable that some students perform poorly, it is reasonable to presume that most students would perform well. As such, you would expect the distribution to have a left skew, as Figure 5.9 illustrates.

FIGURE 5.9   Left skewed distribution

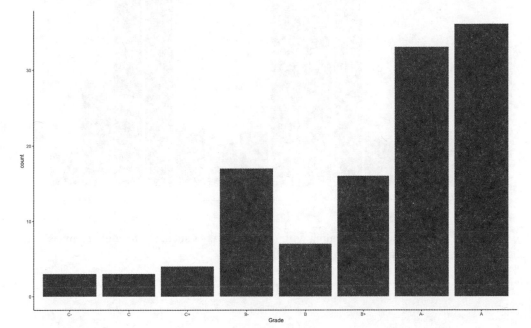

Bimodal Distribution

A *bimodal distribution* has two distinct modes, whereas a multimodal distribution has multiple distinct modes. When you visualize a bimodal distribution, you see two separate peaks. Suppose you are analyzing the number of customers at a restaurant over time. You would expect to see a large numbers of customers at lunch and dinner, as Figure 5.10 illustrates.

Variance

Variance is a measure of dispersion that takes the values for each observation in a dataset and calculates how far away they are from the mean value. This dispersion measure indicates how spread out the data is in squared units. Mathematically, σ^2 signifies population variance, which you calculate by taking the average squared deviation of each value from the mean, as follows:

$$\sigma^2 = \frac{\sum(x_i - \mu)^2}{N}$$

FIGURE 5.10   Bimodal distribution

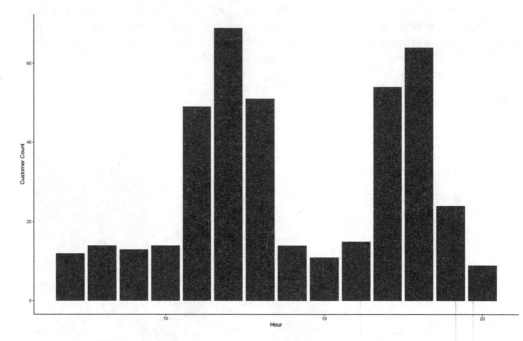

However, you will usually be dealing with sample data. As such, the formula changes slightly when calculating sample variance, as follows:

$$s^2 = \frac{\sum\left(x_i - \bar{x}\right)^2}{n - 1}$$

The slight difference in the denominator between the formulas for calculating population and sample variance is due to a technique known as Bessel's correction. *Bessel's correction* specifies that when calculating sample variance, you need to account for bias, or error, in your sample. Recall that a sample doesn't fully represent the overall population. When you have sample data and use the degrees of freedom in the denominator, it provides an unbiased estimate of the variability.

When the variance is large, the observations' values are far from the mean and thus far from each other. Meanwhile, a small variance implies that the values are close together.

Consider Figure 5.11, which shows histograms of temperature data for Chicago, Illinois, and San Diego, California. As a city in the Midwest, Chicago is known for having cold winters and hot summers. Meanwhile, San Diego has a must more stable climate with minor fluctuations in temperature. Using the data behind Figure 5.11, the variance for Chicago temperature is 517.8, while the variance for San Diego is 98.6.

FIGURE 5.11   Temperature variance

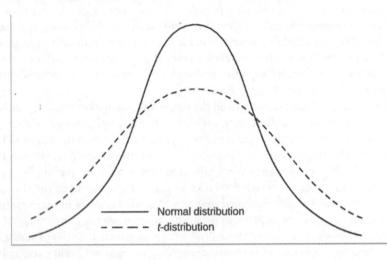

Normal distribution
— — — — t-distribution

Variance can be a useful measure when considering financial investments. For example, a mutual fund with a small variance in its price is likely to be a more stable investment vehicle than an individual stock with a large variance.

Standard Deviation

Standard deviation is a statistic that measures dispersion in terms of how far values of a variable are from its mean. Specifically, standard deviation is the average deviation between individual values and the mean. Mathematically, σ signifies population standard deviation, which you calculate by taking the square root of the variance, as follows:

$$\sigma = \sqrt{\sigma^2} = \sqrt{\frac{\Sigma\left(x_i - \mu\right)^2}{N}}$$

Similar to the difference between population and sample variance, the formula for sample standard deviation uses Bessel's correction:

$$s = \sqrt{s^2} = \sqrt{\frac{\Sigma\left(x_i - \bar{x}\right)^2}{n-1}}$$

As you can see from these formulas, calculating variance is an important step on the way to determining standard deviation.

Similar to variance, the standard deviation is a measure of volatility, with a low value implying stability. Standard deviation is a popular statistic because of the empirical rule. Also known as the three-sigma rule, the *empirical rule* states that almost every observation falls within three standard deviations of the mean in a normal distribution. Specifically, the empirical rule states that approximately 68 percent of values are within one standard deviation of the mean, 95 percent of values fall within two standard deviations, and 99.7 percent fall within three standard deviations.

Combining the central limit theorem and the empirical rule makes standard deviation a common way of describing and discussing variability. For example, using the data behind Figure 5.12, the San Diego temperature mean is 64, and the standard deviation is 10. Using the empirical rule, this implies that 68 percent of the time, the temperature in San Diego is between 54 and 74 degrees. Similarly, using two standard deviations, the implication is that the temperature in San Diego is between 44 and 84 degrees 95 percent of the time.

Standard deviation is a widely accepted measure of quality control in manufacturing processes. Large manufacturers implement programs to improve the consistency of their manufacturing processes. The goal of these programs is to ensure that the processes operate within a certain number of standard deviations, or sigmas. Quality control literature frequently uses the word *sigma* instead of *standard deviation* due to sigma being the mathematical symbol for population standard deviation.

One quality control program is known as Six Sigma, which sets the goal for a production process to six standard deviations. Achieving that degree of consistency is difficult and expensive. However, considering the data in Table 5.6, achieving six standard deviations of consistency implies a process that has almost no defects.

TABLE 5.6   Standard deviation performance levels

Standard deviations	Defects per million	Percent correct
1	691,462	30.85
2	308,538	69.146
3	66,807	93.319
4	6,210	99.379
5	233	99.9767
6	3.4	99.9997

Each Sample Is Unique

Keep in mind that each sample from a population is unique. Suppose you take two different samples from a population. The variance and standard deviation for each sample will be different.

Special Normal Distributions

The Central Limit Theorem and empirical rule combine to make the normal distribution the most important distribution in statistics. There are two special normal distributions that have broad applicability and warrant a deeper understanding.

Standard Normal Distribution

The *standard normal distribution*, or *Z-distribution*, is a special normal distribution with a mean of 0 and a standard deviation of 1. You can standardize any normal distribution by converting its values into Z-scores. Converting to the standard normal lets you compare normal distributions with different means and standard deviations.

Calculating Standardized Scores

If you are curious about the math behind calculating the Z-score's value, the formula is as follows:

$$Z = \frac{x - \mu}{\sigma}$$

It is common to use tables like Table 5.10 to look up the critical value for the desired confidence interval instead of calculating it manually.

Student's t-distribution

The *Student's t-distribution*, commonly known as the *t-distribution*, is similar to the standard normal distribution in that it has a mean of 0 with a bell-like shape. One way the t-distribution differs from the standard normal distribution is how thick the tails are since you can use the t-distribution for sample sizes of less than 30. Consider Figure 5.12, which overlays a normal distribution and a t-distribution. Note that there is more area under the tails of the t-distribution than of the normal distribution.

FIGURE 5.12   Standard normal distribution and t-distribution

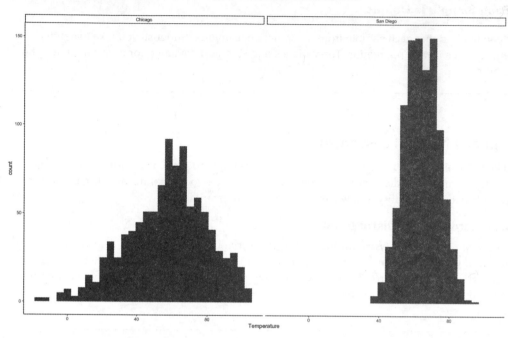

It's crucial to note that the height of the bell and the thickness of the tails in t-distributions vary due to the number of degrees of freedom. Numerically, the value for *degrees of freedom* is 1 less than the number of observations in your sample data. The degrees of freedom represent the number of values that can vary when calculating a statistic.

For example, consider the data in Table 5.7. In each row, there are three observations, and the value of the mean calculates to 50. In this example, if the first two observations are known, the value of the third observation must be fixed in order to calculate a mean of 50.

TABLE 5.7   Illustrating degrees of freedom

x_1	x_2	x_3	Mean
49	50	51	50
40	50	60	50
20	50	a	50
20	b	c	50

Consider the third row of Table 5.7. Since the mean is 50, the value of a must be 80:

Initial Equation: $\qquad\qquad\dfrac{20 + 50 + a}{3} = 50$

Multiply both sides by 3: $\qquad 20 + 50 + a = 150$

Subtract 70 from both sides: $\quad a = 80$

Now consider the last row of Table 5.7, where b and c represent unknown values:

Initial Equation: $\qquad\qquad\dfrac{20 + b + c}{3} = 50$

Multiply both sides by 3: $\qquad 20 + b + c = 130$

Subtract 20 from both sides: $\quad b + c = 130$

In this case b and c can be any combination of values that add up to 130, meaning that the values are free to vary. Since there are two observations that can have variable values, this sample data has 2 degrees of freedom.

Recall that by definition, the number of degrees of freedom increases as the sample size goes up, affecting the shape of the curve. The greater the degrees of freedom, the more the t-distribution looks like the standard normal distribution.

Measures of Position

Understanding a specific value for a variable relative to the other values for that variable gives you an indication of the organization of your data. Statisticians commonly use quartiles to describe a specific observation's position. The process of obtaining quartiles is similar to that of determining the median. You first sort a numeric dataset from smallest to largest and divide it positionally into four equal groups. Each grouping is known as a *quartile*. The first quartile is the group that starts with the minimum value, whereas the fourth quartile is the group that ends with the maximum value.

Figure 5.13 visualizes a dataset containing the sales price for 30,000 homes. To better understand the specific values for this data, you calculate an initial set of summary statistics, including the minimum, median, and maximum values, as well as the quartiles. Table 5.8 illustrates these summary statistics for this data.

FIGURE 5.13   Sales prices for 30,000 homes

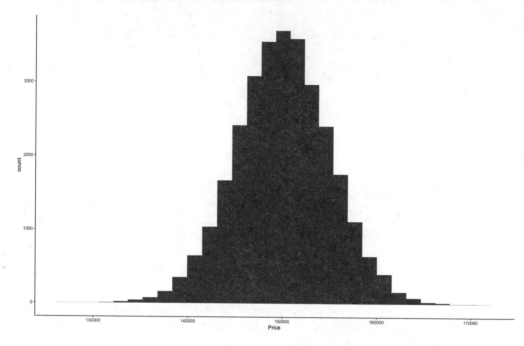

TABLE 5.8   Illustrating interquartile range

Positional statistic	Value
Minimum	128,246
First Quartile	146,657
Median	150,069
Third Quartile	153,420
Maximum	172,197

Once you've calculated these summary statistics, you have a better understanding of the position of your data, as shown in Table 5.9.

TABLE 5.9   Illustrating lower and upper limits for interquartiles

Quartile	Lower bound	Upper bound	Range
First	128,246	146,657	18,411
Second	146,657	150,069	3,412
Third	150,069	153,420	3,351
Fourth	153,420	172,197	18,777

The *interquartile range* (*IQR*) is the combination of the second and third quartiles and contains 50 percent of the values in the data. When exploring a dataset, recall that outliers can have a significant impact on mean and range. Using the IQR as a dispersion indicator, in addition to the range, improves your perspective since the IQR excludes outliers.

Inferential Statistics

Inferential statistics is a branch of statistics that uses sample data to draw conclusions about the overall population. For example, suppose you are trying to quantify the weight of college students in the United States. With more than 20 million college students, getting a complete census is not feasible. By combining balanced, representative sample data with inferential statistical techniques, you can confidently make assertions about the broader population.

Confidence Intervals

Each time you take a sample from a population, the statistics you generate are unique to the sample. In order to make inferences about the population as a whole, you need a way to come up with a range of scores that you can use to describe the population as a whole. A *confidence interval* describes the possibility that a sample statistic contains the true population parameter in a range of values around the mean. When calculating a confidence interval, you end up with a *lower bound* value and an *upper bound* value. Given the confidence interval range, the lower bound is the lower limit, and the upper bound is the upper limit.

Confidence Interval Considerations

While it is possible to develop a confidence interval for a skewed distribution, our conversation will focus on a normal distribution and presume the sample mean, population standard deviation, and sample size are known.

When calculating a confidence interval, you need to specify the confidence level in addition to the sample mean, population standard deviation, and sample size. Based on the empirical rule, the *confidence level* is a percentage that describes the range around the mean. The wider the confidence level, the more confident one can be in capturing the true mean for the sample. High confidence levels have a wide confidence interval, while low confidence levels have a narrower confidence interval.

The *critical value* is a Z-score you specify to denote the percentage of values you want the confidence interval to include. Since deriving critical values is beyond the scope of this book, Table 5.10 illustrates commonly used confidence levels and their corresponding critical values. When looking at the mathematical formula for calculating confidence intervals, z is the symbol for the critical value associated with a particular confidence level.

TABLE 5.10   Confidence level and critical value for normally distributed data

Confidence level	Critical value (2-tail) (Z-score)
80%	1.282
85%	1.440
90%	1.645
95%	1.960
99%	2.575
99.5%	2.807
99.9%	3.291

In addition to the critical value, you need the standard error. The *standard error* measures the standard deviation of the distribution of means for a given sample size. You calculate the standard error by taking the population standard deviation divided by the square root of the sample size.

Now that you know all the components, you need to calculate a confidence interval. Here is the formula:

$$CI = \bar{x} \pm z \frac{\sigma}{\sqrt{n}}$$

Let's look at a practical example of why understanding confidence intervals is crucial when working with sample data. Suppose you are working with a population of 10,000 people and have a sample size of 100. If you take 20 different samples, the specific observations in each sample will vary across each of the 20 samples, as Figure 5.14 illustrates. Looking at Figure 5.14, the outer circle represents the population and the small circles denote individual samples. Since the sample membership is random, they should be representative of the overall population. However, it is statistically possible for a group of extreme values to make up a sample.

FIGURE 5.14   Samples in a population

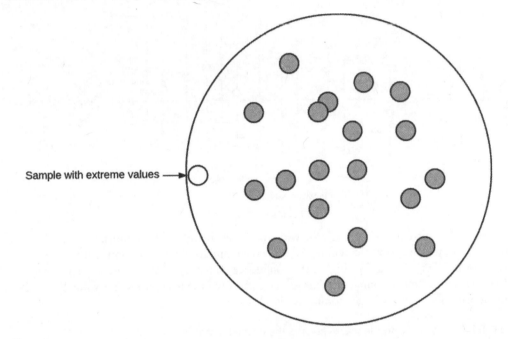

Samples taken from a population

Now, suppose you want to estimate the population mean using the mean of your samples. The likelihood that the mean of a given sample is the actual mean of the population is low, so you build a buffer of numbers around the sample mean in the hopes of capturing the true value of the population. Start by specifying a confidence level. A 95 percent confidence level indicates that 95 percent of the time, the range of values around the sample mean will contain the population mean. That implies that in 5 percent of the samples, or 1 in 20, the range around the sample mean will not contain the population mean.

Consider Figure 5.15, which shows a different depiction of the 20 samples from Figure 5.14. Figure 5.15 also shows that this population has a mean of 50. The population mean value is fixed and doesn't change. As such, a given sample may or may not contain the actual population mean. In Figure 5.15, you see a population mean of 50 and 20 samples at a 95 percent confidence level. Notice that the second sample doesn't contain the population mean because the line indicating the range of values around the sample mean doesn't cross the line for the population mean.

FIGURE 5.15   Samples at a 95 percent confidence level and population mean

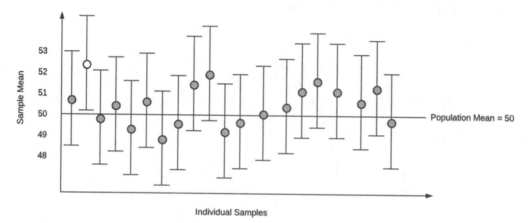

The higher the confidence level, the wider the range of values it contains. Consider Figure 5.16, which shows the width of a 95 percent and a 99 percent confidence interval on a normal distribution. The higher the confidence interval, the more values it contains; thus, we can be "more confident" that we have captured the true parameter value within its boundaries if we have a larger confidence level.

FIGURE 5.16   Confidence levels and the normal distribution

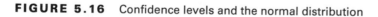
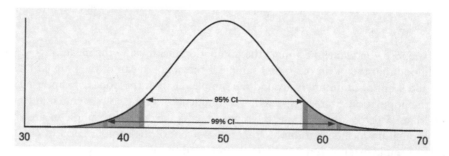

When using confidence intervals, you need to balance what's good enough for the situation at hand. For example, a 95 percent confidence interval may be appropriate for

estimating the average weight of adult females in the United States. However, if you are trying to achieve a Six Sigma manufacturing process, you need greater accuracy than a 95 percent confidence interval.

Substituting Sample Standard Deviation for Population Standard Deviation

When calculating confidence intervals, you need to have the standard deviation of the entire population. However, since getting measures about the whole population is challenging, the population standard deviation is likely unknown. In that case, while it's more precise to use the t-distribution, if your sample size is greater than 30, it's reasonable to use the normal distribution and substitute the sample standard deviation as follows:

$$CI = \bar{x} \pm z\frac{s}{\sqrt{n}}$$

Hypothesis Testing

Data analysts frequently need to build convincing arguments using data. One of the approaches to proving or disproving ideas is hypothesis testing. A *hypothesis test* consists of two statements, only one of which can be true. It uses statistical analysis of observable data to determine which of the two statements is most likely to be true.

For example, suppose you are a pricing analyst for an airline. One question you might want to explore is whether or not people over 75 inches tall are willing to pay more for additional legroom on roundtrip flights between Chicago and San Francisco. By conducting a hypothesis test on a sample of passengers, the analyst can make an inference about the population as a whole.

Exam Tip

As you prepare for the Data+ exam, keep in mind that when hypothesis testing, the null and alternative hypothesis describe the effect in terms of the total population. To perform the hypothesis test itself, you need sample data to make inferences about characteristics of the overall population.

A hypothesis test consists of two components: the null hypothesis and the alternative hypothesis. When designing a hypothesis test, you first develop the null hypothesis. A *null hypothesis* (H_0) presumes that there is no effect to the test you are conducting. When hypothesis testing, your default assumption is that the null hypothesis is valid and that you have to have evidence to reject it. For instance, the null hypothesis for the airline example is that people over 75 inches tall are not willing to pay more for additional legroom on a flight.

You also need to develop the alternative hypothesis. The *alternative hypothesis* (H_a) presumes that the test you are conducting has an effect. The alternative hypothesis for the airline pricing example is that people over 75 inches are willing to pay more for more legroom. The ultimate goal is to assess whether the null hypothesis is valid or if there is a statistically significant reason to reject the null hypothesis.

To determine the statistical significance of whether to accept or reject the null hypothesis, you need to compare a test statistic against a critical value. A *test statistic* is a single numeric value that describes how closely your sample data matches the distribution of data under the null hypothesis. In the airline pricing example, you can convert the mean price people are willing to pay for additional legroom into a test statistic that can then be compared to a critical value, ultimately indicating whether you should reject or retain the null hypothesis.

In order to get the right critical value, you need to choose a significance level. A *significance level*, also known as *alpha* (α), is the probability of rejecting the null hypothesis when it is true. Alpha levels are related to confidence levels as follows:

$$\alpha = 100\% - C$$

For example, suppose you specify a confidence level of 95 percent. You calculate the significance level by subtracting the confidence level from 100 percent. With a confidence level of 0.95, the significance level is 0.05, meaning that there is a 5 percent chance of concluding that there is a difference when there isn't one. The significance level is something you can adjust for each hypothesis test.

Consider Figure 5.17, where the population mean is 50. The unshaded area represents the confidence level. The shaded areas are the critical regions. A *critical region* contains the values where you reject the null hypothesis. If your test statistic falls within a critical region, there is sufficient evidence to reject the null hypothesis. Since the area of the critical regions combined is alpha, each tail is half of alpha. For example, if alpha is 5 percent, each critical region in Figure 5.17 is 2.5 percent of the area under the curve.

FIGURE 5.17   Visualizing alpha

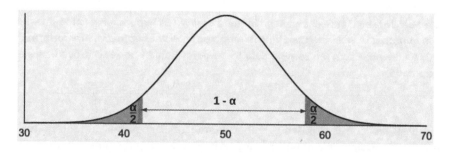

Once you have a test statistic, you can calculate a p-value. A *p-value* is the probability that a test statistic is as or more extreme as your actual results, presuming the null hypothesis is true. You can think of the p-value as the evidence against the null hypothesis. The range for p-values falls between 0 and 1. The lower the p-value, the less likely the test statistic results from random chance. When you compare your p-value with your significance level, it is generally accepted that if a p-value is less than 0.05, you may consider the results "statistically significant."

How you define your null and alternative hypotheses determines whether you are conducting a one-tailed or a two-tailed test. A *one-tailed test* is when the alternative hypothesis is trying to prove a difference in a specific direction. If your alternative hypothesis is trying to determine if a value is lower than the null value, you use a one-tailed test. Similarly, if your alternative hypothesis is assessing whether a value is higher than the null value, a one-tailed test is appropriate. Since the airline example assesses whether a person is willing to pay more for additional legroom, it is a one-tailed test. Specifically, to reject the null hypothesis, you want the average price people are willing to pay to be in the shaded area in Figure 5.18.

FIGURE 5.18   One-tailed test

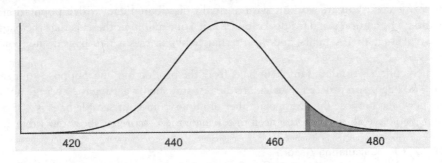

A *two-tailed test* is when the alternative hypothesis seeks to infer that something is not equal to the assertion in the null hypothesis. For example, suppose you manufacture and sell bags of individually wrapped mints. Each bag should contain an average of 100 mints within a range of 95 to 105. In this case, the production process is defective if bags contain on average either less than 95 or more than 105 mints. To determine whether or not this is the case, you use a two-tailed test with the critical regions shaded in Figure 5.19. To conduct a hypothesis test for this example, you select a sample of bags from your production line and then determine if the average number of mints from the sample bags falls within the range from 95 to 105. The larger the sample size, the more reliable your inference will be. You need to carefully balance the number of samples and the proportion of those samples to the population with the cost of obtaining them.

FIGURE 5.19   Two-tailed test

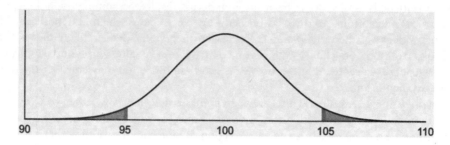

Hypothesis Testing with the *Z*-test

Hypothesis testing with the *Z-test* is appropriate when you have a sample size over 30 and a known population standard deviation, and you are using the normal distribution. When performing a two-tailed *Z*-test, you can use the *Z*-score from Table 5.10 to specify your confidence level. The *Z-score* describes how far away from the mean a given value is.

Let's walk through the bag of mints example in detail. Let's say you choose an alpha value of 95 percent. You are working with normally distributed data with a population mean of 100 and a population standard deviation of 2.5. Your null hypothesis is that the bags contain an average of 100 mints, and the alternative hypotheses is that bags do not contain 100 mints.

You then collect a random sample of bags from the production line. Suppose your sample contains 100 bags. You proceed to calculate the test statistic by getting the average number of mints per bag. Suppose the average number of mints from your sample bags is 105.5. At this point, you have all the data you need to calculate the Z-score, as shown in Table 5.11.

TABLE 5.11   Calculating Z-score

$x =$	105.5
$\mu =$	100
$\sigma =$	2.5
$Z = \dfrac{105.5 - 100}{2.5} =$	2.2

Once you have your Z-score of 2.2, you can compare it to the confidence levels in Table 5.10. A Z-score of 2.2 falls between 95 percent and 99 percent. With an alpha of 95 percent, the Z-score of 2.2 indicates that your sample mean falls within the critical region, providing evidence that you should reject the null and conclude that, on average, a bag does not contain 100 mints.

Continuing this example, let's explore precisely where 105.5 falls in the critical region by looking at its probability value, or p-value. Recall that a p-value of less than 0.05 is considered statistically significant. In Figure 5.20, we see that the p-value for 105.5 is 0.028. With a p-value of 0.028, this means that there is only a 2.8 percent probability that a bag contains 100 mints due to random chance. Since 2.8 percent is less than 5 percent, you would say the results of this hypothesis test are statistically significant. Once again, it is a good idea to capture more than one sample to account for your chosen confidence level.

FIGURE 5.20   Sample statistic and p-value

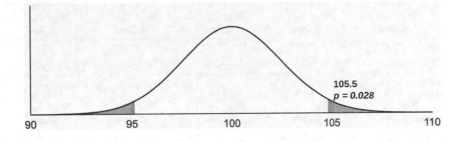

Exam Tip

As you prepare for the Data+ exam, keep in mind the concept of p-values and statistical significance. When the p-value is less than or equal to 0.05, you should reject the null hypothesis. Alternatively, when the p-value is greater than 0.05, you should retain the null hypothesis as there is not enough statistical evidence to accept the alternative hypothesis. Remember this saying:

"When the p is low, the null must go.

When the p is high, the null must fly!"

Hypothesis Testing with the t-test

Frequently, the standard deviation of the population is unknown. It's also possible that you will have a sample size of less than 30. In either of those cases, the Z-test is not an option. In this case, you can perform a t-test. A *t-test* is conceptually similar to a Z-test, but uses the t-distribution instead of the standard normal distribution. You interpret the results of a t-test the same way you interpret a Z-test in terms of critical regions, confidence levels, and p-values.

For example, suppose you want to have the same situation in terms of determining whether or not people over 75 inches tall are willing to pay for additional legroom on a flight. However, due to time constraints, you are only able to collect a sample of 10. You also don't have precise data on the standard deviation on the payment variability for the population of flyers who are over 75 inches in height. As such, you can use a t-test to evaluate your null and alternative hypotheses. Consider the flowchart in Figure 5.21 when determining whether to use a Z-test or t-test.

FIGURE 5.21   Hypothesis testing flowchart

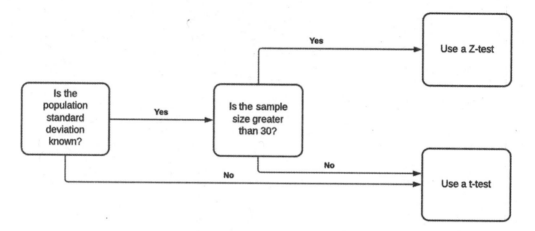

Assessing Hypothesis Tests

Recall that retaining or rejecting the null is based on probabilities. Even with a very low p-value, it is still possible that your sample data won't accurately describe the population, as shown in Figure 5.15. As such, you can end up making a Type I or Type II error, mistakenly rejecting either the null or the alternative hypothesis.

A *Type I error* happens when you have a false positive, rejecting the null hypothesis when it is true. Continuing with the mint bag example, suppose your sample mean is 105.5. However, despite the low p-value, the actual population mean of the number of mints per bag is 100, which falls outside the critical range as shown in Figure 5.19. Therefore, you end up rejecting the null hypothesis even though it is true and commit a Type I error.

A *Type II error* happens when you have a false negative, retaining the null hypothesis when it is false. In this case, suppose you calculate a sample mean of 104. As Figure 5.22

shows, the p-value for 104 is 0.11. Leaning on your statistics knowledge, you retain the null hypothesis and conclude that there are an average of 100 mints per bag. If the actual population mean is 107, falling outside the critical regions, you are committing a Type II error. Table 5.12 is a matrix that describes the possible outcomes when conducting hypothesis tests.

TABLE 5.12 Potential hypothesis test outcomes

When the null hypothesis is:	True	False
Rejected	Type I error: False positive	Correct decision
Accepted	Correct decision	Type II error: False negative

FIGURE 5.22 Insignificant sample mean

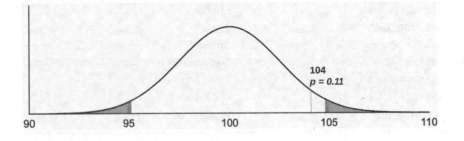

Hypothesis Testing with Chi-Square

Z-tests and t-tests work well for numeric data. However, there are times when you want to compare the observed frequencies of categorical variables against what was expected. The *chi-square test* is available when you need to assess the association of two categorical variables. In this case, the null hypothesis asserts that there is no association between the variables, and the alternative hypothesis states that there is an association between them.

For example, suppose you want to determine whether a statistically significant association exists between a person's eye color and their favorite music genre. To test this, you survey 100 random people, record their eye color, and ask them their favorite movie genre. After obtaining the data, you perform a chi-square test to assess whether there is a statistically significant relationship between eye color and movie genre. If the results suggest you retain the null, the two variables are independent. If the results suggest you reject the null, then some sort of relationship exists between eye color and favorite movie genre.

Another example where the chi-square test is appropriate is if you want to understand the relationship between a person's favorite sport to watch and where they attend university, as shown in Table 5.13. To test this, you would survey 10 random people from each university and ask them to select their favorite sport. Once you have the data, you perform a chi-square test to determine whether there is a statistically significant association between each person's university and their favorite sport.

TABLE 5.13   Categorical variables

Options for university	Options for favorite sport
Indiana University	Baseball
University of Michigan	Basketball
Michigan State University	Football
The Ohio State University	Rugby
Pennsylvania State University	Soccer
University of Illinois	Softball
University of Iowa	Swimming
University of Minnesota	Track and field
Purdue University	Volleyball
University of Wisconsin	Water polo

Simple Linear Regression

Simple linear regression is an analysis technique that explores the relationship between an independent variable and a dependent variable. You can use linear regression to identify whether the independent variable is a good predictor of the dependent variable. You can perform a regression analysis in spreadsheets like Microsoft Excel and programming languages, including Python and R. When plotting the results of a regression, the independent variable is on the x-axis and the dependent variable is on the y-axis.

Simple linear regression has many applications. For example, you might use simple linear regression to assess the impact of a marketing promotion on a company's sales. In healthcare, you might explore the relationship between a person's age and body mass index (BMI).

Consider the graph in Figure 5.23, which explores the relationship between a person's age and BMI. In this case, age is the independent variable and BMI is the dependent variable. Each point on the plot is an observation of a given person, their age, and their BMI. The line in Figure 5.23 represents the regression line that best fits the data, minimizing the distance between the points and the line itself. Since the regression line inclines to the right, it has a *positive slope.* If the line declines to the right, it would have a *negative slope.* The positive slope of the regression line implies that as age increases, BMI increases as well. Since the slope is so slight, BMI doesn't increase dramatically as a function of age.

FIGURE 5.23 Simple linear regression of age and BMI

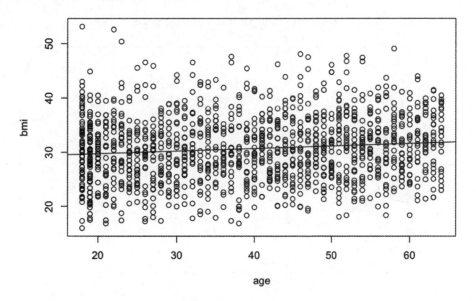

Using simple linear regression, you want to determine if the dependent variable truly depends on the independent variable. Figure 5.24 shows the output of a linear model generated with R. Examining Figure 5.24, the Pr(>|t|) column represents the p-value. Since the p-value for age in this output is 0.0000619, you can reject the null hypothesis and conclude that BMI does depend on age.

FIGURE 5.24 Linear model output of age and BMI

```
Call:
lm(formula = bmi ~ age, data = insurance)

Residuals:
    Min      1Q  Median      3Q     Max
-13.791  -4.359  -0.240   4.127  23.472

Coefficients:
            Estimate Std. Error t value             Pr(>|t|)
(Intercept) 28.80389    0.49158  58.595 < 0.0000000000000002 ***
age          0.04743    0.01180   4.018            0.0000619 ***
---
Signif. codes:  0 '***' 0.001 '**' 0.01 '*' 0.05 '.' 0.1 ' ' 1

Residual standard error: 6.064 on 1336 degrees of freedom
Multiple R-squared:  0.01194,  Adjusted R-squared:  0.0112
F-statistic: 16.15 on 1 and 1336 DF,  p-value: 0.00006194
```

Consider Figure 5.25, which examines the relationship between a vehicle's speed and its ability to come to a complete stop. Although there are relatively few observations, the regression line has a positive slope. Since the slope of the line is steeper in Figure 5.25 than in Figure 5.23, you conclude that every increase in miles per hour has a more significant impact on stopping distance than a comparative increase in age has on BMI.

FIGURE 5.25   Simple linear regression of speed and distance

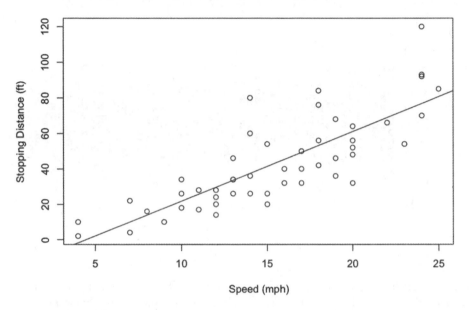

From Simple to Multiple Linear Regression

Note that you explore the relationship between two variables using simple linear regression. Multiple linear regression builds on that concept by examining the effect of numerous independent variables on a dependent variable. For example, Figure 5.24 shows the impact of vehicle speed on braking distance. However, there are many different types of tires, including winter, all-season, and high performance. The type of tire on a vehicle may also affect braking distance. You can use multiple linear regression to assess the impact of tire composition and speed on braking distance.

A crucial aspect of linear regression is the correlation between how far the observations are from the regression line. *Correlation* is a measurement of how well the regression line fits the observations. The *correlation coefficient* (r) ranges between –1 and 1 and indicates the strength of the correlation. The stronger the correlation, the more tightly the points wind around the line of best fit. Perfect correlation is when r has a value of either –1 or 1, implying that every data point falls directly on the regression line. Interpreting correlation strength depends on the industry. Table 5.14 provides an example of guidelines for interpreting correlation strength in medical research.

TABLE 5.14   Medical research correlation coefficient guidelines

Association strength	Positive *r*	Negative *r*
Negligible	0.0 – 0.3	0.0 – –0.3
Low	0.3 – 0.5	–0.3 – –0.5
Moderate	0.5 – 0.7	–0.5 – –0.7
High	0.7 – 0.9	–0.7 – –0.9
Very High	0.9 – 1.0	–0.9 – –1.0

In Figure 5.23, the correlation is low since many observations are not close to the regression line. Correlation improves in Figure 5.25, since the points are not as widely scattered. Figure 5.26 illustrates a highly correlated relationship. As you can imagine, the better the correlation, the stronger the relationship between the independent and dependent variables.

FIGURE 5.26   Highly correlated data

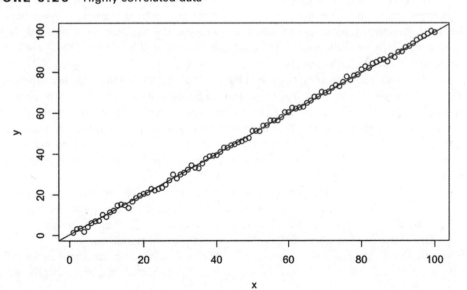

When evaluating the correlation between variables, one thing to keep in mind is that it does not imply causation. For example, consider the turbine speed of a hydroelectric dam on a river. After heavy rain, the river's flow increases, as does the speed of the turbine, making turbine speed and water flow highly correlated. An incorrect conclusion is that an increase in the turbine's speed causes an increase in water flow.

Analysis Techniques

Data analysts have an abundance of statistical tools available to explore data in the pursuit of insights. While you need to understand when to use the appropriate tool or statistical test, it is crucial to identify and apply techniques that help you structure your approach. When assessing techniques, you should identify and adopt frameworks that help improve the consistency of how you approach new data challenges.

Determine Type of Analysis

When embarking on a new analytics challenge, you need to understand the business objectives and desired outcomes. This understanding informs the type of analysis you will conduct. The first step to understanding the objectives is to ensure that you have clarity on the business questions at hand. Recall that the goal of answering a business question is to develop an insight that informs a business decision.

Business questions come in many forms. You may receive questions informally through hallway conversations, text messages, or emails. More significant initiatives should have written requirements documents defining the business questions that are in scope. Regardless of the form your requirements are in, you need to review the business questions and identify any points that require additional clarification. This clarity will help you identify the data you need as well as the data sources.

While reviewing requirements, develop a list of clarifying questions. This list can help define the scope of your analysis. Your clarification list can also identify any gaps between what is achievable given data source and time constraints. For example, one of the requirements may be to analyze sales data for the past 10 years. However, due to a change in the system that records sales, you only have access to seven years of historical information. The absence of data over a three-year period is a gap you need to discuss with your business partner.

Once you have your list of questions, review it with the business sponsor to ensure you agree on expectations. Recognize that reviewing and refining business questions is an iterative process. While you need to have initial clarity, you will likely have to return to your business leader for additional clarification as you conduct your analysis.

When you have consensus on the scope of your analysis, have clarity about outstanding questions, and know what data you need and where it is coming from, you can proceed confidently with conducting your analysis. It's a good idea to maintain your requirements document as you go about your work. Use the document to track new issues that impact the project timeline and any adjustments to project scope or ultimate deliverables. A running log identifying any scope changes is a valuable aid that can help you make sure you deliver your analysis on time. It can also help you after your work is complete as you reflect on what went well and what would make future endeavors more successful.

Types of Analysis

With a clear scope and access to the data you need, you can get on with your analytical work. One of the types of analysis you may be asked to perform is trend analysis. *Trend analysis* seeks to identify patterns by comparing data over time. Suppose you work for a hospitality company with properties in the United States, and one of your goals is to evaluate corporate performance. To advance that goal, you examine the total sales for each state over the past five years. In conducting trend analysis, you can identify whether sales are declining, remaining consistent, or growing in every state. Understanding sales trends may influence the company to sell unprofitable properties and invest in areas that show signs of sustained growth.

In addition to trend analysis, you may also conduct performance analysis. *Performance analysis* examines defined goals and measures performance against them and can inform the development of future projections. Continuing with the hospitality example, the company may have average occupancy goals for each property in its portfolio. Performance analysis can identify whether properties are achieving those goals. Combining performance analysis with trend analysis can help develop projections for the future.

For example, suppose one of the company's properties is a hotel in Chicago. The sales trend for that property has been going up over the past five years. However, the data shows that this property has been inconsistent in achieving its occupancy target. The results of this analysis are that hotel management has found a way to grow sales despite inconsistent occupancy performance. The company could then follow up with local management to understand why this is true and if any local tactics are applicable to other properties.

Suppose another of the company's properties is a hotel in Des Moines, Iowa. The data shows that this property's sales and occupancy numbers are growing. With no obvious location factors influencing this growth, the company can follow up with local management to better understand this location's success. While past performance doesn't guarantee future success, the results of this analysis can help the company establish basic occupancy and sales projections for the coming year.

If you need to explore patterns in the connection between individual observations, it may be necessary to perform a link analysis. *Link analysis* is a technique that uses network theory to explore the relationship between data points. In 2015, the International Consortium of Investigative Journalists (ICIJ) received one of the most sizable data leaks in history, known as the Panama Papers. Over 11.5 million documents consisting of 40 years' worth of data are in this leak. By conducting a link analysis, the ICIJ analyzed these documents and uncovered patterns of illicit financial behavior, including tax evasion and money laundering.

Exploratory Data Analysis

At the onset of your analysis, you will encounter many datasets for the first time. When first exploring a dataset, it's a good idea to perform an exploratory data analysis. An *exploratory data analysis (EDA)* uses descriptive statistics to summarize the main characteristics of a dataset, identify outliers, and give you context for further analysis. While there are many approaches to conducting an EDA, they typically encompass the following steps:

- **Check Data Structure:** Ensure that data is in the correct format for analysis. Most analysis tools expect data to be in a tabular format, so you need to confirm that your data has defined rows and columns.

- **Check Data Representation:** Become familiar with the data. In this step, you validate data types and ensure that variables contain the data you expect.

- **Check if Data Is Missing:** Check to see if any data is missing from the dataset and determine what to do next. While checking for null values, calculate the proportion of each variable that is missing. If you discover that most of the data you need is missing, you need to either categorize it as missing or impute a value for the missing data. You can also go back to the source and remediate any data extraction issues.

- **Identify Outliers:** Recall from Chapter 4 that an outlier is an observation of a variable that deviates significantly from other observations of that variable. As shown in this chapter, outliers can dramatically impact some descriptive statistics, like the mean. It would be best to determine the cause of outliers and consider whether you want to leave them in the data before proceeding with any ongoing analysis.

- **Summarize Statistics:** Calculate summary statistics for each variable. For numeric variables, examples of summary statistics include mean, median, and variance. For categorical data like eye color, you could develop a table showing the frequency with which each observation occurs.

- **Check Assumptions:** Depending on the statistical method you are using, you need to understand the shape of the data. For example, if you are working with numeric data, you should choose a normal or t-distribution for drawing inferences. If you are working with categorical data, use the chi-square distribution.

Summary

Wielding statistical techniques to analyze data is a cornerstone ability of the modern data analyst. It is imperative to appreciate the difference between census and sample data. A census consists of an observation for every member of the population, whereas a sample is data about a specific subset. Since it is frequently prohibitive to obtain a census, analysts typically work with sample data. Whether you are working with census or sample data, you end up using statistics.

Descriptive statistics is a branch of statistics that describes a dataset. Descriptive statistics help you understand the data's characteristics and can help understand events that have already happened. One category of descriptive statistics is measures of frequency. Measures of frequency shed light on recurring values in your data. Count is the most common measure of frequency. For example, one of the first things an analyst does when encountering a new table in a database is to get the total number of rows by issuing the following SQL statement:

```
SELECT COUNT(*) FROM <table_name>
```

Once you understand the total number of rows you are dealing with, it is common to understand proportions in the data to check for bias. For example, if the population you are studying is split evenly between men and women, you would expect that any random sample from the population would have an equal proportion of men and women.

Measures of central tendency are descriptive statistics that help you understand how tightly or widely distributed your data is. Mean, median, and mode are all measures of central tendency. Exploring how far apart the mean and median values are can tell you whether you are working with data that follows a normal distribution. If the mean and median are close, the distribution is likely normal. If the mean and median are far apart, the data is skewed to one side.

Measures of dispersion help you understand how widely distributed your data is. The range, or difference between maximum and minimum values, establishes the upper and lower limits for numeric variables in your data. Variance is a dispersion measure that calculates how far each observation in a dataset is from its mean value and is most often used as a path to calculating standard deviation. Standard deviation, or the square root of variance, is a frequently referenced statistic due to the empirical rule, stating that almost every observation falls within three standard deviations from the mean in a normal distribution.

Measures of position help identify where a specific value for an observation is relative to other values. The interquartile range is a valuable measure of position, as it places all values of a variable into one of four quartiles where 50 percent of the values in a dataset are in the second and third quartiles.

Inferential statistics differs from descriptive statistics in that you can use inferential statistics from a sample to draw conclusions about the population. Making generalizations about the population using sample data is a powerful concept that enables impactful decisions.

When performing statistical inference, you have a degree of uncertainty as inferential statistics are based on probabilities. Confidence intervals help you understand how a test statistic relates to its corresponding population parameter. A confidence interval provides the upper and lower limits for a given confidence level that the population parameter falls within the confidence interval's range. The higher the confidence level, the wider the range of values fall within the confidence interval.

You also use statistics to conduct hypothesis tests. Hypothesis tests assert two mutually exclusive statements in the form of the null and alternative hypotheses. When hypothesis testing, you seek to reject the status quo of the null hypothesis by using statistics to assert that the alternative hypothesis is plausible.

The sample size impacts the distribution you use when conducting hypothesis tests. When working with numeric data, you can use the normal distribution if you know the population standard deviation and have a sample size greater than 30. However, if the population standard deviation is unknown or the sample size is less than 30, you use the t-distribution. If you are working with categorical data, you use the chi-square distribution for comparison purposes.

You have to account for potential mistakes when hypothesis testing. A Type I error is a false positive, when you reject the status quo when it is true. A Type II error is a false negative, when you accept the status quo when it is false.

Regardless of the statistics you use, it is crucial to have a systematic approach when conducting an analysis. Having a clearly defined scope that the business representative agrees on is imperative. You also need to have access to good sources of data. With these two things in place, you initiate an analytics project by performing an exploratory data analysis (EDA). The EDA will inform you about the type of data you are working with and whether you have any missing data or outlier values, and it will provide summary statistics about each variable in your dataset.

Exam Essentials

Differentiate between descriptive and inferential statistics.   Descriptive statistics help you understand past events by summarizing data and include measures of frequency and measures of dispersion. Inferential statistics use the powerful concept of concluding an overall population using a sample from that population.

Calculate measures of central tendency.   Given a dataset, you should feel comfortable calculating the mean, median, and mode. Recall that the mean is the mathematical average. The median is the value that separates the lower and higher portions of an ordered set of numbers. The mode is the value that occurs most frequently. While mean and median are applicable for numeric data, evaluating the mode is particularly useful when describing categorical data.

Explain how to interpret a p-value when hypothesis testing.   Recall that p-values denote the probability that a test statistic is as extreme as the actual result, presuming the null hypothesis is true. The lower the p-value, the more evidence there is to reject the null hypothesis. Generally speaking, it is safe to consider p-values under 0.05 as being statistically significant. With p-values greater than 0.05, there is less evidence supporting the alternative hypothesis.

Explain the difference between a Type I and Type II error.   When hypothesis testing, a Type I error is a false positive, while a Type II error is a false negative. Suppose you have a null hypothesis stating that a new vaccine is ineffective and an alternative hypothesis stating that the vaccine has its intended impact. Concluding that the vaccine is effective when it isn't is a Type I error. A Type II error is a false conclusion that the vaccine doesn't work when it does have the intended effect.

Describe the purpose of exploratory data analysis (EDA).   One of the first things you should perform with any new dataset is EDA, a structured approach using descriptive statistics to summarize the characteristics of a dataset, identify any outliers, and help you develop your plan for further analysis.

Review Questions

1. Sandy is studying silverback gorillas and wants to determine the average weight for males and females. What best describes the dataset she needs?

    A. Observation

    B. Population

    C. Sample

    D. Variable

2. James wants to understand dispersion in his dataset. Which statistic best matches his needs?

    A. Median

    B. Mode

    C. Mean

    D. Interquartile range

3. Yunqi is collecting data about people's preferred automotive color. Which statistic will help her identify the most popular color?

    A. Mean

    B. Median

    C. Mode

    D. Range

4. Jenny is an occupancy analyst for a hotel. Using a hypothesis test, she wants to assess whether people with families are willing to pay more for rooms near the swimming pool. What should Jenny's null hypothesis be?

    A. Families are willing to pay more for rooms near the swimming pool.

    B. Families are willing to pay less for rooms near the swimming pool.

    C. Families are not willing to pay more for rooms near the swimming pool.

    D. Families are not willing to pay less for rooms near the swimming pool.

5. Suppose that Mars Candy, the company that makes M&Ms, claims that 10 percent of the total M&Ms they produce are green, no more, no less. Suppose you wish to challenge this claim by taking a large random sample of M&Ms and determining the proportion of green M&Ms in the sample. What is the alternative hypothesis?

    A. The proportion of green M&Ms is 10 percent.

    B. The proportion of green M&Ms is less than 10 percent.

    C. The proportion of green M&Ms is more than 10 percent.

    D. The proportion of green M&Ms is not 10 percent.

6. The sales of a grocery store had an average of $8,000 per day. The store introduced several advertising campaigns in order to increase sales. To determine whether the advertising campaigns have been effective in increasing sales, a sample of 64 days of sales was selected, and the sample mean was $8,300 per day. The correct null and alternative hypotheses to test whether there has been a significant increase are:

A. Null: Sample mean is 8,000; Alternative: Sample mean is greater than or equal to 8,000.

B. Null: Sample mean is 8,000; Alternative: Sample mean is greater than 8,000.

C. Null: Population mean is 8,000; Alternative: Population mean is greater than or equal to 8,000.

D. Null: Population mean is 8,000; Alternative: Population mean is greater than 8,000.

7. What is the mean of the following numbers: 1, 1, 2, 3, 3, 4, 5, 6, 7, 8

A. 1

B. 3

C. 3.5

D. 4

8. What is the range of the following numbers: 1, 1, 2, 3, 3, 4, 5, 6, 7, 8.

A. 1

B. 3

C. 7

D. 8

9. What is the median of the following numbers: 1, 1, 2, 3, 3, 4, 5, 6, 7, 8.

A. 1

B. 3

C. 3.5

D. 4

10. A hypothesis test sometimes rejects the null hypothesis even if the true value of the population parameter is the same as the value in the null hypothesis. This type of result is known as:

A. A Type I Error

B. A Type II Error

C. A correct inference

D. The confidence level of the inference

11. Bashar is using a t-test for hypothesis testing. His sample data contains 28 observations. What value should he specify for degrees of freedom are there?

   A. 0

   B. 1

   C. 27

   D. 28

12. Ari is studying the impact of a rural or urban childhood and the degree to which people support parks in their local community. Presuming that people can indicate a low, medium, or high level of support for parks, what should Ari use to determine the existence of a statistically significant relationship between childhood environment and park support?

   A. Z-test

   B. t-test

   C. Simple linear regression

   D. Chi-square test

13. Katsuyuki is exploring how an athlete's weight impacts their time in a 400-meter run. What should Katsuyuki use to determine whether or not weight has an impact on the time it takes to run 400 meters?

   A. Z-test

   B. t-test

   C. Simple linear regression

   D. Chi-square test

14. Zach is interpreting a left skewed distribution of test scores. Enzo scored at the mean, Alfonso scored at the median, and Jezebel scored at the end of the tail. Who had the highest score?

   A. Zach

   B. Enzo

   C. Alfonso

   D. Jezebel

15. Gregory is examining the following sample data:

   5, 12, 6, 8, 5, 9, 7, 5, 12, 4, 9, 8, 9, 10, 11, 11

   What is the median?

   A. 8

   B. 8.5

   C. 8.125

   D. 9

16. Odin wants to understand patterns in a social network. Which is the most appropriate type of analysis technique to conduct this analysis?

    A. Trend

    B. Performance

    C. Exploratory data

    D. Link

17. Loki is studying global warming by examining temperature data. What type of analysis is Loki conducting? (Choose the best answer.)

    A. Trend

    B. Performance

    C. Exploratory data

    D. Link

18. Balder wants to understand how well his team measures up against corporate sales goals. What type of analysis will give Balder the perspective he needs?

    A. Trend

    B. Performance

    C. Exploratory data

    D. Link

19. According to the empirical rule, what percent of the values in a sample fall within two standard deviations of the mean in a normal distribution?

    A. 68 percent

    B. 90 percent

    C. 95 percent

    D. 99.7 percent

20. Vidar has been asked to determine whether snowboard sales are trending higher over time. Vidar is given two datasets, one with 10 years of precipitation data, and the other with 10 years of snowboard sales from multiple manufacturers. What should he do next? (Choose the best answer.)

    A. Trend

    B. Performance

    C. Exploratory data

    D. Link

Chapter

6

Data Analytics Tools

THE COMPTIA DATA+ EXAM TOPICS COVERED IN THIS CHAPTER INCLUDE:

✓ **Domain 3.0: Data Analysis**

   ■ 3.4. Identify common data analytics tools

Analytics professionals use a wide variety of tools in their work. From simple spreadsheets to complex business intelligence suites, we have many different tools available to help us meet both generalized and specialized analytics needs.

When you're selecting a tool, there are a few important considerations. First, you need the right tool for the job. Just as a carpenter wouldn't use a screwdriver to drive a nail, an analytics professional wouldn't use a spreadsheet to create a machine learning model. Second, you need to choose from the tools available to you. Many analytics tools come with hefty price tags and organizations only license a small subset of them to control costs. Standardizing on a subset of tools also helps improve the ability of teams to work together. If every team in an organization uses different analytics tools, it makes it very difficult for them to collaborate!

Spreadsheets

The *spreadsheet* is the most widely used tool in the world of analytics. It's hard to imagine anyone who doesn't use spreadsheets as part of their work because they provide an intuitive way to organize our data into rows and columns. Spreadsheet software is installed on pretty much every computer in the modern work environment, and web-based spreadsheets are freely available to anyone.

Spreadsheets are productivity software packages that allow users to create documents that organize any type of data into rows and columns. Users may place any data they like in the spreadsheet and then quickly and easily perform mathematical calculations, such as finding the sum of the values in a row or searching out the minimum, maximum, mean, and median values in a dataset.

Spreadsheets lack any of the constraints of a relational database. While you can certainly organize data in a spreadsheet, there's no requirement that you do so. If you'd like, you can mix numbers, text, dates, and other data elements all in the same column. That does, of course, reduce the usefulness of the spreadsheet, but the user of spreadsheet software has total flexibility in how they organize their data.

The power of spreadsheets comes from the fact that virtually anybody can use one. The barrier to entry is low because they're readily accessible and easy to use. If you need to perform a quick ad hoc data analysis on a fairly small set of data, spreadsheets offer an easy way to do that and then share your work with others.

More formal business needs often stress the capabilities of a spreadsheet. Once the number of people needing to access data grows and you have the desire to keep a centralized and managed data store, these requirements often drive a move of that application from a spreadsheet to a relational database.

Microsoft Excel

Microsoft Excel is the most commonly used desktop spreadsheet application. It's available as a component of the widely deployed Microsoft Office productivity suite and most modern knowledge workers have access to it.

As with any spreadsheet, you can store data of any kind in an Excel spreadsheet. Figure 6.1 shows an example of an Excel spreadsheet containing data on restaurant inspections conducted by the city of Chicago. This spreadsheet is organized in the same way you might organize a database table—each column represents a particular data element recorded about each inspection and each row represents a single inspection event.

FIGURE 6.1   Table of data in Microsoft Excel

	Inspection ID	DBA Name	AKA Name	License #	Facility Type	Risk	Address	City	State	Zip
1	Inspection ID	DBA Name	AKA Name	License #	Facility Type	Risk	Address	City	State	Zip
2	1995829	SUBWAY	SUBWAY	1679112	Restaurant	Risk 1 (High)	8711 S ASHL/	CHICAGO	IL	60620
3	1995817	VENEZUELAN	VENEZUELAN	2424110	Restaurant	Risk 1 (High)	2436 N LINC(	CHICAGO	IL	60614
4	1995822	SEVEN TEN	SEVEN TEN	1172093	Restaurant	Risk 1 (High)	1055 E 55TH	CHICAGO	IL	60615
5	1995814	CHISME EXPF	CHISME EXPF	1334960	Restaurant	Risk 1 (High)	5955 S PULA!	CHICAGO	IL	60629
6	1995811	THE NILE RE!	THE NILE RE!	2334190	Restaurant	Risk 1 (High)	1162 E 55TH	CHICAGO	IL	60615
7	1995752	WINGSTOP	WINGSTOP	2517730	Restaurant	Risk 1 (High)	850 W 63RD	CHICAGO	IL	60621
8	1995226	JOY AND JAN	JOY AND JAN	2073555	Restaurant	Risk 1 (High)	4701 W LAW	CHICAGO	IL	60630
9	1995808	SUSHI MON	SUSHI MON	2517725	Restaurant	Risk 1 (High)	2441 N CLAR	CHICAGO	IL	60614
10	1995807	JEANE KENN	JEANE KENN	2215708	Daycare Com	Risk 1 (High)	7600 S PARN	CHICAGO	IL	60620
11	1995802	PEPE'S MEXI(	PEPE'S MEXI(	48820	Restaurant	Risk 1 (High)	1310 E 53RD	CHICAGO	IL	60615
12	1995801	CHILI'S GRILL	CHILI'S GRILL	1937623	Restaurant	Risk 1 (High)	1750 W 119T	CHICAGO	IL	60643
13	1995795	LA FIESTA BA	LA FIESTA BA	1488177	Restaurant	Risk 1 (High)	6424 S PULA!	CHICAGO	IL	60629
14	1995790	DENOVA FRE	MARTHA'S F(	2517805	Grocery Store	Risk 3 (Low)	4459 W DIVE	CHICAGO	IL	60639
15	1995725	UNCLE JOE'S	UNCLE JOE'S	1145333	Restaurant	Risk 1 (High)	10210 S VIN(	CHICAGO	IL	60643
16	1973223	TABO SUSHI	PLUM MARK	2252682	Restaurant	Risk 1 (High)	1233 N WELL	CHICAGO	IL	60610
17	1995781	RED SNAPPE	RED SNAPPE	2350305	Restaurant	Risk 1 (High)	1418 E 53RD	CHICAGO	IL	60615
18	1995779	SAMMY'S BR	SAMMY'S BR	2247014	Restaurant	Risk 1 (High)	250 E 103RD	CHICAGO	IL	60628
19	1995776	MONICA'S PI	MONICA'S PI	2522031	Restaurant	Risk 1 (High)	6446-6448 S PULASKI RD	IL	
20	1995773	A WHIZZ KID!	A WHIZZ KID!	2215488	Daycare Abo	Risk 1 (High)	2600 E 83RD	CHICAGO	IL	60617
21	1995769	MONICA'S PI	MONICA'S PI	2326731	Restaurant	Risk 1 (High)	6448 S PULA!	CHICAGO	IL	60629
22	1995766	KENTUCKY F	KFC	2442911	Restaurant	Risk 1 (High)	5852 S WEST	CHICAGO	IL	60636
23	1995777	CREME DE L/	CREME DE L/	2216029	Daycare Com	Risk 1 (High)	2230 N DOM	CHICAGO	IL	60614
24	1995768	BRIDGEPORT	COFFEE HYD	2277827	Restaurant	Risk 1 (High)	5020 S CORN	CHICAGO	IL	60615
25	1995765	FERNANDEZ	FERNANDEZ	1222819		Risk 3 (Low)	6446 S PULA!	CHICAGO	IL	60629
26	1995751	AKIBA-SCHE(	JEWISH DAY	2275647	School	Risk 1 (High)	5235 S CORN	CHICAGO	IL	60615
27	1995750	LITTLE NEST	LITTLE NEST	2492597	Children's Se	Risk 1 (High)	5426 W DEV(	CHICAGO	IL	60646

Excel then allows users to perform calculations and visualizations on their data. You might want to count the total number of restaurant inspections, determine the average length of time that an inspection takes, or compute the number of inspections conducted each day. You can perform almost any simple analysis you might need right in the Excel spreadsheet. Figure 6.2 shows an example of a quick visualization showing the results of inspections conducted by the city.

FIGURE 6.2 Data visualization in Microsoft Excel

Count of Inspection Data	Column Labels			
Row Labels	Risk 1 (High)	Risk 2 (Medium)	Risk 3 (Low)	Grand Total
Business Not Located	0.02%	0.05%	0.00%	0.03%
Fail	18.80%	18.67%	17.46%	18.69%
No Entry	4.89%	3.95%	2.41%	4.55%
Not Ready	1.04%	1.81%	5.35%	1.45%
Out of Business	5.33%	10.27%	17.23%	7.02%
Pass	57.95%	53.87%	55.20%	56.98%
Pass w/ Conditions	11.98%	11.38%	2.35%	11.27%
Grand Total	100.00%	100.00%	100.00%	100.00%

Risk 1 (High)

- Business Not Located
- Fail
- No Entry
- Not Ready
- Out of Business
- Pass
- Pass w/ Conditions

Microsoft Excel has long held a dominant market share in the spreadsheet market, but competitors do exist. For example, Apple's Numbers spreadsheet software is available to Mac users. Cloud-based spreadsheets such as Google Sheets are also quite popular because they make it easy for multiple people to collaborate on the same spreadsheet. While these other spreadsheets are interesting, you won't need to know about them on the Data+ exam because they're not mentioned in the exam objectives.

Programming Languages

In many cases, business analysts and data scientists need a way to be able to load, manipulate, and analyze data outside of the constraints of software written by another organization. In those cases, they might develop their own software to meet a specific need. In fact, many skilled analysts find it easier to write their own code to perform many analytics tasks than to work within another analytics package.

Programming languages allow skilled software developers to write their own instructions to the computer, allowing them to directly specify the actions that should take place during the analytics process.

Exam Tip

You do not need to know *how* to program on the Data+ exam, and you shouldn't expect any questions that ask you to write or interpret code. You should instead focus on the *purpose* of programming languages and where they might fit into an analytics environment.

R

The *R* programming language is extremely popular among data analysts because it is focused on creating analytics applications. R originally appeared in the 1990s as a statistical programming language that was popular among a niche audience. More than two decades later, the language has evolved into one of the most popular languages used by statisticians, data scientists, and business analysts around the world.

R gained rapid traction as a popular language for several reasons. First, it is available to everyone as a free, open source language developed by a community of committed developers. This approach broke the mold of past approaches to analytic tools that relied on proprietary, commercial software that was often out of the financial reach of many individuals and organizations.

R also continues to grow in popularity because of its adoption by the creators of machine learning methods. Almost any new machine learning technique created today quickly becomes available to R users in a redistributable *package*, offered as open source code on the Comprehensive R Archive Network (CRAN), a worldwide repository of popular R code.

One of the most important advances in the R language was the creation of a set of R packages known as the *tidyverse* by Hadley Wickham and other developers. The tidyverse approach to data analysis simplifies the use of the language and makes it accessible to anyone willing to invest a few hours in learning some basic syntax.

Most modern R developers choose to write, test, and deploy their code using an integrated development environment (IDE) called RStudio. This graphical interface, shown in Figure 6.3, provides a well-designed environment to manage your code, monitor its progress, and troubleshoot issues that might arise in your R scripts.

FIGURE 6.3   Data analysis using R and RStudio

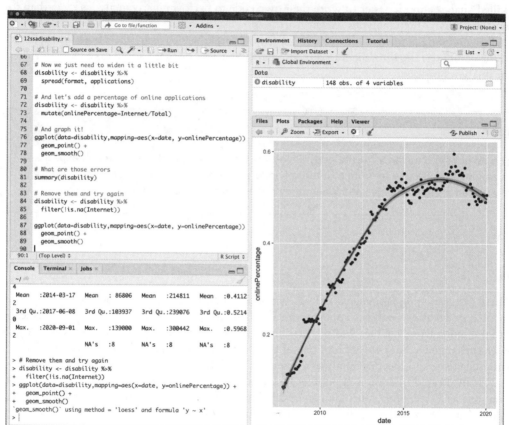

Python

The *Python* programming language is arguably the most popular programming language in use today. Python is about the same age as R, but the major difference between Python and R is that Python is a general-purpose programming language. This means that it is capable of creating software to meet just about any need you might imagine. You can do everything from code a video game to perform a complex data analysis in Python.

With that flexibility, however, comes some complexity. While R is quite popular because of its ease of use, writing software in Python requires some more expertise. Python developers usually have a more formal background in computer science and are familiar with many coding concepts, such as looping and branching, that aren't necessary in most R code.

Python also has specialized libraries that focus on the needs of analysts and data scientists. In particular, the Python Data Analysis Library (pandas) provides a set of tools for structuring and analyzing data. Figure 6.4 shows an example of Python code performing data analysis.

FIGURE 6.4   Data analysis using Python and pandas

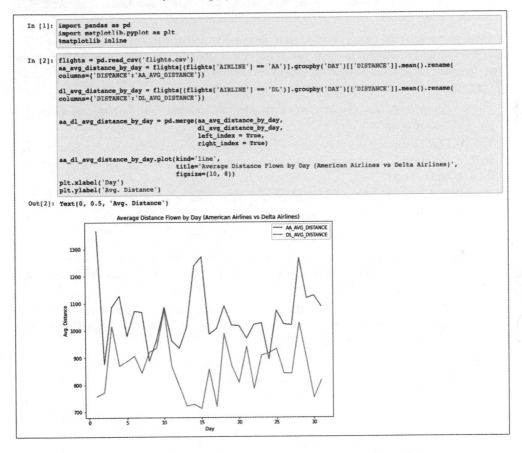

Structured Query Language (SQL)

The *Structured Query Language (SQL)* is the language of databases. Any time a developer, administrator, or end user interacts with a database, that interaction happens through the use of a SQL command. SQL is divided into two major sublanguages:

- The *Data Definition Language (DDL)* is used mainly by developers and administrators. It's used to define the structure of the database itself. It doesn't work with the data inside a database, but it sets the ground rules for the database to function.

- The *Data Manipulation Language (DML)* is the subset of SQL commands that are used to work with the data inside of a database. They don't change the database structure, but they add, remove, and change the data inside a database.

As you prepare for the exam, you'll need to be familiar with the major commands used in SQL. It's important to understand that you're not responsible for writing or reading SQL commands. You just need to know what the major commands are and when you would use them.

There are three DDL commands that you should know:

- The *CREATE* command is used to create a new table within your database or a new database on your server.

- The *ALTER* command is used to change the structure of a table that you've already created. If you want to modify your database or table, the ALTER command lets you make those modifications.

- The *DROP* command deletes an entire table or database from your server. It's definitely a command that you'll want to use with caution!

There are also four DML commands that you should know:

- The *SELECT* command is used to retrieve information from a database. It's the most commonly used command in SQL as it is used to pose queries to the database and retrieve the data that you're interested in working with.

- The *INSERT* command is used to add new records to a database table. If you're adding a new employee, customer order, or marketing activity, the INSERT command allows you to add one or more rows to your database.

- The *UPDATE* command is used to modify rows in the database. If you need to change something that is already stored in your database, the UPDATE command will do that.

- The *DELETE* command is used to delete rows from a database table. Don't confuse this command with the DROP command. The DROP command deletes an entire database table, whereas the DELETE command just deletes certain rows from the table.

Users, administrators, and developers access databases in different ways. First, a developer, administrator, or power user who knows SQL might directly access the database server and send it a SQL command for execution. This often happens through a graphical user interface, such as the Azure Data Studio interface shown in Figure 6.5. This tool allows you to write database queries in SQL, send them to the database, and then view the results.

Utilities like Azure Data Studio can do more than just retrieve data. They also offer a graphical way for database administrators to reconfigure a database. You can click through

FIGURE 6.5   SQL query using Azure Data Studio

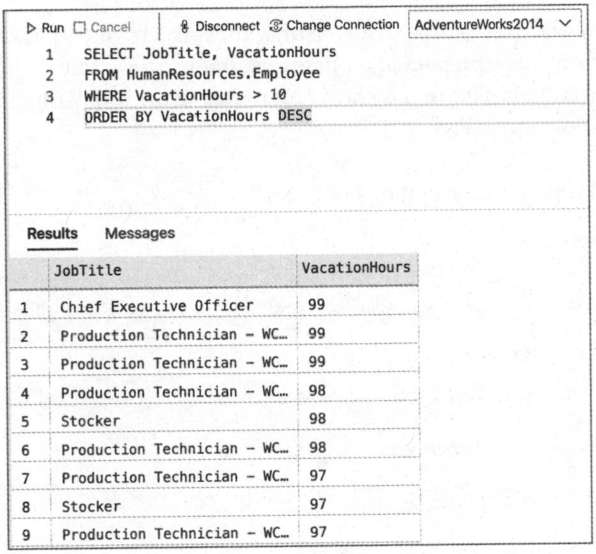

a series of menus to choose the changes you'd like to make to the database and the utility writes SQL commands that carry out your requests and sends them to the database.

Similarly, many query and report builder tools are available that simplify database access for end users, allowing them to click through a series of menus and drag objects around on the screen to retrieve data from a database. The tool then translates those actions into a SELECT statement that retrieves the desired information from the database.

Finally, computer software can interact with databases programmatically. This just means that software can send SQL commands to the database as part of its activity. For example, when you fill out a form on a company's website, chances are that software is processing that form and then storing a record of your activity in a database.

Statistics Packages

Of course, not everyone has the ability or desire to write their own software. It's often far simpler to work within software packages that provide the capabilities that we need. Statistics packages are a great example of this. These software packages go beyond the simple statistical analyses that are possible in spreadsheets and provide access to advanced statistical environments that are accessible through a graphical user interface and/or a built-in scripting language.

These software packages may be used by anyone interested in data analysis, but the reality is that they are mainly the domain of professional statisticians. Generally, data analysts with a computer science background tend to prefer using programming languages to write their own code, while those who do not have a strong background in statistics generally prefer some of the more visually oriented tools discussed later in this chapter.

IBM SPSS

One of the most popular pieces of statistical software is IBM's *SPSS* package. SPSS is one of the oldest statistical software packages, first released in 1968, but it continues to be used today by many statisticians. Figure 6.6 shows an example of calculating the correlations between a set of variables using SPSS.

FIGURE 6.6 Calculating correlations in SPSS

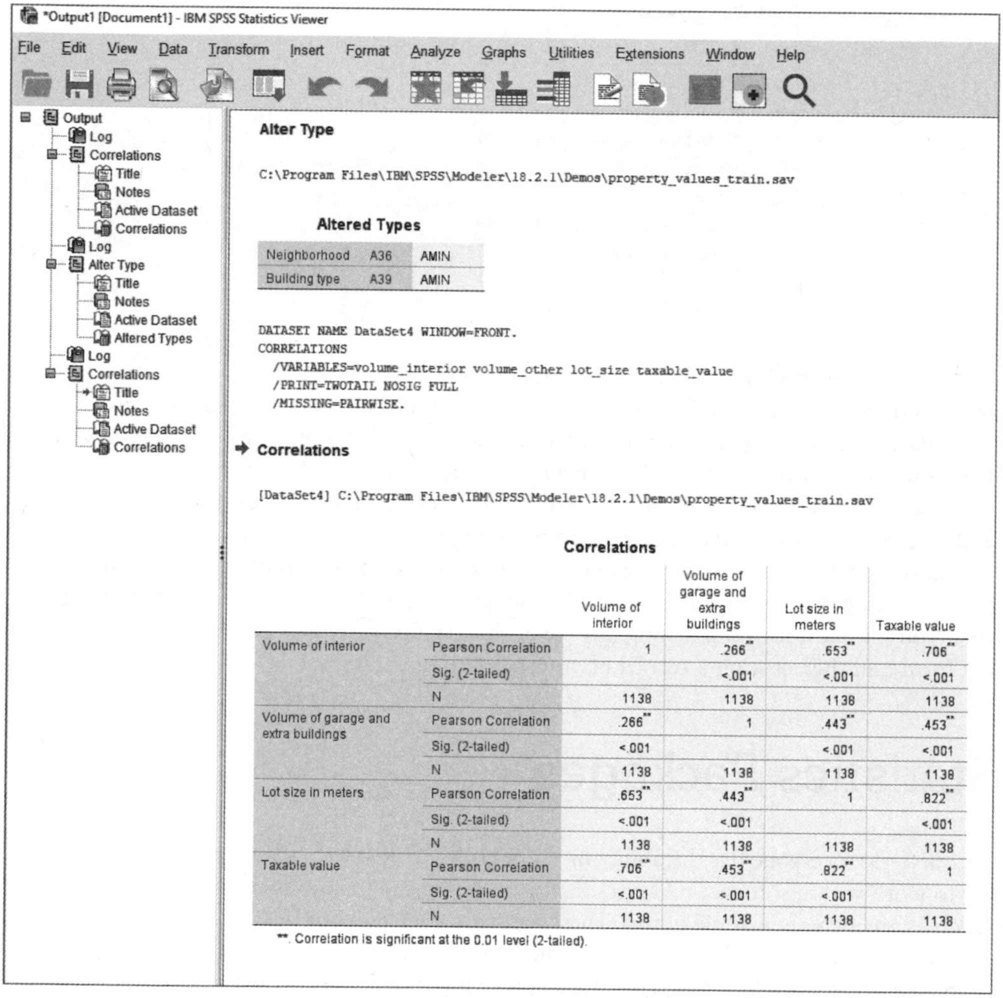

		Volume of interior	Volume of garage and extra buildings	Lot size in meters	Taxable value
Volume of interior	Pearson Correlation	1	.266**	.653**	.706**
	Sig. (2-tailed)		<.001	<.001	<.001
	N	1138	1138	1138	1138
Volume of garage and extra buildings	Pearson Correlation	.266**	1	.443**	.453**
	Sig. (2-tailed)	<.001		<.001	<.001
	N	1138	1138	1138	1138
Lot size in meters	Pearson Correlation	.653**	.443**	1	.822**
	Sig. (2-tailed)	<.001	<.001		<.001
	N	1138	1138	1138	1138
Taxable value	Pearson Correlation	.706**	.453**	.822**	1
	Sig. (2-tailed)	<.001	<.001	<.001	
	N	1138	1138	1138	1138

**. Correlation is significant at the 0.01 level (2-tailed).

SAS

SAS is a statistical package that is quite similar in function and form to SPSS. Like SPSS, SAS is a long-standing pillar of the statistical software community. It was first released in 1976 and also continues to be widely used today. Figure 6.7 shows an example of a simple data analysis being performed in SAS.

FIGURE 6.7 Analyzing data in SAS

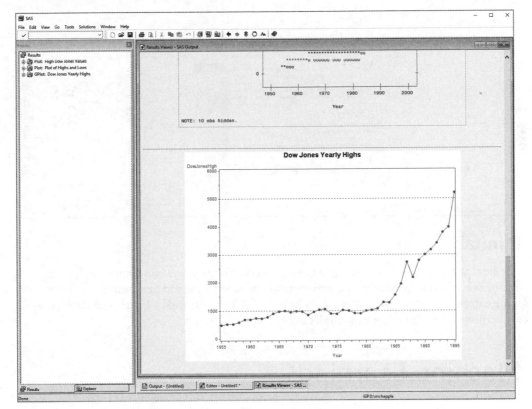

Stata

Stata is yet another statistical analysis package that dates back to the 1980s and continues to be updated today. It offers essentially the same features as SPSS and SAS and provides users with both a graphical interface and a command-line interface depending on their personal preference. Stata is less widely used than the more popular SAS and SPSS tools. Figure 6.8 shows an example of building and visualizing a linear regression model in Stata.

FIGURE 6.8   Building a simple model in Stata

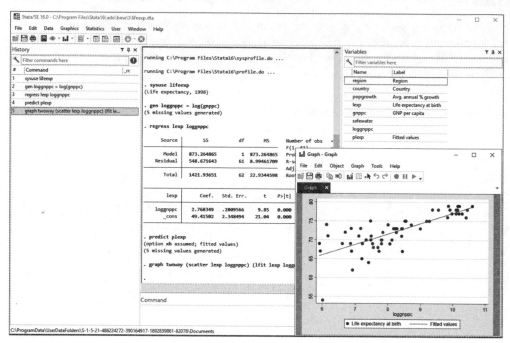

Minitab

The final statistical software package covered on the Data+ exam is *Minitab*. And, once again, Minitab shares most of the same features as SPSS, SAS, and Stata but fits into the same category as Stata—an older tool that is not widely used today. Figure 6.9 shows the evaluation of a linear regression model in Minitab.

Machine Learning

Moving on from statistics-focused tools, the industry also makes use of a set of graphical tools designed to help analysts build machine learning models without requiring them to actually write the code to do so. These machine learning tools aim to make machine learning techniques more accessible. Analysts may still tune the parameters of their models but do not necessarily need to write scripts to do so.

FIGURE 6.9   Evaluating a regression model in Minitab

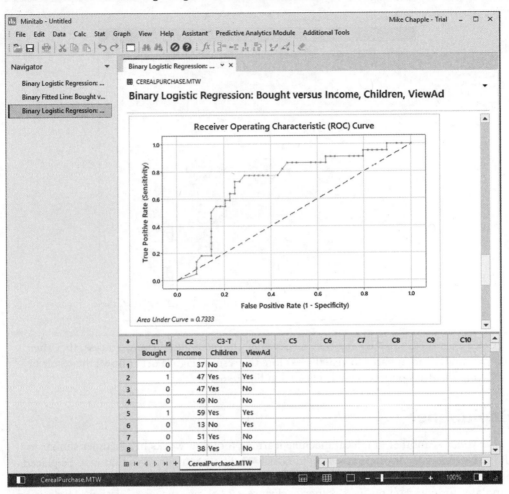

IBM SPSS Modeler

IBM's *SPSS Modeler* is one popular tool for building graphical machine learning models. Instead of requiring that users write code, it provides an intuitive interface where analysts can select the tasks that they would like the software to carry out and then connect them in a flowchart-style interface. Figure 6.10 shows an example of this interface being used to create a decision tree model of consumer credit data.

FIGURE 6.10   Designing a machine learning task in SPSS Modeler

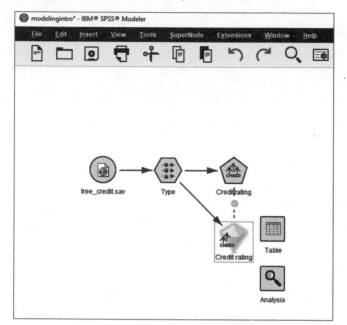

Once the user is satisfied that they've designed the machine learning process, they then run the model and are able to visually explore the results. Figure 6.11 shows the result of executing the decision tree model specified in Figure 6.10.

RapidMiner

RapidMiner is another graphical machine learning tool that works in a manner similar to IBM SPSS Modeler. It offers access to hundreds of different algorithms that may be placed in a visually designed machine learning workflow. RapidMiner also offers prebuilt analytic templates for common business scenarios. Figure 6.12 shows the visual design of a decision tree task in RapidMiner.

FIGURE 6.11   Exploring a data model in SPSS Modeler

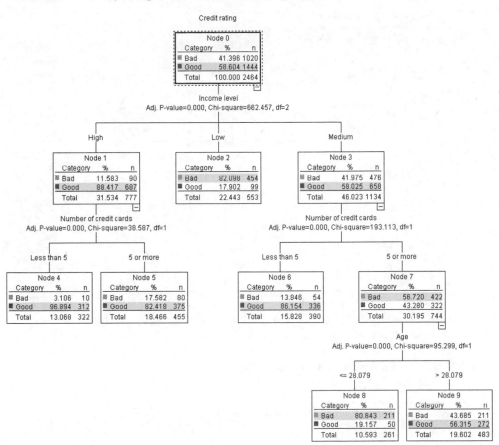

Figure 6.13 shows the result of creating this decision tree in RapidMiner. The presentation of results is not quite as visually appealing as the decision tree in SPSS Modeler, but it provides similar information to the analyst.

FIGURE 6.12 Designing a machine learning task in RapidMiner

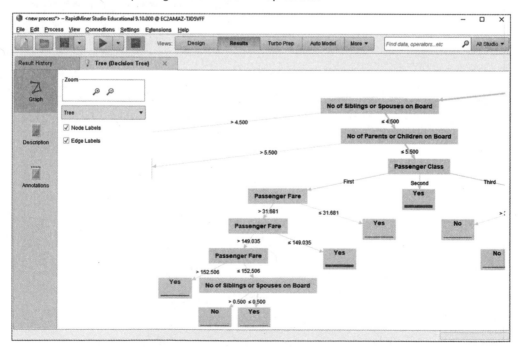

FIGURE 6.13 Exploring a data model in RapidMiner

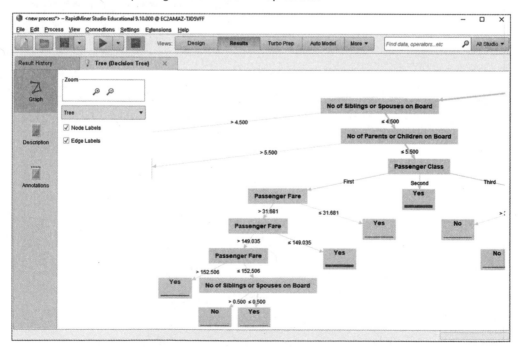

Analytics Suites

Up until this point in the chapter, we've discussed analytics tools that fit into two basic models: programming languages that allow skilled developers to complete whatever analytic task faces them and specialized tools, such as spreadsheets, statistics packages, and machine learning tools that focus on one particular component of the analytics process.

Today, most organizations choose to adopt an *analytics suite* that provides powerful capabilities that cross all phases of an analytics process. These tools allow analysts to ingest and clean data, perform exploratory statistical analysis, visualize their data, produce models, make predictions, and communicate and report their results. These packages are normally more expensive than the other tools we've discussed, but they also provide an end-to-end environment where all of an organization's analysts and developers may work together on analytics projects.

IBM Cognos

IBM *Cognos* is an example of one of these integrated analytics suites. It uses a web-based platform to offer analysts within an organization access to their data and is backed by IBM's Watson artificial intelligence capability. The major components of Cognos include the following:

- **Cognos Connection** is a web-based portal that offers access to other elements of the Cognos suite.

- **Query Studio** provides access to data querying and basic reporting tools.

- **Report Studio** offers advanced report design tools for complex reporting needs.

- **Analysis Studio** enables advanced modeling and analytics on large datasets.

- **Event Studio** provides real-time data monitoring and alerting, allowing business leaders to be immediately notified when certain events take place and/or providing automated responses to those events.

- **Metric Studio** offers the ability to create scorecards for business leaders to quickly analyze key metrics from across the organization.

- **Cognos Viewer** allows stakeholders to easily interact with data and analyses prepared using Cognos.

Figure 6.14 shows an example of IBM Cognos's data exploration capabilities.

FIGURE 6.14   Exploring data in IBM Cognos

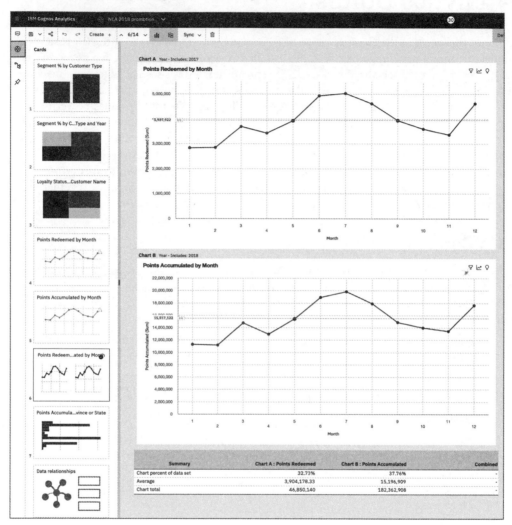

Power BI

Power BI is Microsoft's analytics suite built on the company's popular SQL Server database platform. Power BI is popular among organizations that make widespread use of other Microsoft software because of its easy integration with those packages and cost-effective bundling within an organization's Microsoft enterprise license agreement.

The major components of Power BI include the following:

- **Power BI Desktop** is a Windows application for data analysts, allowing them to interact with data and publish reports for others.

- The **Power BI** service is Microsoft's software-as-a-service (SaaS) offering that hosts Power BI capabilities in the cloud for customers to access.

- **Mobile apps** for Power BI provide users of iOS, Android, and Windows devices with access to Power BI capabilities.

- **Power BI Report Builder** allows developers to create paginated reports that are designed for printing, email, and other distribution methods.

- **Power BI Report Server** offers organizations the ability to host their own Power BI environment on internal servers for stakeholders to access.

Figure 6.15 shows an example of a complex visual dashboard built within the Microsoft Power BI environment to display important information about groundwater quality.

FIGURE 6.15 Communicating a story with data in Microsoft Power BI

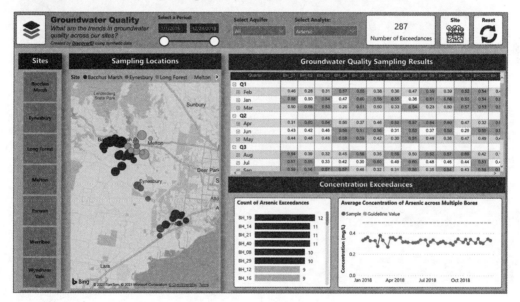

MicroStrategy

MicroStrategy is an analytics suite that is less well-known than similar tools from IBM and Microsoft, but it does have a well-established user base. MicroStrategy offers many of the same tools as its counterparts, making it easy for users to build dashboards and reports and apply machine learning techniques to their business data.

Figure 6.16 provides an example of a dashboard built within the MicroStrategy tool to analyze the performance of a business against its goals.

FIGURE 6.16   Building a dashboard in MicroStrategy

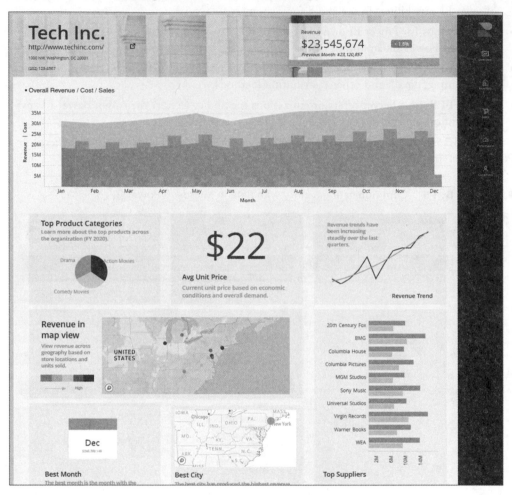

Domo

Domo is a software-as-a-service (SaaS) analytics platform that allows businesses to ingest their data and apply a variety of analytic and modeling capabilities. It is not a very widely used tool, but knowledge of it is included in the objectives for the Data+ exam.

Figure 6.17 shows the use of Domo to analyze a dataset of information about restaurant health inspections performed by the city of Chicago.

FIGURE 6.17   Analyzing a dataset in Domo

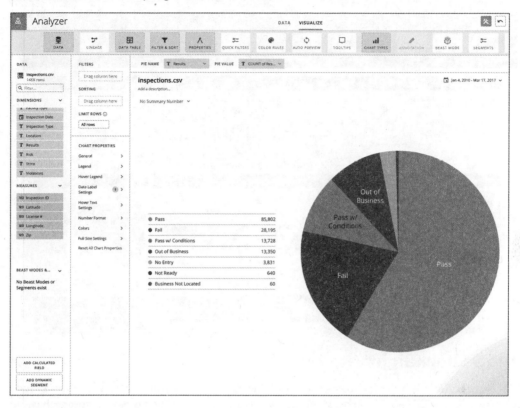

Datorama

Salesforce *Datorama* is an analytics tool that focuses on a specific component of an organization's business: sales and marketing. It's not a general-purpose analytics tool but is instead focused on applying machine learning, visualization, and other analytics techniques to the sales and marketing process.

Figure 6.18 shows an example of an analysis of an organization's marketing efforts performed within Datorama.

FIGURE 6.18   Communicating a data story in Datorama

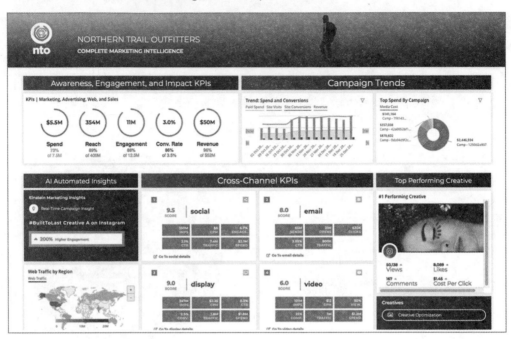

AWS QuickSight

AWS QuickSight is a dashboarding tool available as part of the Amazon Web Services cloud offering. This tool's power comes from the fact that it is available on a pay-as-you-go basis and its integration with the powerful data storage, data warehousing, machine learning, and artificial intelligence capabilities offered by the Amazon cloud.

Figure 6.19 shows an analysis of an organization's sales pipeline performed within AWS QuickSight.

Tableau

Tableau is arguably the most popular data visualization tool available in the market today. The focus of this tool is on the easy ingestion of data from a wide variety of sources and powerful visualization capabilities that allow analysts and business leaders to quickly identify trends in their data and drill down into specific details.

Figure 6.20 shows an example of obesity data for the United States visualized by county using Tableau.

FIGURE 6.19   Building a dashboard in AWS QuickSight

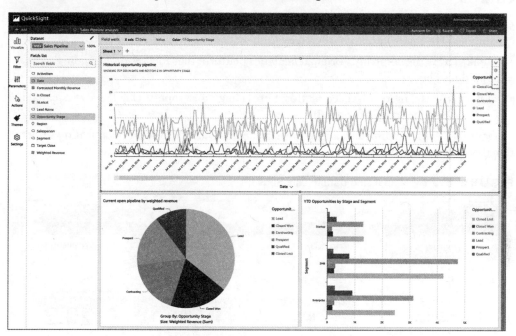

FIGURE 6.20   Visualizing data in Tableau

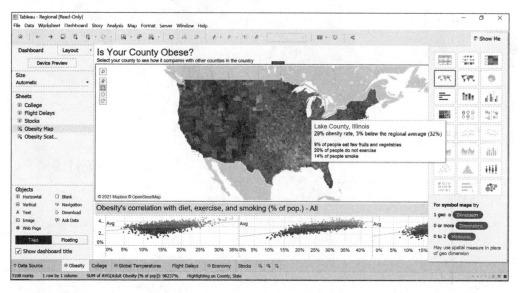

Qlik

Qlik is another popular SaaS analytics platform, offering access to cloud-based analytics capabilities. The major products offered by Qlik include the following:

- **QlikView** is the company's original analytics platform that focuses on providing rapid insights.

- **Qlik Sense** is a more advanced platform providing more sophisticated analytics capabilities (at a higher cost, of course!).

Figure 6.21 offers a financial analysis performed in Qlik Sense of an organization's operational processes from orders placed through fulfillment, billing, and receivables.

FIGURE 6.21   Visualizing data in Qlik Sense

BusinessObjects

BusinessObjects is an enterprise reporting tool from SAP that is designed to provide a comprehensive reporting and analytics environment for organizations. One of the strengths of this suite is the ability to integrate BusinessObjects reports with other applications, allowing organizations to integrate analytics into other portions of their workflow.

Summary

Data professionals have many different categories of tools at their disposal as they seek to achieve their organization's analytics goals. Spreadsheets are the simplest of these tools, offering a personal productivity solution that is quite flexible and easy to learn. For this reason, spreadsheets remain an indispensable tool in every organization. At the other end of the spectrum, programming languages, such as R and Python, provide software developers with the ability to create their own customized analytics tools.

The reality is that most organizations and analysts want tools that reside somewhere between these extremes. They want tools that are more powerful than spreadsheets, but they don't want to develop those tools themselves. That's where specialized packages that perform statistical analysis and machine learning as well as full-fledged analytics suites enter the picture. The modern analytics organization typically has one or more of these tools at their disposal as they standardize on a set of tools.

Exam Essentials

Describe the role of the spreadsheet in the modern organization.   Spreadsheets are productivity software packages that allow users to create documents that organize any type of data into rows and columns. They are extremely flexible analytics tools that are available on most modern office computer systems and are very easy to use. The most commonly used spreadsheet software package is Microsoft Excel.

Understand how analytics teams use programming languages.   Data professionals with coding skills often turn to programming languages to create their own software analysis tools. This approach frees them of the constraints of other packages and allows them to create software that directly meets their needs. The R programming language is designed specifically for analytics use and is quite easy to learn. Python is a general-purpose programming language that is more difficult to learn but can create virtually any software package.

Know how analysts and developers interact with databases.   Relational databases are the primary data stores used in the modern organization. Analysts and developers may interact directly with databases using the Structured Query Language (SQL). SQL has two subcomponents. The Data Definition Language (DDL) defines the structure of the database and contains commands to create, alter, and destroy databases and tables. The Data Manipulation Language (DML) interacts with the data stored in a database and contains commands to add, retrieve, modify, and delete data.

Describe the role of statistical analysis software.   Statistical analysis software provides access to advanced statistical environments that are accessible through a graphical user interface and/or a built-in scripting language. These software packages are commonly used by professional statisticians in their work. The statistical analysis software packages covered on the Data+ exam include IBM SPSS, SAS, Stata, and Minitab.

Describe the role of machine learning software.   Machine learning packages offer a set of graphical tools designed to help analysts build machine learning models without requiring them to actually write the code to do so. These machine learning tools aim to make machine learning techniques more accessible. Analysts may still tune the parameters of their models but do not necessarily need to write scripts to do so. The machine learning software packages covered on the Data+ exam include IBM SPSS Modeler and RapidMiner.

Describe the role of data analytics suites.   Data analytics suites provide powerful capabilities that cross all phases of an analytics process. These tools allow analysts to ingest and clean data, perform exploratory statistical analysis, visualize their data, produce models, make predictions, and communicate and report their results. The data analytics suites covered on the Data+ exam include IBM Cognos, Microsoft Power BI, MicroStrategy, Domo, Datorama, AWS QuikSight, Tableau, Qlik, and BusinessObjects.

Review Questions

1. Ricky is a data analyst looking to begin developing his own applications to simplify some reporting and modeling tasks. He does not have experience programming and would like to use a language that will meet his analytics needs but be easy to learn. What language would best meet his needs?

   A. Python

   B. Ruby

   C. C++

   D. R

2. Ann is using the Structured Query Language to retrieve information stored in a relational database table. What DML command should she use to specify the records she would like to retrieve?

   A. INSERT

   B. UPDATE

   C. SELECT

   D. CREATE

3. Which one of the following statements about spreadsheets is incorrect?

   A. Spreadsheet software is available on most modern business computers.

   B. Spreadsheet software is easy to use.

   C. Spreadsheet software provides powerful machine learning capabilities.

   D. Microsoft Excel is the most common example of a spreadsheet.

4. Kevin is helping prepare a computer for a professional statistician who will be performing some quality control analyses for his organization. Which one of the following tools is most likely to meet the statistician's needs?

   A. Tableau

   B. SPSS

   C. Cognos

   D. Excel

5. Vincent is looking for a software package that will allow his team to create machine learning workflows by visually designing them. Which one of the following approaches would best meet his needs?

   A. Using RapidMiner

   B. Designing software in Python

   C. Designing software in R

   D. Using SAS

6. Carla works for an organization that relies heavily on the machine learning and analytics tools offered by Amazon Web Services. She would like to select a dashboarding tool that will easily integrate with those other tools. What product would best meet her needs?

A. QuickSight

B. Cognos

C. MicroStrategy

D. Power BI

7. Simone works for an organization that uses the Cognos analytics suite. What component of the suite could she use to best create scorecards for business leaders?

A. Query Studio

B. Report Studio

C. Analysis Studio

D. Metric Studio

8. Lisa is an IT technician with a large organization that uses the Power BI analytics suite. A new data analyst is joining the organization and would like to have a tool installed on their laptop to create paginated reports. What tool would best meet this need?

A. Power BI Desktop

B. Power BI Report Server

C. Power BI Report Builder

D. Power BI service

9. Xavier is a new data analyst who would like to learn a data visualization package. He would like to use software that specializes in data visualization, integrates with a large number of data sources, and is widely used across organizations. What tool would best meet his needs?

A. Tableau

B. Excel

C. QuickSight

D. Stata

10. Bob is exploring analytics tools available from Qlik and would like to use a tool that is cost-effective and will get him up and running quickly. What tool would best meet his needs?

A. Qlik Sense

B. QlikCreate

C. QlikView

D. Qlik Suite

11. Which one of the following is an enterprise reporting tool available from SAP?

    A. RapidMiner

    B. BusinessObjects

    C. Stata

    D. MicroStrategy

12. Paul accidentally created a database table and would like to remove the entire table from the database. What Structured Query Language command would best meet his needs?

    A. DELETE

    B. ALTER

    C. UPDATE

    D. DROP

13. Ty works for a sales organization that uses the Salesforce customer relationship management platform. He would like to produce some sales analytics quickly and needs a tool that would have the fastest integration time. What tool should he select?

    A. Qlik Sense

    B. QuickSight

    C. SPSS Modeler

    D. Datorama

14. What Python library provides data analysts with access to tools that allow them to better structure data?

    A. Numpy

    B. TensorFlow

    C. pandas

    D. Keras

15. Which one of the following is not a standard way for a relational database to receive commands?

    A. SQL query created within a graphical interface

    B. SQL query written directly by an end user

    C. Natural language query written by a customer

    D. SQL query created by software written in Python

16. Wanda is selecting a tool to present analytics reports to business leaders. Which one of the following tools is most likely to meet her needs?

    A. Minitab

    B. SAS

    C. Power BI

    D. Stata

17. Amanda works for an organization that uses the Cognos analytics suite. She would like to set up automated alerting that notifies leaders when one of the organization's stores experiences an out-of-stock situation. What component of Cognos would best meet her needs?

    A. Query Studio

    B. Event Studio

    C. Metric Studio

    D. Analysis Studio

18. Gwen would like to modify the structure of an existing database table. What SQL command would best meet her needs?

    A. UPDATE

    B. MODIFY

    C. DROP

    D. ALTER

19. Kelly is looking for a statistical analysis package for use by her organization's statisticians. Which one of the following tools would be least suitable for this purpose?

    A. Stata

    B. Minitab

    C. SPSS Modeler

    D. SAS

20. Which one of the following commands would not be considered part of the Data Manipulation Language (DML)?

    A. INSERT

    B. SELECT

    C. UPDATE

    D. CREATE

Chapter 7

Data Visualization with Reports and Dashboards

THE COMPTIA DATA+ EXAM TOPICS COVERED IN THIS CHAPTER INCLUDE:

✓ **Domain 4.0: Visualization**

✓ **4.1. Given a scenario, translate business requirements to form a report**

✓ **4.2. Given a scenario, use appropriate design components for reports and dashboards**

✓ **4.3. Given a scenario, use appropriate methods for dashboard development**

✓ **4.4. Given a scenario, apply the appropriate type of visualization**

✓ **4.5. Compare and contrast types of reports**

In Chapter 5, "Data Analysis and Statistics," you learned about various techniques for analyzing data. In Chapter 6, "Data Analytics Tools," you explored a selection of software packages and programming languages that facilitate analysis. While the analytical process aims to derive insights from data, it is crucial to communicate those insights to the appropriate people at the right time. As raw data evolves into usable information, reports and dashboards are essential tools for sharing the results of analytical work.

Every day, businesses rely on data to inform decisions. While it is desirable to have beautiful, visually appealing reports and dashboards, the essence of visualizing data is to tell a story, giving the appropriate information to the right people at the right time. If a report or dashboard fails to facilitate effective communications, it will diminish the organizational impact of the analysis behind the visualization.

This chapter will develop an understanding of considerations to think through when translating business requirements into a visualization. We will first understand why it is vital to understand the business needs before creating visualizations. We will then explore design considerations to keep in mind when creating reports and dashboards. We will then explore considerations that influence dashboard development methods and the process to build a dashboard.

There are a wide variety of visualizations from which to choose. In this chapter, you will learn about several different types of visualization and the considerations for their use. Finally, we will compare and contrast different types of reports, always keeping in mind the needs of the business and the objective to communicate clearly and efficiently.

Understanding Business Requirements

Reports and dashboards both summarize data for end users, but they distribute those summaries in different ways. A *report* is a static electronic or physical document that reflects information at a given point in time. On the other hand, a *dashboard* is an interactive visualization that encourages people to explore data dynamically. Both reports and dashboards are ideal tools for visualizing data content.

The most important thing to define when developing a report or dashboard is answering the question, "Who is the audience?" For example, a custodial supervisor might want to track the remaining cleaning products' daily levels to inform restocking decisions. Alternatively, a chief executive officer (CEO) may wish to understand revenue by brand and global region. You shouldn't begin creating a report or dashboard until you clearly understand who your audience is and how they will use the product.

Once you clearly understand the audience and their needs, you can turn your attention to identifying the data sources that will satisfy the requirements of your audience. For instance, you may need to combine data across multiple subject areas. For example, if you are working with corporate executives, you may need to combine data from various divisions within the organization. Sourcing this data can be a challenge, as when a corporation grows inorganically through acquisition, it can end up with multiple redundant systems to accomplish a single business objective. As an analyst, your job is to ensure that you have access to the appropriate data sources.

As you identify data sources, you'll need to consider how old the data can be while satisfying the needs of your audience. Suppose you are working with the chief financial officer (CFO) of a consumer products company to develop a historical report on corporate sales revenue for the past five fiscal years. In that case, you don't need real-time sales information and can instead focus on obtaining high-quality historical data. It is most likely that views within a data warehouse or data mart, as described in Chapter 3, "Databases and Data Acquisition," would serve as the data source for this type of report, as Figure 7.1 illustrates.

FIGURE 7.1 Historical reporting

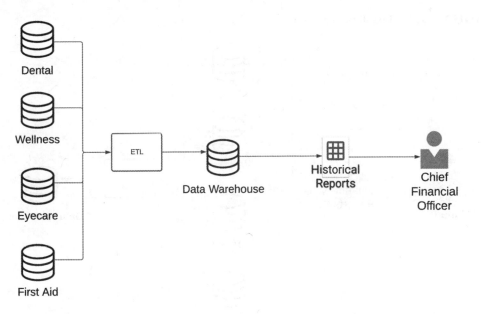

As you consider the needs of the CFO, you will want to think through the parameters of the report and how that affects data sources and report design. Report parameters let you define data range limits for the data elements in your report. For instance, even if you think the CFO will want to see six years of historical sales, you'll want to avoid limiting the report to a specified number of years. Instead of restricting the report generation process, accommodate the ability to filter data by date range. Filtering data in this manner provides you with more flexibility down the road if the CFO later decides that they want to see 10 years of sales data.

In most reports, you'll want to filter by more than one parameter. For example, suppose the CFO wants to share eyecare-related sales data with the person who leads the eyecare division. In that case, you would want to enable the ability to filter the data by content so that the eyecare leader only sees the section of the report that is relevant to their operations.

Alternatively, suppose you are working with a regional sales manager in the dental division who wants to understand the progress of their staff against their sales goal. In this scenario, you need to ask the sales manager how frequently they need the report updated. That frequency may change depending on the time of year. For example, the sales manager may only check this report every month for much of the year. However, as the end of a fiscal quarter approaches, they may want to see updates weekly, daily, hourly, or in real time. In this case, you want to design your report to accommodate when they need updates most frequently, which influences your data source. To satisfy the need for real-time data, you use the transactional system for recording dental sales instead of relying on older data from a data warehouse, as shown in Figure 7.2.

FIGURE 7.2   Real-time reporting

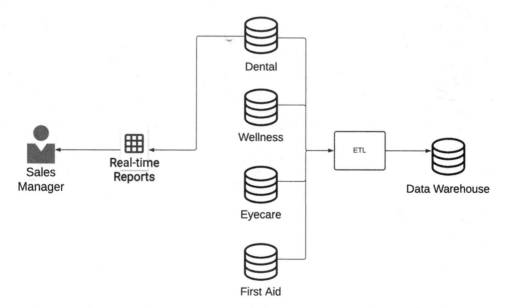

Once you identify who needs what data and when they need it, you can focus on how people access the report. If people will access the report digitally, one way to solve the distribution challenge is with a pull approach. With a *pull approach*, you publish a report to a known location, like a web page, and let people know the frequency and timing of when the report updates. With this approach, people can go to the website when they want to use the report.

Alternatively, you could implement a push approach. With a *push approach*, the report is automatically sent to the appropriate people as it becomes available. When designing a push approach, you need to think through distribution considerations. For example, a report may prove to be too large to distribute via email. In that case, you could use a blended distribution approach. With a *blended approach*, you store the report centrally and let people know when the report has been updated and is ready for use. With the blended approach, you inform people that the report is available while maintaining central control of the report itself.

If you go with a push or blended approach for informing people about the readiness of a given report, be sure to think through the maintenance of the distribution list of people to notify. With all organizations, people rotate in and out of roles. As people transition out of a position, you want to ensure that they no longer receive notifications about reports that are no longer relevant to their job role. On the other hand, as a new person joins the organization, you need to get that person the reports they require to be effective in their role.

However, suppose you are creating a printed report that will be distributed physically to its recipients. In this case, the distribution challenge is entirely different. If the recipients are within your organization, you can use existing distribution channels to distribute the printed report. However, if the recipients are in other locations across the country, you need to ensure that you have the appropriate mailing address for each recipient. You also need to ensure you have enough lead time to send the report through the mail. Alternatively, you could speed up distribution by paying more for overnight delivery.

Understanding Report Design Elements

Whenever you give people a tool, it should be approachable and easy to use. When creating a report or a dashboard, you can use existing design principles as guideposts. These design principles, known as the "five Cs" of creating visualizations, will help ensure that your reports and dashboards communicate clearly and efficiently. When thinking visually, the five Cs are control, correctness, clarity, consistency, and concentration.

Control has to do with how you focus the attention of your audience. When someone encounters a dashboard for the first time, one of your goals is to deliver the pertinent information quickly. For instance, if there is a place where people can adjust parameters and have the dashboard respond, use visual highlights to focus attention on this capability.

Correctness makes sure that your information is accurate and that there are no spelling mistakes. Pay close attention to correctness when using corporate names and logos. For example, Procter & Gamble is a large consumer goods corporation. Misspelling the company name as "Proctor & Gamble" is embarrassing as it displays a lack of correctness.

Clarity refers to selecting the right visualization tool for communicating your message, making sure the visualization is easy to interpret and visually crisp and uses fonts and sizes that are easy to read. For example, consider Figure 7.3, which uses an ornate font. While the diagram conveys the same information as Figure 7.2, the font compromises clarity and makes it hard to read.

FIGURE 7.3   Poor font choice

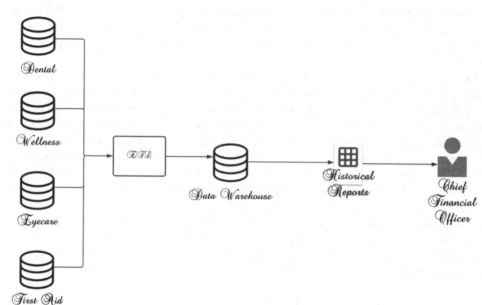

Consistency refers to using the same design and documentation elements throughout your report or dashboard to give your visualization a cohesive and complete feel. Using the same font, page layout, and web page design are all techniques for ensuring consistency.

Concentration refers to using visuals to focus your audience's attention on the most relevant information without overwhelming them with details. Concentration, along with clarity and control, helps you focus your audience by reducing clutter and removing unnecessary details. Use a layout that increases concentration, and remove distracting visual elements from charts. For example, suppose you are creating a report that summarizes quarterly sales performance. To improve concentration, only show the necessary summary statistics instead of including the raw daily sales data.

Report Cover Page

When developing a printed report, keep in mind that the first thing people see is the cover page. Since the cover page is the first thing a person sees, it is vital that it sets expectations about the observations and insights the reader will find within. Effective cover pages have a concise title that describes the contents of the report. Ideally, a cover page will also communicate a significant insight from the report itself. As the saying goes, you never get a second chance to make a good first impression. In that vein, a cover page has to entice a person into turning the page and diving into the report. Figure 7.4 shows the cover page for the 2020 Porsche AG Annual Report. It incorporates product imagery with text on the right detailing what the reader can expect to find within.

FIGURE 7.4   Porsche AG Annual Report cover page

Source: Copyrighted by Dr. Ing. h. c. F. Porsche AG.

Accompanying the title page should be clear instructions on how to use the report. For example, if the report analyzes five years' worth of data, the range of years should stand out on the cover. Excluding the range of years demonstrates a lack of clarity and control.

Executive Summary

Following a report's cover page is an executive summary. The executive summary provides an overview of the report's contents. When crafting an executive summary, you should begin with the end in mind, summarizing crucial observations and insights. With time an executive's most precious resource, the summary needs to convey the big ideas, while the body of the report details the analysis that led to those ideas. Figure 7.5 illustrates a compelling executive summary taken from the 2020 Porsche AG Annual Report.

FIGURE 7.5 Porsche AG Annual Report executive summary

Dear Reader,

The year 2020 was a very challenging year. The coronavirus pandemic has severely tested human co-existence. Meanwhile, the global economy was subjected to a stress test. Porsche too was affected. We were forced to halt production for six weeks in the spring, and our dealership operations also had to temporarily close.

Our response to these challenges was rapid, flexible and pragmatic. We introduced targeted measures to protect our workforce. And we engaged in systematic crisis management, successfully shoring up our liquidity and stabilising our results. In this way we steered Porsche strategically and robustly through the crisis.

With good results. With deliveries of new vehicles totalling 272,162, we were a mere three per cent down on the record figure set in 2019. Our company remains highly profitable. Operating profit: 4.2 billion euros. Return on sales: 14.6 per cent. Figures that are unmatched in our sector. Figures that represent a great success for our entire team. In a difficult environment, that team has remained united, shown fighting spirit, and been dedicated to the task at hand.

This success is founded on our fresh and attractive product range. 911 Turbo, 911 Targa, 718 GTS – thoroughbred sports cars, and the stuff of our customers' dreams. Then there are our attractive best-sellers: the Cayenne and the Macan. Not forgetting our powerful Gran Turismo, the Panamera.

Our electric mobility strategy has also provided a strong tailwind, noticeably gaining momentum in 2020. In Europe, one third of our new deliveries were already electrified, with an equal split between all-electric and hybrid vehicles. This figure will rise to 50 per cent by 2025. What this shows is that our electrification strategy is taking hold.

Our success is driven by our innovative power. The technological strength that has always set Porsche apart has been concentrated in the Taycan, our first all-electric sports car. Its innovative 800-volt architecture already has a proven track record, used in our winning race cars at Le Mans. This architecture means that it is not only fast on the road, but also quick to recharge. In a further success story, the Taycan was voted the most innovative vehicle in the world in 2020. Internationally, it has picked up more than 50 awards – more than any other Porsche model has ever achieved in the space of one year.

Porsche is clearly committed to the goals of the Paris Agreement, and is a trailblazer in this area. We are pursuing a consistent electrification and sustainability strategy. And we are setting ourselves ambitious decarbonisation targets, including in comparison with the rest of the industry. Porsche is also setting new standards in sustainable production.

Our original plant in Zuffenhausen has been CO_2-neutral since 2020, with the Leipzig plant following suit in January 2021. This is also where the all-electric Macan will come off the production line in future. This underlines our credentials as a sustainable mobility pioneer. Our goal is ambitious: Porsche will be completely CO_2-neutral as early as 2030.

We see ourselves as a partner in society and embrace the responsibilities that this involves – towards the environment, social issues and the economy. Porsche has, for example, supported countless social activities in 2020, the year of coronavirus. These have all been targeted and well coordinated, with a significantly increased volume of donations and a voluntary commitment from many employees.
In addition, we supported the state governments of Baden-Württemberg and Saxony in the procurement of Personal Protective Equipment and made our expertise available to the crisis teams. Porsche has also been involved in many aid activities with an international aspect. This has greatly advanced our understanding of sustainability and carries us into the future.

And we are also investing in our employees. Employees who work hard every day to inspire our customers – with pioneering spirit and passion. Last year, we signed works agreements to secure jobs at our locations until 2030, sending out a clear signal of our future intentions. Our team is highly motivated. With that team, we are successfully shaping the future of sustainable mobility.

The new Porsche Strategy 2030 shows us the way forward. This also applies to the further expansion of our digital capabilities: we are systematically stepping up the efficiency, precision and quality of our processes. Making us even faster and even more flexible. We are undertaking considerable efforts to succeed in our goals: between now and 2025, Porsche will be investing 15 billion euros in electromobility, sustainable production and digitalisation. This is money well spent, not least because it will strengthen our commercial success and profitability in the long term. Even in an age of transformation, we remain as focused as ever on our strategic return target of 15 per cent.

In 2020, Porsche showed impressively: our business model is robust and flexible. Our brand has never had such a positive appeal. Strategically, we remain firmly on course. Sustainability, innovation and digitalisation will determine our future path. We are also strongly and profitably positioned for the future. Our good performance in terms of return and capital value allows us to look to that future with confidence: we will embrace our opportunities with self-confidence and a down-to-earth approach.

The Executive Board of
Dr. Ing. h.c. F. Porsche AG

Letter from the Executive Board of Porsche AG The figures for fuel consumption, energy consumption and CO_2 emissions are found on pages 212–213. 5

Source: Copyrighted by Dr. Ing. h. c. F. Porsche AG.

Design Elements

When developing a report or dashboard, you need to incorporate design elements into your thinking. Color schemes, page layout, font size and style, charts, and corporate standards are among the many design elements you should consider. These considerations apply if you are enhancing an existing report or creating a new dashboard.

Color Schemes

A *color scheme* is a limited selection of colors you use when creating a report or a dashboard. The first decision to make is whether you need to use a monochromatic color palette or have the flexibility to use more than one color. A *monochromatic* palette limits you to working with shades of a single color, as shown in Figure 7.6. One use case where a black monochromatic palette is an appropriate choice is creating physical reports. For example, suppose you are designing a less formal printed report for frequent, high-volume distribution. Given the distribution needs, printing in full color could be prohibitively expensive. When distributing electronically, consider whether the recipient has access to a color printer.

FIGURE 7.6   Black monochromatic color palette

If you have the luxury of working with more than one color, selecting a complementary color palette is a sound choice. A *complementary* palette starts with two contrasting colors. Examples of complementary colors are red and green, orange and blue, and yellow and purple. Suppose you are creating a corporate annual report for broad distribution. This kind of report has a high impact and annual distribution, making the cost of color printing insignificant. Whether you are working in monochrome or multiple colors, ensure that the font color contrasts with the background color to ensure readability.

Layouts

The *layout* of a report or dashboard determines the arrangement of its component parts. It is crucial to consider approachability when thinking about the design. When developing the layout for a report, begin with a summary before diving into the supporting detail. For a long, multipage report, use a table of contents so that the reader can efficiently navigate to a topic of interest, as well as headings for sections and subsections.

Use brief paragraphs and bullet points to focus the reader's attention. Ensure parallel construction when developing bullet points. *Parallel construction* is when all bullet points use the same form and have the same style and approximate length. Figure 7.7 shows nonparallel construction, where the second bullet point has a different format than the other three. Figure 7.8 fixes the construction issue by changing the phrasing of the second bullet point.

FIGURE 7.7 Nonparallel construction

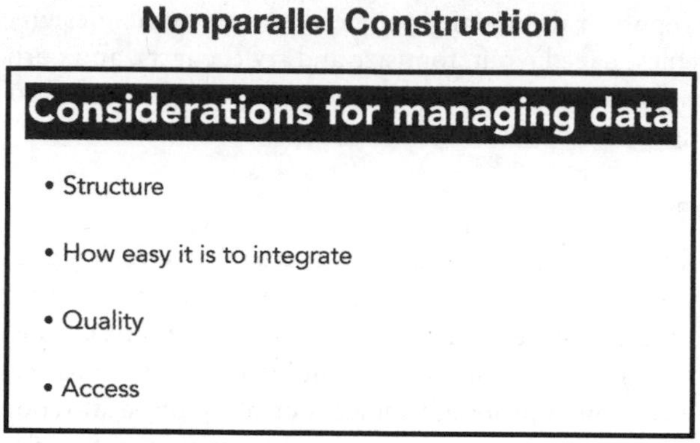

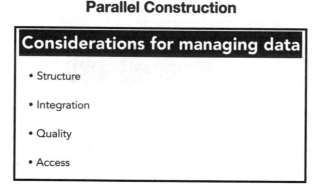

FIGURE 7.8 Parallel construction

Fonts

When choosing a font style, pick one that is easy for people to read by avoiding ornate fonts. After excluding ornate options, you need to decide between a serif or sans serif font style. In typography, a *serif* is a finishing detail for each letter in a typeface. A *serif font style* includes serifs, whereas a *sans serif font style* does not. Consider the capital T at the start of each sentence in Figure 7.9. For all the sans serif font styles, the horizontal component of the capital T is a straight line. On the other hand, all serif style fonts have a finishing flourish at either end of the horizontal line.

Studies show that using a serif font instead of a sans serif font makes text easier to read. Times New Roman, Garamond, and Courier New are all examples of serif fonts, while Helvetica, Arial, and Geneva do not have serifs. Spend some time studying all the letters in Figure 7.9 to compare these popular fonts and see the stylistic difference for each serif and sans serif letter.

FIGURE 7.9   Serif and sans serif fonts

Serif and Sans Serif Fonts

Serif	Sans Serif
Times New Roman: The quick brown fox jumped over the lazy dog.	**Helvetica:** The quick brown fox jumped over the lazy dog.
Garamond: The quick brown fox jumped over the lazy dog.	**Arial:** The quick brown fox jumped over the lazy dog.
Courier New: The quick brown fox jumped over the lazy dog.	**Geneva:** The quick brown fox jumped over the lazy dog.

After selecting a font style, determine the appropriate font size for your title, table of contents, headings, subheadings, and body text. You measure font sizes in points, with each point representing 1/72 of an inch. Start with your body text when determining font sizes. The body text makes up most of what a person reads, so you want to make sure you don't pick a font size that is too small. It is common for body text to range between 12 and 14 points. After selecting a font size for your body text, use progressively larger sizes for subheadings, headings, and titles. Figure 7.10 illustrates a sample style guide that specifies layout elements and their font size.

FIGURE 7.10   Sample layout elements and font sizes

Layout Element	Font Size
Title	30 points
Heading Level 1	26 points
Heading Level 2	20 points
Heading Level 3	16 points
Body Text	13 points

Remember that selecting an appropriate font size is crucial for printed reports, as the size becomes fixed during printing. However, font size is less critical when distributing electronically, as recipients may adjust the overall font size on a computer, tablet, or mobile device.

Graphics

Using graphics to present summary information is a practical choice, whether creating a report or developing a dashboard. As the saying goes, a picture is worth a thousand words, and visually conveying information with charts helps focus your audience's attention. Think through the key chart elements when designing charts, including the chart's title, labels, and legends.

When developing a chart, make sure you specify a chart title. A *chart title* uses a large font size and concise wording to clearly describe what the chart depicts. If necessary, you can use a subtitle to supplement your title with additional information to add clarity.

When using a chart, be sure to use labels appropriately. In a chart with an x-axis and a y-axis, a *label* describes what each axis represents. Consider Figure 7.11, which shows how a vehicle's engine displacement on the x-axis relates to its highway efficiency in miles per gallon on the y-axis. If the axes did not have labels and the title was missing, a person wouldn't know what information the chart conveys.

FIGURE 7.11   Sample chart

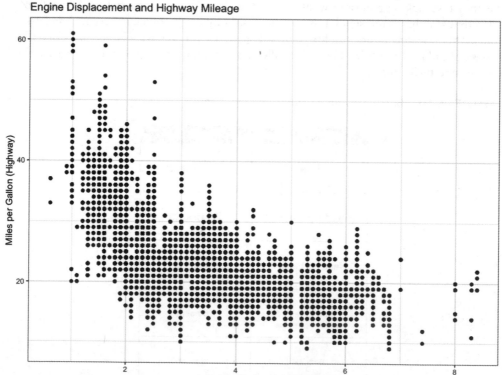

Source: Environmental Protection Agency National Vehicle and Fuel Emissions Laboratory

When a chart shows multiple categories, use a *legend* to help the reader distinguish between categories. For example, consider Figure 7.12, which shows Ford's and Volkswagen's corporate average highway fuel economy in miles per gallon. The legend indicates that the data in the chart for Ford uses circles, whereas the data for Volkswagen uses triangles.

FIGURE 7.12   Sample chart with legend

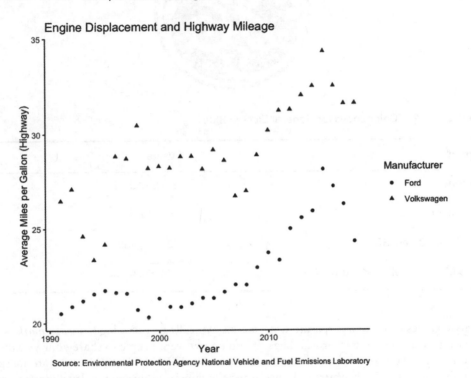

Source: Environmental Protection Agency National Vehicle and Fuel Emissions Laboratory

Corporate Reporting Standards

When developing any type of visualization, be mindful of any existing corporate reporting standards. For instance, your organization may have a style guide for reporting. A *style guide* is a set of standards that drives consistency in communication. As a means of enforcing structure and consistency, style guides define the use of a variety of branding elements, including page layout, font selection, corporate color codes, logos, and trademarks.

Imagine that you work for General Electric and are developing a new visualization. Figure 7.13 shows the logo for General Electric. The logo is quite recognizable. Incorporating the logo into a report or dashboard communicates an association with the brand. If you are working in color, you also want the appropriate color code from Table 7.1 to use the "General Electric Blue" elsewhere in your visualization. Using consistent colors is one way to give your visualizations a cohesive look.

FIGURE 7.13   General Electric logo

TABLE 7.1   Color codes for General Electric Blue

Format	Value
Pantone	PMS 4151 C
HEX Color	#026CB6
Red Green Blue(RGB)	(2, 108, 182)
Cyan Magenta Yellow Key(CMYK)	(89, 56, 0, 0)

Style guides can also incorporate watermarks. Typically text or a logo, a *watermark* is superimposed over a report or web page. If you do not want people to share your visualization outside your organization, you could use an "INTERNAL USE ONLY" watermark, as shown in Figure 7.14. Watermarks are especially important during the development process. For example, using a "DRAFT" watermark allows you to circulate a report to ensure it meets expectations while letting people know it is a work in progress.

Larger organizations have a communications department responsible for developing brand standards. When creating visualizations, make sure you work with your communications colleagues to ensure you are doing your part to project your organization's brand consistently.

Documentation Elements

People must trust the information in your visualizations. To help establish trust, you can incorporate documentation elements, including version numbers, reference data sources, and reference dates. Reference dates include the initial creation date, report run date, and data refresh date.

FIGURE 7.14 Sample chart with watermark

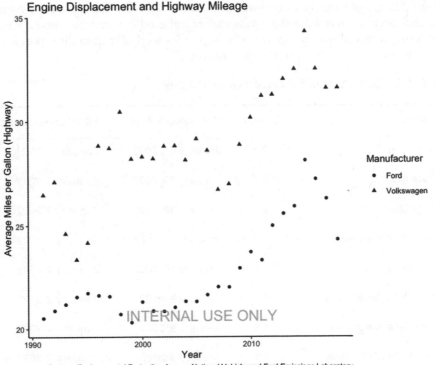

Source: Environmental Protection Agency National Vehicle and Fuel Emissions Laboratory

Version Number

A version number is a numeric value that refers to a specific version of a report. Version numbers help you keep track of changes to content and layout over time. Reference data sources identify where data in the report originates. For example, if you are using a data mart to create a visualization for colleagues in the finance division, specify the name of the data mart.

Reference Data Sources

Reference dates help people understand what to expect in terms of data recency. For example, if a report has a daily refresh cycle, the report run date helps people realize when the last data refresh date was. If they see that the refresh date is from a week ago, they know the report is missing a week's worth of data.

Consider the version history for a daily sales report as shown in Table 7.2. Note that a significant change happens on January 12, 2022. The source for this report becomes the Sales Data Mart, replacing the Corporate Data Warehouse. Note that the version numbering scheme changes to acknowledge the significance of using a different data source. With this level of transparency about the report's origins, people's level of trust in the report increases. It also underscores the integrity of the data sources.

TABLE 7.2   Sample daily sales report version history

Data sources	Version	Data refresh date	Initial creation date
Sales Data Mart	2.3	January 14, 2022	January 7, 2022
Sales Data Mart	2.2	January 13, 2022	January 7, 2022
Sales Data Mart	2.1	January 12, 2022	January 7, 2022
Corporate Data Warehouse	1.5	January 11, 2022	January 7, 2022
Corporate Data Warehouse	1.4	January 10, 2022	January 7, 2022
Corporate Data Warehouse	1.3	January 9, 2022	January 7, 2022
Corporate Data Warehouse	1.2	January 8, 2022	January 7, 2022
Corporate Data Warehouse	1.1	January 7, 2022	January 7, 2022

Frequently Asked Questions

When developing a report or a dashboard, it is good to maintain a set of frequently asked questions (FAQs). A FAQ provides answers to people's most common questions. If the dashboard is available online, the FAQ can contain links to a glossary of unique terms, cross-references to other dashboards or reports, and contact information if there are additional questions.

Appendix

When developing a report, use an appendix to include supporting details that are inappropriate to include in the main body. For example, suppose you use statistical analysis to derive the central insight for a report. Recall that one of the goals of creating a report is to convey insights. Instead of detailing each calculation in the main report body, move them to an appendix. That way, the general reader will not feel overwhelmed by the details, while the informed reader can explore the calculations in detail.

Understanding Dashboard Development Methods

Recall that dashboards are dynamic tools that help people explore data to inform their decision-making. Since dashboards are dynamic, their design, development, and delivery mechanisms are more complex than the considerations for developing reports. Let's explore the dashboard considerations that you should keep in mind.

Consumer Types

As with developing a report, it is crucial to identify who will be interacting with the dashboard you create. For example, *C-level executives*, with titles like chief executive officer and chief financial officer, have the most senior leadership positions in an organization. Your dashboard needs to consolidate critical performance metrics with the ability to get additional detail on an as-needed basis to assist people with C-level responsibilities in making strategic decisions. Ensure you spend sufficient time identifying the *key performance indicators* (*KPIs*) crucial to senior leaders. A KPI is a metric that leadership agrees is crucial to achieving the organization's business objectives. As you identify *what* leaders want to see, you can locate *where* to get the relevant data.

A large organization typically has external stakeholders who serve on its board of directors. While the board's needs closely align with the needs of C-level executives, you need to incorporate any of the board's unique requirements in your dashboard so that board members can fulfill their oversight and corporate management duties effectively.

Lower levels of management focus on a different set of metrics than senior leadership. Although the information needs differ from the C-suite, they are no less critical to organizational success. To ensure your dashboard will add value, make sure to work with managers to identify the KPIs that provide the information they need to lead their portion of the organization effectively.

You may be developing dashboards for people external to your organization. Your organization may enter into a *service level agreement (SLA)* that describes the level of service an external vendor or partner can expect. Violating an SLA can result in financial and reputational damages. To help communicate clearly and with transparency, a dashboard that is available to the general public provides a single source of information for anyone interested in the status of your services. For example, Figure 7.15 shows a publicly accessible dashboard for Amazon Web Services, one of the world's leading cloud service providers. Examining this dashboard, we see a list of services and their operational status. In addition to showing the current status, you can opt into receiving status updates for a particular service.

FIGURE 7.15   Sample public-facing dashboard

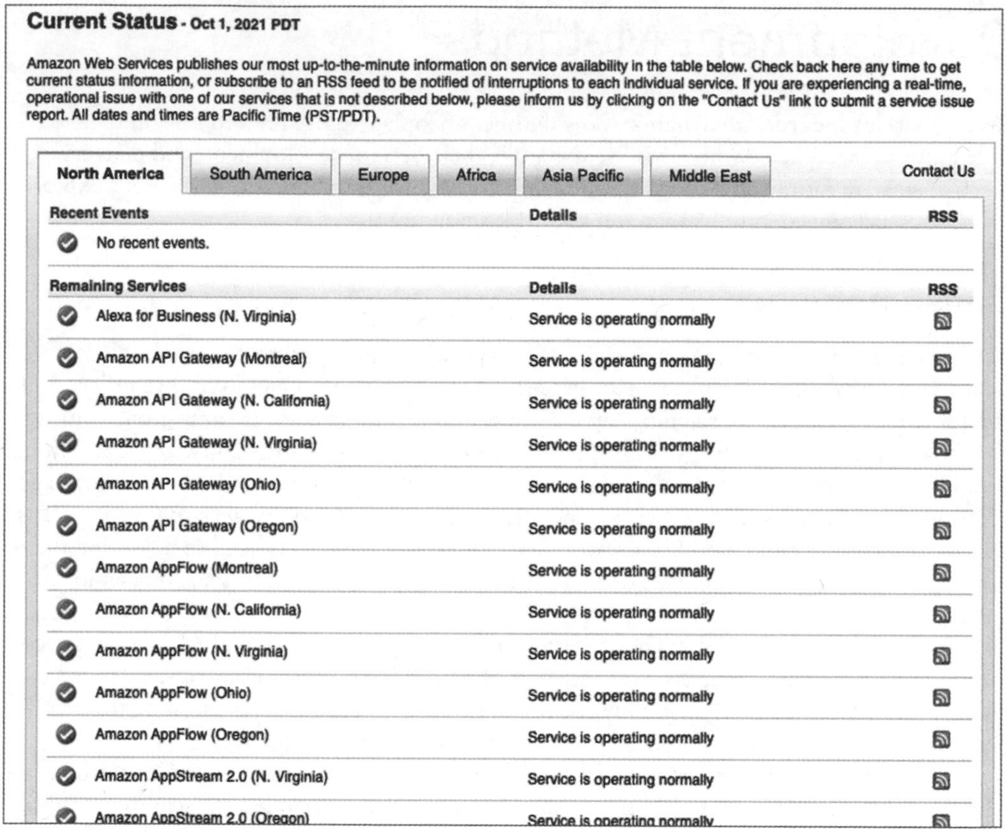

You may need to develop a dashboard for technical experts. For instance, the people who use the dashboard in Figure 7.15 could have functional or technical responsibilities. A person with financial responsibility might only want to know when the outage violates an SLA, which triggers a service credit. However, a technical expert using the service wants to learn more about the specifics of an outage and how that impacts the services they provide.

Data Source Considerations

With clarity on what your dashboard needs to contain, you can proceed with identifying data sources. The most vital determination you make about data sources hinges on whether or not the dashboard needs to incorporate live data. *Static data* is data that refreshes at some regular interval. A typical design pattern is for operational databases to update a data warehouse every night. *Continuous data*, also known as *live data*, typically comes directly from an operational database that people use to perform their daily duties. The operational database provides a *live data feed* to the dashboard.

For example, as the senior leader responsible for an organization's finances, a CFO has many needs. Since people are among an organization's most expensive assets, one of the KPIs a CFO tracks is employee count. Suppose the CFO expects their dashboard to reflect how many employees an organization has up to the minute. In that case, you need to source data directly from the operational human resources database.

However, if it is sufficient to have the employee count updated at the end of each business day, you can pull data from a data warehouse. Figure 7.16 visualizes the process for determining whether you need to connect with an operational database. Depending on the needs of the dashboard consumer, you may end up with connections to both operational and reporting databases.

FIGURE 7.16   Data sourcing flowchart

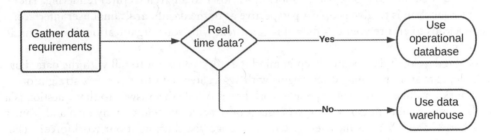

Data Type Considerations

One thing that differentiates dashboards and reports is the fact that dashboards use software as the delivery mechanism. As such, you have to have a deeper understanding of your source data than when you are creating a report. Whether you use packaged software like Tableau or Qlik or write your own visualization using a programming language like Python or R, you need to ensure you can handle the data type of each attribute.

When creating a dashboard, you use qualitative data to create dimensions. A *dimension* is an attribute that you use to divide your data into categories or segments. To make sure you are representing the source data categories entirely, map the field definitions from the source data to your visualization tool. For example, a geographic dimension lets you look at your data by geographic region. A date dimension enables you to explore data at various levels of time-related granularity. For example, suppose you are creating a sales dashboard and want to allow the flexibility to look at sales by day of the week, week, month, quarter, year, fiscal quarter, and fiscal year. Each date increment is a value within the time dimension.

A *measure* is a numeric, quantitative value that a dashboard user is curious about. For example, a sales executive may wish to examine regional sales of a specific product over time. In this case, the number and dollar value of sales are measures, and region and time are dimensions. When in doubt, recall that a measure contains what a user wants to look at, while a dimension provides ways to segment or subdivide the data.

Development Process

After you identify the data sources that will power your dashboard, you must turn your attention to developing the dashboard itself. Use wireframes and mockups to help build and refine the dashboard's design. A *wireframe* is a blueprint for an application that defines the basic design and functions of a dashboard. Think of a wireframe like a blueprint for a building. Architects develop blueprints to describe the internal structure of a building. Similarly, a wireframe defines the basic structure, functionality, and content of a dashboard. Use wireframes to define the presentation layout and navigation flow to guide how people will interact with the dashboard.

A *mockup* extends a wireframe by providing details about the visual elements of the dashboard, including fonts, colors, logos, graphics, and page styles. While a wireframe is conceptually similar to a blueprint, a mockup is closer to an architectural rendering. The goal of a mockup is to give people a perspective as to the dashboard's final user interface. Use mockups to ensure your dashboard is consistent with your organizational communication standards.

As you develop a dashboard, keep in mind the story you want to tell with the data. For example, data story planning often begins with aggregated data that answers straightforward questions like "How many people work here?" While the answer to that question is a number, you should anticipate follow-on questions, including "How many men and women work here?" and "What is the average tenure and age distribution of our workforce?" The latter question can help inform succession planning. Incorporating wireframes, mockups, and a data story plan help design an optimal *web interface*.

Keep in mind that creating a dashboard is an iterative process. As you develop wireframes and mockups, be sure you deliberately incorporate steps to obtain approval to proceed. One way to ensure you don't lose sight of crucial requirements is to include the voice of the customer during feedback sessions. In these sessions, show your mockups to the people who will be using your dashboard. Most often, people think of additional features and voice other requirements when reacting to the design of a mockup. Document and incorporate this feedback to improve the quality and usefulness of your dashboard. At the end of the development process, the goal is to have a dashboard that informs and delights its users.

Delivery Considerations

Delivery considerations are a crucial part of the development process. Accounting for how you will refresh data is one of the many things to consider. As you document their requirements and develop mockups, you need to determine whether people can subscribe to changes, as seen in Figure 7.12. If *subscription* capability is a requirement, you need to have a system where people can opt in to receive a notification when the underlying data changes.

In addition to offering a subscription service, another delivery consideration is *scheduled delivery*. For example, suppose a portion of your dashboard consists of daily production figures. The leader of a manufacturing facility wants to subscribe to data refresh notifications. However, they also want the daily number of defects to be delivered to their mobile device at six o'clock in the morning to help them prepare for their daily quality control meeting. In this case, you can schedule a notification to provide a link to the relevant data at the appropriate time.

A crucial detail you need to identify as part of the development process is how interactive the dashboard needs to be. The level of interactivity needs to accommodate requirements from the data story plan. Once again, consider the questions an executive might have about the composition of the organization's employees. As the dashboard conveys aggregated data, you need to understand the dimensions where dashboard users will want to explore additional details. That will help you design a dashboard that lets people *drill down* into deeper levels of detail. For example, suppose the dashboard landing page for a chief sales officer (CSO) shows total corporate global sales. The CSO may want to see more detail for a given region, country, or metropolitan area. When the CSO drills down into a specific region, the dashboard filters data to only show details for that region. Similarly, if the CSO further drills into a country, the dashboard only shows the sales data for that country.

Some requirements dictate the ability to *roll up* data. For example, a regional manager wants to know about total sales in their region. In contrast, the CSO wants to roll up, or aggregate, sales activity across all regions. A well-designed dashboard will give the regional manager the data they need while accommodating the needs of the CSO.

Suppose that as the CSO explores sales activity across regions, they become concerned about a specific region. A good dashboard will allow *filtering* on the appropriate dimension to limit the data to only that region.

A CSO pays close attention to the sales funnel, where people progress from lead to customer. A well-designed dashboard provides the number of people at each level in the funnel, as shown in Figure 7.17. However, the CSO may want to see individual details for prospects in the Follow-ups category, as they are one step away from becoming customers. Instead of searching for this information, sound dashboard design allows the CSO to create *saved search* criteria. Once saved, they can re-execute their search as data updates over time without having to reinput the original search criteria. As you can imagine, the dashboard translates this type of search into a SQL query against a database.

FIGURE 7.17   Sales funnel

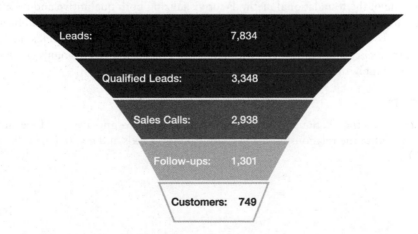

Operational Considerations

Once you have final approval, you proceed with developing the dashboard. Similar to the design stage, make sure you include frequent opportunities to gather feedback. Once dashboard development is complete, test it thoroughly to verify its functionality.

As you build a dashboard, make sure you clearly define the access permissions. *Access permissions* define the data that a given person can access. When defining access permissions, do so in terms of roles instead of people. For example, suppose Megan Trotter is a promising regional sales leader. In that role, Megan needs access to sales performance data in her region but doesn't need access to sales data for other regions. To give Megan only the data she needs, assign access permissions to the regional sales leader role instead of Megan directly since a person can switch roles over time. Suppose that Megan ends up in the CSO role. In that case, she needs access to all sales data. However, if Megan pivots and ends up with a role in Human Resources, she no longer needs access to sales-related data.

As you confirm that the dashboard will serve its intended purpose, you are ready to deploy it to production. Once the dashboard is in active use, your work is not over. You need to ensure the dashboard continues to answer leadership's questions while performing well. As the person responsible for the dashboard itself, you need to pursue ongoing *dashboard optimizations*. A given optimization may improve the performance of a dashboard component or may include a new data source to enable answering new sets of questions.

Exploring Visualization Types

You have many options for presenting information visually. It is vital to select a visualization type that appropriately conveys the story you are telling with your data in a compelling format. Let's examine some of the most widely used shapes for visualizing information.

Charts

Charts are one of the foundational methods for visualizing both qualitative and quantitative data. There are many chart types, including line, pie, bar, stacked, scatter, and bubble charts. As you recall from Chapter 4, "Data Quality," histograms are particularly well suited to illustrating frequency and centrality. With so many options to choose from, it's crucial to know when to apply the appropriate chart shape to the data at hand.

Line Chart

A *line chart* shows the relationship of two variables along an x- and a y-axis. Line charts effectively visualize the relationship between time on the x-axis and a variable on the y-axis.

Consider Figure 7.18, which illustrates how the average duration of Hollywood movies changes between 1927 and 2016. Interpreting the line, the range of the average duration varies significantly between 1927 and the late 1970s. After the late 1970s, the range for the average duration is smaller, converging to around 112 minutes.

FIGURE 7.18   Line chart

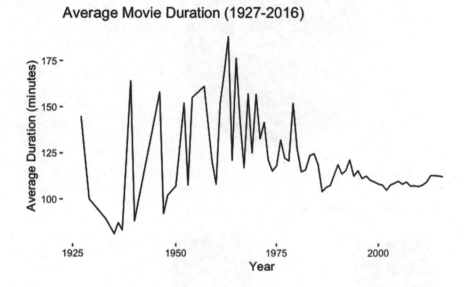

Pie Chart

A *pie chart* gets its name from its circular shape where the circle represents 100 percent, and each slice of the pie is a proportion of the whole. A pie chart presents categorical, or discrete, data as individual slices of the pie. When using a pie chart, ensure that you label each pie slice appropriately, as shown in Figure 7.19. Without the percentage labels, it is a challenge to determine the relative proportions of the Crime and Adventure slices. While pie charts are an option, a bar chart illustrates the same information in a more easily interpreted format.

Bar Chart

Similar to a pie chart, a *bar chart* presents categorical data. Where a pie chart is circular, a bar chart uses rectangular bars to depict each proportion. Bar charts tend to be more interpretable for people than pie charts. For example, Figure 7.20 illustrates the same data as Figure 7.19. Visually, it is straightforward for a person to compare the relative heights of each bar.

FIGURE 7.19   Pie chart

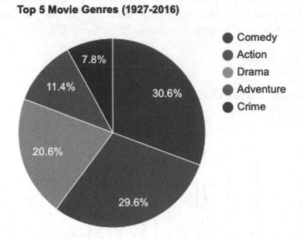

Top 5 Movie Genres (1927-2016)

- ● Comedy
- ● Action
- ● Drama
- ● Adventure
- ● Crime

30.6%
7.8%
11.4%
20.6%
29.6%

FIGURE 7.20   Bar chart by genre

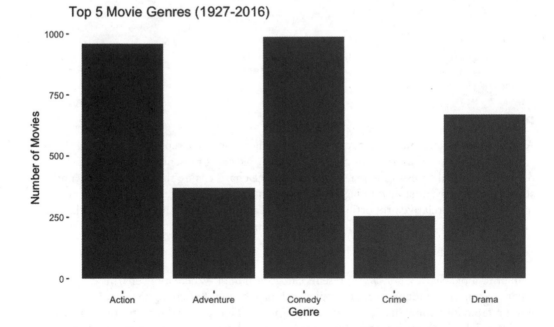

Top 5 Movie Genres (1927-2016)

Keep in mind the information you are trying to convey when using bar charts. If the alphabetic order of the categories is a critical component that your audience will anchor to, then Figure 7.20 is appropriate. However, as the title indicates, the intent is to show the top five movie genres between 1927 and 2016. Arranging the bars according to height is a better way to present the data, as Figure 7.21 illustrates.

FIGURE 7.21   Bar chart by count

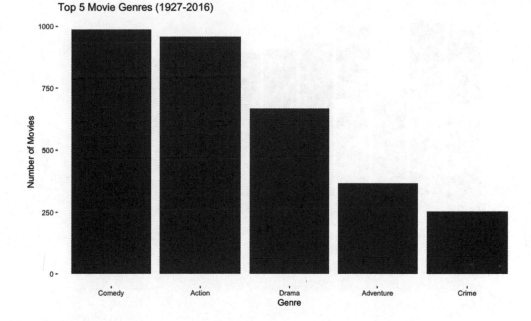

Top 5 Movie Genres (1927-2016)

Stacked Chart

A *stacked chart*, or *stacked bar chart*, starts with a bar chart and extends it by incorporating proportional segments on each bar for categorical data. Suppose that you identify the top movie genres, as shown in Figure 7.21, and want to explore the number of movies in each category over time. Figure 7.22 uses a stacked bar chart to visualize the proportional number of films made over 10 years.

Scatter Chart

A *scatter chart*, or *scatter plot*, uses a dot for each observation in a data set to show the relationship between two numeric variables. Recall the line chart in Figure 7.18, which shows how the average duration for a film changes over the years. Since years are numeric, you can use a scatterplot to visualize the relationship between year and duration, as shown in Figure 7.23.

   Suppose you are a pricing analyst for a movie studio and want to explore the relationship between a film's budget and its gross revenue. Since you can use dollars to measure both budget and revenue, you can use a scatterplot to visualize the relationship, as shown in Figure 7.24.

FIGURE 7.22   Stacked bar chart

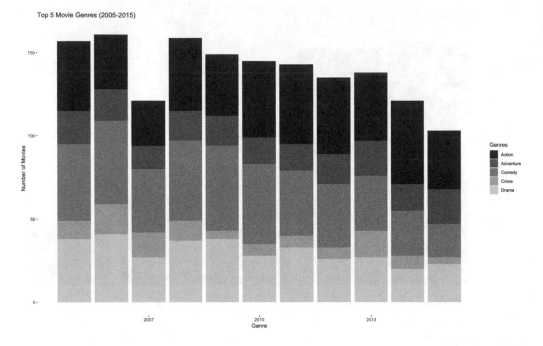

Sometimes it makes sense to layer different charts together to increase a visualization's impact. Considering the scatterplot in Figure 7.24, it appears that the bigger a film's budget is, the higher the box office gross. Combining tools and visualizations, Figure 7.25 adds a linear regression line on top of the scatterplot. Adding a layer with the regression line facilitates conveying the message that there is a positive relationship between a film's budget and its box office gross.

Bubble Chart

A *bubble chart* is a scatterplot where the size of each dot is dependent on a third numeric variable. Consider the density of dots in Figure 7.25. One way to increase the visual appeal of that chart is to add aggregation. Converting the y-axis from actual gross to average gross gives us the graph in Figure 7.26. However, in aggregating this data, you lose the perspective of how many individual observations exist.

FIGURE 7.23   Average duration scatterplot

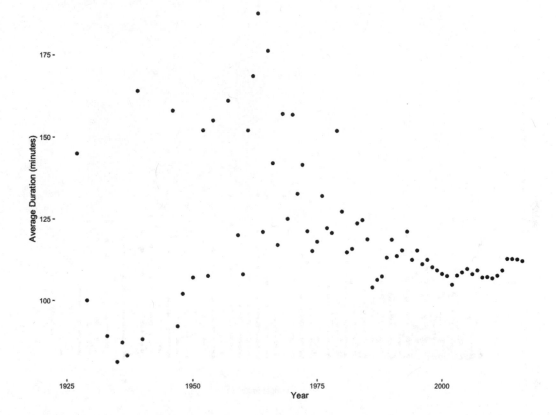

Average Movie Duration (1927-2016)

To illustrate the number of observations without cluttering the scatter chart, create a bubble chart, as shown in Figure 7.27. In this figure, the size of each dot represents the number of movies at that budget level. Using dot size to represent the third numeric dimension of movie count lets you convey additional information without adding clutter.

Histogram

A *histogram* is a chart that shows a frequency distribution for numeric data. When performing an exploratory data analysis, create histograms for numeric data. These histograms illustrate the shape of the distribution and can inform the next stage of analysis. Histograms are also effective for communicating a distribution's shape to stakeholders.

FIGURE 7.24   Budget and box office gross scatterplot

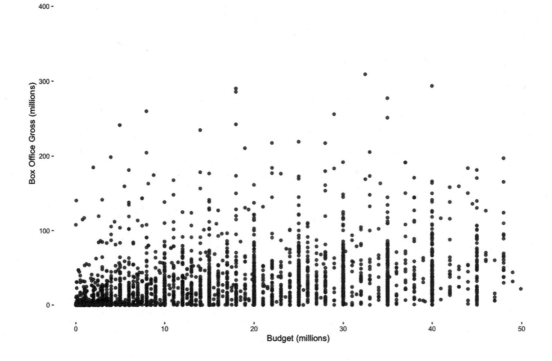

Movie Budget and Box Office Gross (1927-2016)

Considering Figure 7.28, there is a considerable right skew to the distribution and the majority of movies have a box office gross of under $200 million. Meanwhile, Figure 7.29 shows that the duration of films during the same period as Figure 7.28 has a more normal distribution with a slight right skew.

Maps

People frequently use maps to convey the location of a country, town, or individual address. Maps are effective methods orienting a person to a dataset. There are numerous types of maps available to visualize data, including geographic, heat, and tree maps.

FIGURE 7.25   Budget and box office gross scatter and line chart

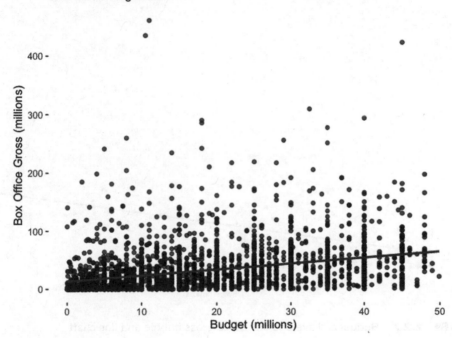

Movie Budget and Box Office Gross (1927-2016)
With Linear Regression

Geographic Maps

Geographic maps are excellent for location-related data. For example, Figure 7.30 shows the location of higher education institutions in the United States where the undergraduate population exceeds 25,000 students. Use geographic maps when location is a component of your data.

Heat Maps

A *heat map* is a visualization that uses color and location to illustrate significance. Heat maps are versatile and apply in many different contexts. For example, you can use a heat map to represent organizational risks, as shown in Figure 7.31. You first assign the risks facing your business a likelihood and impact score. After scoring, you put the risks on the heat map. The higher the probability and impact of a specific risk, the more an organization needs to develop a strategy to manage the risk. Risk heat maps help orient leaders to the challenges they face, especially during times of transition.

FIGURE 7.26 Budget and average box office gross scatter and line chart

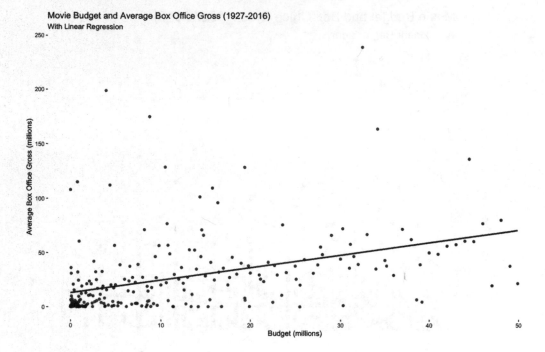

FIGURE 7.27 Budget and average box office gross bubble and line chart

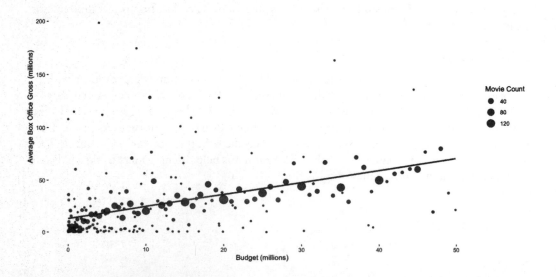

FIGURE 7.28   Histogram of box office gross

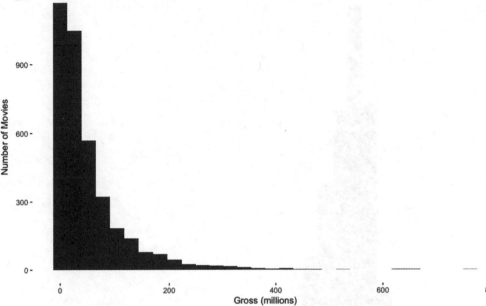

Movie Box Office Gross (1927-2016)

Heat maps can also illustrate the relationship between variables. Figure 7.32 shows the correlation between movie attributes. At one extreme, cast_total_facebook_likes and actor_3_facebook_likes are highly correlated, while movie_facebook_likes and facenumber_in_poster are not. Understanding correlation impacts the variables you would consider for making predictions.

Tree Maps

A *tree map* uses rectangles whose area depicts a proportional representation of hierarchical data. Tree maps are effective at showing the distribution at levels within the hierarchy. For example, Figure 7.33 shows aggregate movie genres from 1927 to 2016, with the area of each rectangle representing the number of films and the color indicating the genre. Looking at the size of the rectangles in Figure 7.33, the most prevalent genres are comedy and action. Figure 7.34 decomposes the comedy genre, where romantic comedies occupy the largest segment.

Consider tree maps when creating interactive visualizations. You can imagine a person opening the Comedy rectangle from Figure 7.33 to see the tree map in Figure 7.34.

FIGURE 7.29   Histogram of movie duration

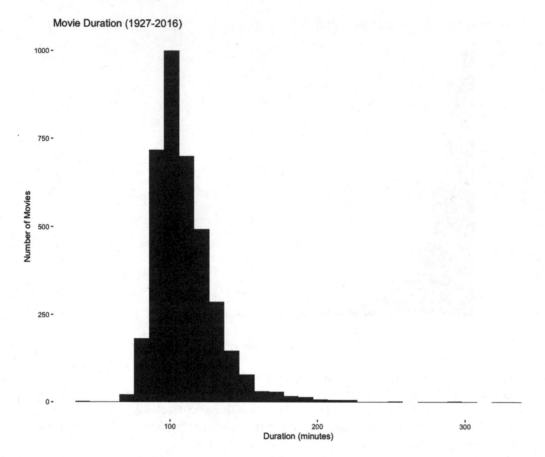

FIGURE 7.30   Large U.S. colleges and universities

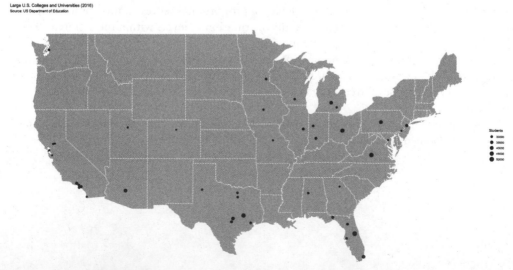

FIGURE 7.31   Risk heat map

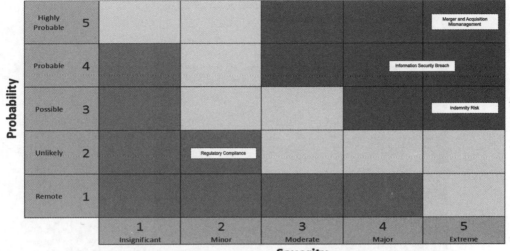

FIGURE 7.32   Correlation heat map

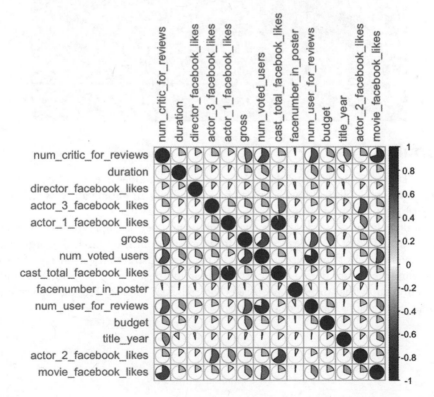

FIGURE 7.33   Tree map of movie genres

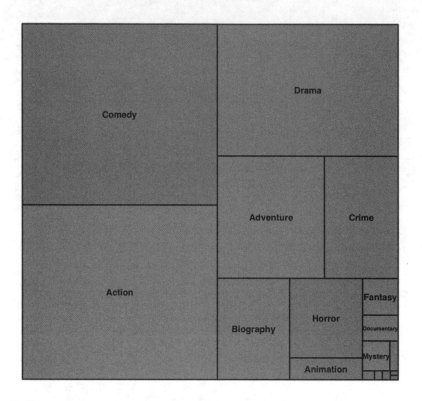

Tree Map of Movie Genres (1927-2016)

Waterfall

A *waterfall chart* displays the cumulative effect of numeric values over time. Waterfall charts facilitate an understanding of how a series of events impact an initial value. Use a waterfall chart any time you want to see how events affect a baseline value.

For example, Figure 7.35 shows the change in the number of employees over a calendar year. Comparing End of Year Headcount to Initial Headcount shows that this organization grew the number of employees. The rest of the bars illustrate how a variety of factors impacted employee count during the year. The color and position for both Internal and External Hires show that these are positive events, whereas Internal Moves, Separations, and Involuntary Separations have a negative impact.

FIGURE 7.34   Tree map of the comedy genre

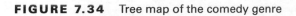

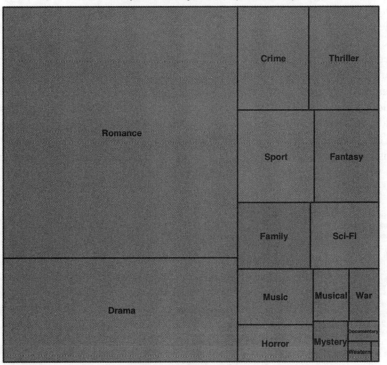

FIGURE 7.35   Headcount waterfall chart

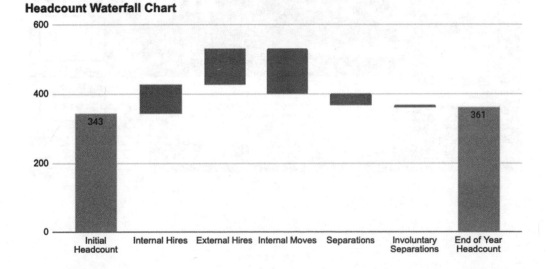

Infographic

An *infographic*, which gets its name from the words "information" and "graphic," is a visualization that presents information clearly and concisely. Infographics minimize text in favor of visual elements to represent a topic in a format that is easy to understand. The goal of an infographic is to convey an insight in a way that minimizes the time to comprehension.

Consider the infographic in Figure 7.36. This infographic conveys how advising and interventions combine to positively affect academic success. The central portion of the infographic illustrates how the design, build, capture, identify, notify, boost, evaluate, and report processes flow together. The detailed phase descriptions on the edges of this infographic provide additional information about how data is collected, analyzed, and assessed. By combining graphics, text, and data, this infographic tells a compelling story about how one university is building the infrastructure and processes to help students realize their potential.

FIGURE 7.36   Infographic

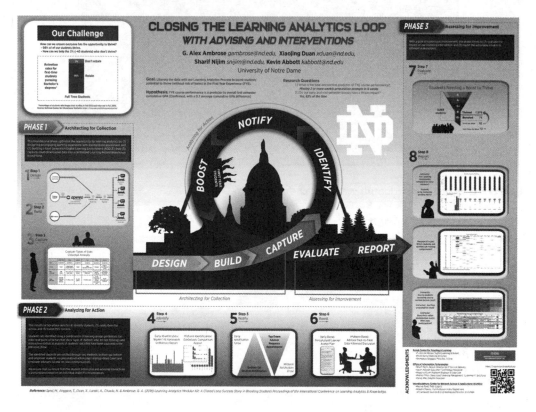

Word Cloud

A *word cloud* is a visualization that uses shape, font size, and color to signify the relative importance of words. Word clouds are effective at visualizing free-form text responses. When creating a word cloud, you eliminate common words and conjunctions as they occur frequently and don't add value in terms of meaning. The heart shape of Figure 7.37 conveys positivity, and the words *system*, *learn*, *data*, *inspired*, *course*, and *think* stand out.

FIGURE 7.37   Positive word cloud

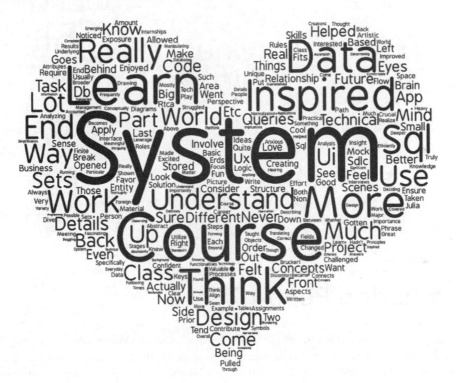

Be deliberate when choosing a word cloud's shape, as it helps convey the overall sentiment. For example, the shape of Figure 7.38 establishes the context that responses about struggle form the basis of the word cloud, with *assignments* standing out as the most significant individual word.

FIGURE 7.38   Negative word cloud

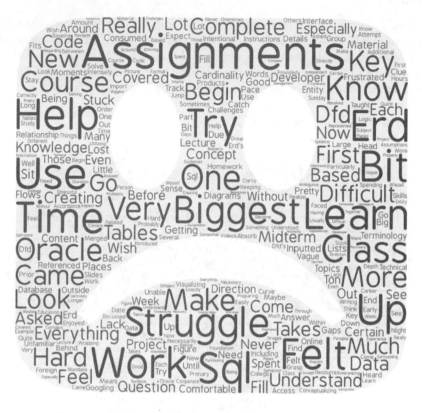

Comparing Report Types

There are several report types to choose from, depending on the information you want to convey. When embarking on any reporting project, recall that you first have to identify the audience and their needs. After clarifying who will consume your report and what information they need to see, it is crucial to determine when they need it.

Static and Dynamic

It is imperative to identify whether a report needs to be static or dynamic, as that difference impacts where you get your data. *Static reports* pull data from various data sources to reflect data at a specific point in time. Suppose you work in a financial services firm and develop a five-year trend report for securities in the automotive sector, including Ford, Volkswagen, and Tesla. To feed your trend report, you need the daily price for each security over five years. Data marts and data warehouses are typical sources for this type of data.

Dynamic reports give people real-time access to information. Using your five-year trend report to inform their analysis, a financial analyst in your company may want to execute a trade. For the analyst to determine the price they are willing to pay for a given security, they need access to real-time pricing data. Data marts and data warehouses are insufficient for providing real-time information. In this case, you require current pricing information from the exchange where the security is actively traded, like the New York Stock Exchange or the Nasdaq. This type of real-time access typically uses an application programming interface (API).

Ad Hoc

Ad hoc reports, or *one-time reports*, use existing data to meet a unique need at a specific point in time. For example, suppose a hospital suffers an information security breach. As a result of the breach, some of their patient data is posted publicly on the Internet. In reaction to this one-time event, hospital administrators commission an ad hoc report to identify the patients they need to notify.

Self-Service (On-Demand)

Self-service reports, or *on-demand reports*, allow individuals to answer questions that are unique to them at a time of their choosing. Instead of having data pushed to them, an attribute of self-service reporting is that individuals can pull a report at the time of their choosing. For instance, consider an organization with 200 salespeople. Each one of those 200 people has a unique sales goal. A self-service progress-to-goal report lets the salespeople check the current state of their sales against their sales objective. Self-service reports can source their data from transactional or analytical systems depending on how up-to-date the data needs to be.

Recurring Reports

Recurring reports provide summary information on a regularly scheduled basis. Typically, recurring reports get delivered to their audience immediately after creation. For example, a company's sales leader will want monthly, quarterly, and annual sales numbers available regularly.

There are numerous types of recurring *operational reports* that organizations use to monitor organizational health and performance. Operational reports typically show the KPIs for an organization. For example, logistics organizations monitor the total number of packages and whether or not they were on time. Airlines monitor on-time departures and arrivals. Manufacturing companies keep track of daily defect rates. Financial KPIs, like the debt-to-equity ratio, apply to virtually every type of organization.

Compliance reports detail how your organization meets its compliance obligations. Depending on where your organization operates in the world, there are country-specific compliance requirements, including financial, health, information technology, and safety.

From a *financial compliance reporting* standpoint, if you are a public company in the United States, you need to document annual compliance with the Sarbanes–Oxley Act (SOX). SOX compliance ensures that your company provides proof of accurate financial reporting. To comply with SOX, you need to document access controls, security controls, your data backup methodology, and the processes by which people become authorized to make financially significant changes.

From a *safety compliance reporting* standpoint, you need to comply with the Occupational Safety and Health Act (OSHA) in the United States to ensure the safety of your employees. There are general industry standards that apply across the manufacturing, retail, and wholesale sectors.

If you process health-related data in the United States, you must meet *health compliance reporting* obligations. These obligations are subject to the U.S. Health Insurance Portability and Accountability Act of 1996 (HIPAA). HIPAA protects sensitive patient health information from being disclosed without a patient's knowledge or consent.

Organizations develop *risk compliance reports* to engender trust. For example, System and Organization Controls (SOC) reports document how an organization maintains its IT systems' security, availability, and confidentiality in the information technology space. These reports also demonstrate how an organization collects, uses, retains, discloses, and disposes of data.

Each industry has its own set of unique regulatory requirements. *Regulatory compliance reports* document how an organization meets those compliance burdens. For example, if you process credit card payments, you must comply with the Payment Card Industry Data Security Standard (PCI DSS). This standard documents rules for storing, processing, or transmitting cardholder or sensitive authentication data.

These compliance obligations are a mere subset of the regulations that exist. Regardless of the type of compliance obligation, you need to produce the appropriate compliance report regularly.

Tactical and Research

It is vital to identify whether the report you create is for tactical or strategic purposes. *Tactical reports* provide information to inform an organization's short-term decisions. Tactical information helps organizations accomplish initiatives like constructing a building, opening a manufacturing plant, or shipping products from one location to another. Data for tactical reports come from various sources, including operational and analytical systems, and enables operational decisions.

A *research report* helps an organization make strategic decisions. To achieve strategic objectives, an organization executes multiple tactical initiatives. Where a tactical report informs a decision with a finite scope and duration, research reports inform the development of an overarching strategy. The implications of strategic decisions are broad, including whether to acquire a competitor, how many component suppliers an organization needs, and whether to diversify and enter an entirely new market. Since the decision implications are broad, strategic reports take more time to create than tactical reports. Strategic reports often combine internal data about an organization's operational performance and risks with data about external forces.

Summary

Communicating data visually is one of the most impactful activities an analyst performs. It is imperative to understand the audience of your visualization clearly. Senior leaders have different information requirements than individual salespeople, and you need to understand what decisions people make using your visualization.

You also need to clarify the business objectives for each visualization and the appropriate vehicle for distribution. If the situation requires static information, a report is a suitable choice. However, if people need to interact with the data, you need to create a dynamic dashboard that enables exploration.

As you identify requirements, make sure that you understand the limitations of the data or its use. If someone wants to look at 10 years' worth of data but you only have data for seven years, you need to communicate that shortcoming and work with the business user to determine a viable path forward. Similarly, some circumstances require you to restrict access to specific data elements. Take data sensitivity into account as you consider distribution options.

In addition to any unique data-specific circumstances, you need to establish the publishing and distribution frequency. For instance, if people need a report in their email by 7 a.m. to start their day, you need to ensure that you have updated data sources and enough time to produce and distribute the report.

There are numerous visual elements to consider when designing a report. More formal reports need a cover page with instructions for use and an executive summary that provides a synopsis of insights. In the body of the report, ensure you use consistent, legible font sizes and styles. Make sure the chart titles, axes, and legends have clear labels. If you work with a large organization, work with corporate communications to incorporate corporate branding and style guides as appropriate.

From a change management perspective, make sure you update the publish date, version number, data sources, and refresh date when distributing a report. Careful change management helps ensure that people have the same data when contemplating decisions.

Dashboards are more complex than reports, as they are interactive and can reflect real-time information. When building a dashboard, keep dimensional modeling in mind when gathering business requirements. Understanding the dimensions that people want to use for segmenting data helps ensure you bring in the appropriate data sources. Keep in mind that the objective is to communicate essential information while minimizing clutter.

The key to an impactful dashboard is an iterative development process. Use wireframes to define the structure of your dashboard, and get mockups of the interface into the hands of the dashboard consumers as early as possible. If you have access to user experience professionals, tap into their knowledge to create a dashboard design that is intuitive and easy to use.

Just as you have different recipients for different reports, consider the types of roles that will access your dashboard. Work with your information security and application administration teams to identify the best way to implement role-based permissions.

There are many different types of charts that can help convey information visually. Keep in mind the situation where different chart types apply. For example, when presenting categorical data, you should choose between a bar, stacked bar, and pie chart, and histograms are ideal for showing a frequency distribution.

Make sure you can compare and contrast the different types of reports. For example, static reports provide a snapshot of information at a point in time, whereas dynamic reports incorporate real time data. Ad hoc reports tend to be tactical and helpful for a limited time, whereas research reports take longer to compile, include more data sources, and are valuable for a longer time.

Organizations have many different reporting obligations. These recurring reports can address internal and external audiences and satisfy compliance, risk, regulatory, and operational commitments.

Exam Essentials

Describe the most crucial first steps when developing a visualization.   The most important first steps when developing a visualization are identifying the audience and understanding their needs. If you don't know who will use a visualization or understand its purpose, your creation will have a limited impact.

Compare reports and dashboards.   Reports are static documents that get distributed physically or electronically. As static documents, they reflect data at the time of creation. Dashboards are dynamic and encourage data exploration. Typically delivered as a web interface, dashboards can integrate real-time data and enable users to explore segment data along multiple dimensions.

Identify the best type of chart for a given scenario.   Given a specific scenario, select the type of chart that is most appropriate. Bar and pie charts work well for categorical data, whereas line charts are excellent for illustrating the relationship between two variables. Scatter charts show all of the points in a data set, whereas bubble charts use size to show the effect of a third numeric attribute. Maps are good for spatial data, waterfall charts show positive and negative impacts over time, and infographics convey a message. A word cloud is an optimal choice for displaying the relative significance of words when dealing with unstructured data.

Identify the type of report that should be used in a given scenario.   Given a specific scenario, identify the type of report that would meet the requirement. For example, you need a recurring report on a regular schedule to meet various compliance objectives. On the other hand, self-service reports enable individuals to answer a specific question at the time of their choosing.

Describe considerations for maintaining data security.   When working with static reports, having tight control over how reports get distributed is one approach to ensuring the security of the data in the report. Dashboards are more complicated, as they are accessible in an interactive manner. Work closely with information security and application administrators to map people's various roles to the appropriate dashboard sections. Restrict sensitive data access only to the functions that require it.

Review Questions

1. Igor is creating an inventory report for the manager of a local convenience store. On average, replacement items are delivered within 3 days after the manager places an order. What is the most appropriate frequency for this report? (Choose the best answer.)

   A. Real-time

   B. Hourly

   C. Daily

   D. Weekly

2. Jasmine is developing a daily report that will be posted at the entrances to 700 different franchise locations. What is the most appropriate color scheme?

   A. Black monochrome palette

   B. Red and green complementary palette

   C. Blue and orange complementary palette

   D. Yellow and purple complementary palette

3. Bowen is developing a report that explores how consumer sentiment about his company's products changes over time. Where should he put a paragraph describing the most profound insight in the report? (Choose the best answer.)

   A. Title page

   B. Executive summary

   C. Report body

   D. Appendix

4. Javier wants to illustrate the relationship between height and weight. What type of chart should he use?

   A. Bar

   B. Scatter

   C. Line

   D. Histogram

5. John's CEO wants to be able to explore how retail sales have been changing over time. What is the best way to present the information to the CEO? (Choose the best answer.)

   A. Historical report

   B. Recurring report

   C. One-time report

   D. Interactive dashboard

6. Ron is a recent hire at a large organization and is developing his first report. What should he do first? (Choose the best answer.)

    A. Check with the communications division to see whether any corporate style guides exist.

    B. Work with his supervisor to identify distribution mechanisms.

    C. Work with operations to develop a delivery schedule.

    D. Check with his colleagues to determine the best way to get his completed report to the appropriate people.

7. Kelly wants to get feedback on the final draft of a strategic report that has taken her six months to develop. What can she do to get prevent confusion as she seeks feedback before publishing the report? (Choose the best answer.)

    A. Distribute the report to the appropriate stakeholders via email.

    B. Use a watermark to identify the report as a draft.

    C. Show the report to her immediate supervisor.

    D. Publish the report on an internally facing website.

8. Maggie is a new analyst tasked with developing a dashboard. What should she focus on to obtain an understanding of requirements for internal senior leaders? (Choose the best answer.)

    A. Service credits

    B. Service level agreements

    C. Key performance indicators

    D. Defect rate

9. Cian is mapping dashboard requirements to data sources. What should he use to ensure the structure is in place to deliver the dashboard successfully?

    A. Mockup

    B. Wireframe

    C. Data warehouse

    D. Data mart

10. Zakir wants to visualize aggregate sales data over time. What type of chart should he select?

    A. Pie chart

    B. Tree map

    C. Histogram

    D. Line chart

11. Celine wants to visualize annual precipitation in South America. What type of chart would create the greatest impact?

    A. Geographic heat map

    B. Stacked bar chart

    C. Word cloud

    D. Waterfall chart

12. Luciana is an analyst for a sporting venue. She wants to distill post-event free-response survey data to inform leadership what respondents have on their minds. What type of visualization should she choose?

    A. Pie chart

    B. Bar chart

    C. Word cloud

    D. Dashboard

13. Aubree wants to visualize the correlation between 15 different variables. What type of chart should she select?

    A. Tree map

    B. Bar chart

    C. Infographic

    D. Heat map

14. Appa wants to tell a story about the effect of climate change on coastal cities with a single, static visualization. Which of the following should he choose?

    A. Tree map

    B. Bar chart

    C. Infographic

    D. Heat map

15. Kingston wants to create an interactive visualization that allows people to explore brand sales by category and subcategory. What type of visualization should he choose for his dashboard?

    A. Tree map

    B. Bar chart

    C. Infographic

    D. Heat map

16. Rita wants to illustrate the relationship between per capita GDP, life expectancy, and population size. What type of visualization should she choose?

    A. Bubble chart

    B. Bar chart

    C. Infographic

    D. Heat map

17. Sanjay's company has three primary brands that drive corporate profitability. If Sanjay wants to visualize the contribution of each brand over time, what type of chart should he choose?

    A. Bubble chart

    B. Stacked bar chart

    C. Infographic

    D. Heat map

18. Adeline is developing a poster to raise awareness about climate change. What type of visualization should she use?

    A. Bubble chart

    B. Stacked bar chart

    C. Infographic

    D. Heat map

19. Abbas's CFO wants to drill down on cost centers across the organization. What type of visualization should Abbas create?

    A. Bubble chart

    B. Stacked bar chart

    C. Infographic

    D. Dashboard

20. Shivang's CEO wants to visualize the relationship between height and 100-meter sprint time for 200 individuals. What type of chart should he choose?

    A. Bubble chart

    B. Stacked bar chart

    C. Infographic

    D. Scatter chart

Data Governance

Recall from Chapter 4, "Data Quality," that high-quality data is the foundation for all things analytical. In Chapter 4, you learned about methods for assessing data quality. We also explored various manipulation techniques for improving data quality. While the tactical approaches in Chapter 4 are vital to ensuring high-quality data, this chapter explores the strategic, process, and regulatory considerations that organizations need to consider to safeguard their data.

In this chapter, we will explore guardrails for accessing, securing, storing, and using data. Revisiting techniques from Chapter 3, "Databases and Data Acquisition," will illustrate how structuring relational data can enforce data quality standards. Regulatory requirements directly impact data governance, especially how those requirements drive the need for data classification standards. Legal or contractual requirements also impact organizational obligations in the event of a data breach.

We will then consider processes and standards that create an operating environment continuously focused on ensuring data quality before concluding this chapter with a survey of master data management and how it can promote data quality during organic and inorganic organizational growth.

Data Governance Concepts

Data governance is the set of policies, procedures, and controls that an organization develops to safeguard its information while making it useful for transactional and analytic purposes. As the name implies, data governance is primarily a business function. Governments have a method for creating, interpreting, and enforcing laws. Part of this process ensures that these laws are known to the citizenry. For organizations, data governance is an umbrella term covering the creation, interpretation, and enforcement of data use.

Organizations develop numerous policies to govern their data. These policies promote data quality, specify the use of data attributes, and define access to different data domains. Additional governance policies identify how to secure data, comply with regulations, protect data privacy, and deal with data over time. Just as countries enforce laws, organizations implement procedural and technical controls to comply with data governance standards.

Strong executive support is vital to any data governance effort. An organization invests a significant amount of time and resources to define, develop, implement, and control access to data. For data governance to succeed, all levels of an organization must appreciate the importance of well-governed data. While technology is a critical component to facilitating adherence to policies, an information technology organization can't drive data governance efforts on its own. You need executive support across the organization for data governance efforts to succeed.

Data Governance Roles

It takes multiple people fulfilling a variety of roles for data governance to thrive. A crucial concept relating to data governance is data stewardship. Stewardship denotes looking after something, like an organization or property. *Data stewardship* is the act of developing the policies and procedures for looking after an organization's data quality, security, privacy, and regulatory compliance. The most vital role for effective data stewardship is that of the organizational data steward. An *organizational data steward*, or *data steward*, is the person responsible for data stewardship.

The data steward is responsible for leading an organization's data governance activities. As the link between the technical and nontechnical divisions within an organization, a data steward works with many people, from senior leaders to individual technologists. To establish policies, a data steward works with various data owners.

A *data owner* is a senior business leader with overall responsibility for a specific data domain. A *data domain*, or *data subject area*, contains data about a particular operational division within an organization. Finance, human resources, and physical plant are all examples of operational divisions. Data owners work with the data steward to establish policies and procedures for their data domain.

In large, complex organizations, data owners may choose to delegate day-to-day governance activities to subject area data stewards. A *subject area data steward* works in the data owner's organization and understands the nuances that apply within that organizational unit. A subject area data steward works on behalf of their data owner to handle daily tasks. For example, processing access requests as people rotate in and out of roles is a responsibility a data owner may delegate to their subject area data steward. The need for subject area data stewards arises from the intricacies of different data domains. To implement data governance policies, data stewards work with data custodians.

A *data custodian* is a role given to someone who implements technical controls that execute data governance policies. Data custodians are frequently information technology employees who configure applications, dashboards, and databases.

For example, unique laws govern an organization's finances, people, and physical plant. Figure 8.1 visualizes how an organizational data steward works both vertically and horizontally with the various data owners, subject area data stewards, and data custodians to actively steward, or take care of, the organization's data.

Access Requirements

One crucial component of data governance defines the access requirements for data. *Data access requirements* determine which people need access to what data. Access requirements differ by data subject area and can be as granular as a single field. For example, managers

FIGURE 8.1 Organizational example

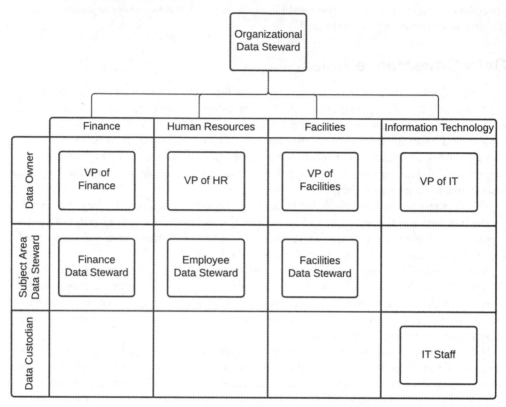

need access to details about their employees, including their names and contact information. Since managers are responsible for providing feedback, they also need access to performance data. However, no manager has a compelling need to view their employees' Social Security number (SSN). While SSNs are necessary for payroll and tax purposes, malicious actors can also use them for identity theft.

When you're determining access requirements, it is essential to develop a data classification matrix. A *data classification matrix* defines categories, descriptions, and disclosure implications for data. Table 8.1 is an example of a data classification matrix. It is vital to consider data classification when considering access requirements to ensure proper data stewardship.

A data steward works with a data owner to establish broad classifications, with subject area data stewards to develop procedures for granting access to information, and with data custodians to ensure the appropriate technical controls are in place to protect information.

TABLE 8.1   Sample data classification matrix

Classification term	Classification description
Public	Data intended for public consumption. For example, anything on a public-facing website meets this classification. No disclosure implications.
Internal	Data intended for use within an organization. For example, a comprehensive organization chart including names. Disclosure compromises an organization's reputation or operations, but not its privacy or confidentiality obligations.
Sensitive	Data intended for limited use within an organization. For example, a list of employees and their compensation. Disclosure implies a violation of privacy or confidentiality.
Highly Sensitive	Data intended for restricted use, typically due to compliance obligations. Examples include Social Security numbers and bank account numbers. Disclosure implies a legal obligation in the event of a data breach.

Access Permissions

It is a best practice to use role-based access to grant people permissions to access data. *Role-based access* means that instead of giving access to individual people, you grant access to the role they occupy. When you define roles and then assign people to those roles, it simplifies how you manage permissions.

For example, it is common for people to switch jobs within an organization, as it allows for developing new skills and a more comprehensive understanding of the overall business. Figure 8.2 illustrates a specific employee's jobs and how they change over time. In the first year, Ralph works in Finance. During his time in Finance, Ralph has access to data about the organization's finances.

In the second year, Ralph takes a new position in Facilities. Ralph needs access to facilities-related data for his new position and doesn't need to retain access to the Finance system. A data custodian removes Ralph's finance role and assigns him a facilities role to reflect that change.

In the third year, Ralph takes a position in Human Resources. Ralph needs access to human resources data in this new job and no longer needs to see the facilities-related data. A data custodian implements the change to Ralph's access permissions.

A role-based access approach facilitates permissions maintenance and improves consistency. This approach also ensures that Ralph only has access to the data he needs to perform his current duties. Managing permissions with roles also pays dividends when auditing permissions for compliance.

The alternative to role-based access is *user-based access*, which assigns permissions directly to individuals. User-based access is a dangerous practice as it increases operational complexity and the potential for mistakes. Suppose there are both OLTP and OLAP

FIGURE 8.2 Access roles over time

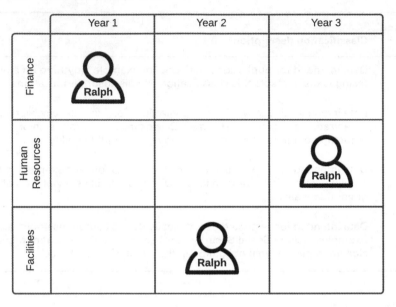

environments for each data subject area. Figure 8.3 illustrates what could happen at the end of Year 3 if the data custodian forgets to remove OLAP permissions at each role transition. In this scenario, Ralph winds up with too much access by the end of Year 3.

FIGURE 8.3 Danger of user-based access

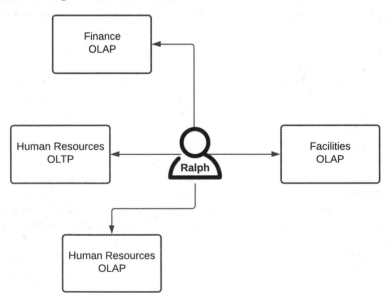

Group Permissions

It's best to start by visualizing people within an organization when creating data access roles. An organization chart documents the reporting structure within an organization. Looking at an organization chart, like the example in Figure 8.4, informs how you develop roles.

FIGURE 8.4 Sample organization chart

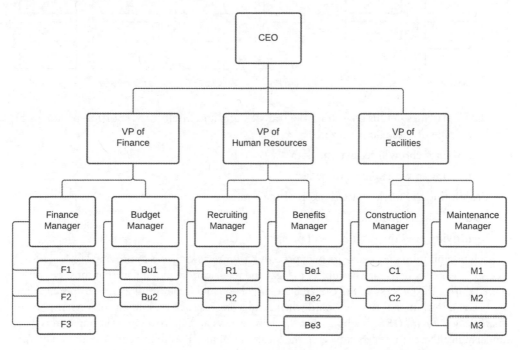

When developing a role-based access strategy, it is common to implement user group-based permissions. Considering the sample organization chart from Figure 8.4, you can imagine vice presidents having broadly permissive access to data within their area of responsibility. Progressing down the organization chart reduces the scope of what someone in that role can access. Figure 8.5 illustrates how roles form naturally around groups of people.

Data Use Agreements

A *data use agreement* (*DUA*) is a contractual document for transferring private data between organizations. You should establish a DUA before sharing data with an outside party. It is essential to understand the classification for each piece of data when crafting a DUA. The more sensitive a data element is, the more critical it is to prepare appropriate sharing-related language. Considering the sample classification matrix from Table 8.1, the data sensitivity level should inform your DUA needs.

FIGURE 8.5   Sample user group–based roles

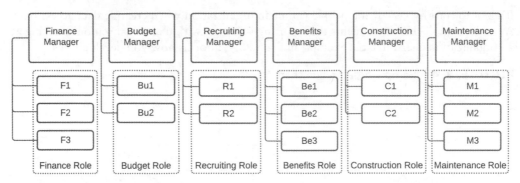

A DUA provides details governing the transfer, use, and disclosure reporting protocols for the data. Some of these details are:

- Identifying who will receive the data
- Identifying how the data can be used
- Prohibiting the further distribution of the data
- Establishing the method of transfer
- Identifying how the recipient will protect the data

Each organization may define its own procedures for reviewing and approving DUAs. However, some organizations may be subject to legal and regulatory requirements that must be considered during this process. In the United States, the Food and Drug Administration specifies that you need an Institutional Review Board when conducting research on human subjects. An *Institutional Review Board* (IRB) is a body that formally reviews and approves any sharing of this data. Similarly, healthcare providers subject to the Health Insurance Portability and Accountability Act (HIPAA) must follow a formal process before sharing any protected health information.

Security Requirements

With data access requirements in place, you need to determine the technical controls for protecting data. In cryptography, *encryption* is the process of encoding data with a key so that only authorized parties can read it. Data encryption is one of the fundamental components of data protection, as the data is unusable without the key to decrypt it. An *encryption key* is a series of letters, numbers, and symbols used during the encoding process to make data unreadable. Once the data is encrypted, you can only access it by decrypting it with a valid key. If you lose the encryption key, any data encrypted with that key becomes useless.

To keep data secure, you must encrypt data at rest as well as data in transit. *Data at rest* is data that exists in permanent storage. The two most common locations for data at rest are databases and flat files. Databases have sophisticated access control mechanisms as part of the database software. Since databases centralize data and require a team of technologists to operate, they are comparatively easy to secure.

For example, both Oracle and Microsoft have *Transparent Data Encryption* (TDE) as part of their database offering. TDE ensures the database files and log files are encrypted.

With TDE, even if an unauthorized party gains access to the database server, the database files themselves are encrypted.

The chance of someone picking up a database server and walking away with it is slight. However, it is much more challenging to secure flat files as you can put them on any device that stores electronic data. Desktop computers, laptops, tablets, mobile phones, and USB thumb drives are all examples of devices that store flat files. Since many of these devices are portable, there is a good chance that one will be lost or stolen. If the device is encrypted, your information is safe if the encryption key isn't lost.

Data in transit is data that is actively moving between one location and another. During data transmission, you must encrypt the connection between the locations to ensure the data's security. When considering data in transit, you need to account for people interacting with computers and computers interacting with other computers.

Transmitting data over the Internet typically uses the Hypertext Transfer Protocol (HTTP). To ensure data security, use *Transport Layer Security* (*TLS*) as the cryptographic protocol for encrypting the connection. Adding TLS on top of HTTP results in *Hypertext Transfer Protocol Secure* (*HTTPS*), as seen in Figure 8.6.

FIGURE 8.6   Encrypted network connection

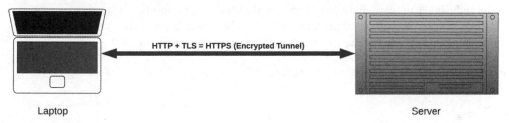

When a person navigates the Internet using a web browser, a padlock shows up in the address bar to indicate an encrypted HTTPS connection. Figure 8.7 illustrates the padlock in three common web browsers. As part of amplifying the security message in the context of data governance, part of your training should include reminders to look for the padlock when putting sensitive information into a browser.

FIGURE 8.7   HTTPS padlock

ETL processes copy data between transactional and analytical systems. When copying files between the transactional and analytical servers, use the *Secure Copy Protocol* (*SCP*) or the *Secure File Transfer Protocol* (*SFTP*). As their names imply, both SCP and SFTP establish an encrypted tunnel to copy data, as shown in Figure 8.8.

FIGURE 8.8   Encrypted ETL process

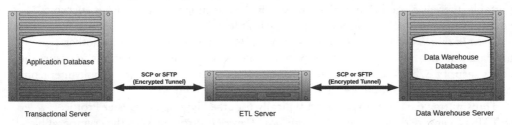

Apart from encryption, you also need to consider whether there is a reason for sensitive data elements, like SSN, to exist in a nonproduction environment. *Data masking*, or *data obfuscation*, replaces sensitive information with a synthetic version. For example, you may use production data to populate your testing and training environments. While testing or training, using a simulated instead of an actual SSN doesn't diminish the testing or training use case. To protect individual privacy and minimize organizational risk, you can implement a data masking strategy for sensitive information, as shown in Figure 8.9.

FIGURE 8.9   Data masking ETL process

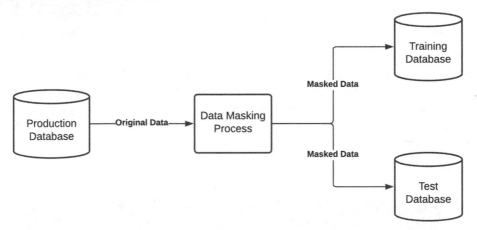

Depending on the use case, you also can deidentify sensitive data to improve security. *De-identifying data* is the process of removing identifiers that can compromise individual privacy. How you deidentify depends on your use case. One way of deidentifying data is to share only aggregated or summarized data. Another way is to remove variables from the data.

Reidentifying data happens when you take deidentified datasets and join them in a way that establishes the identity of individuals. For example, you can identify most Americans by combining their birth date, sex, and zip code. Figure 8.10 illustrates the danger of reidentification, as it shows two separate datasets that share three data elements: birth date, sex, and zip code. Although the medical data set is deidentified, you can reidentify individuals by combining the two datasets using the shared data elements. If the values for those three variables aren't essential to ongoing analysis, the most straightforward path to ensuring the deidentification of the dataset is to remove the variables you don't need. It is especially vital to consider reidentification possibilities when sharing data with an external party.

FIGURE 8.10   Reidentification by combining datasets

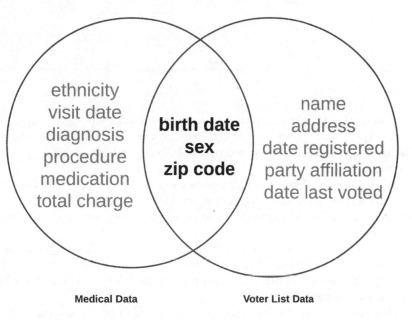

Storage Environment Requirements

There are many environments where data at rest exists, including local storage, a shared drive, and the cloud. Regardless of the storage environment, you need to encrypt all data at rest. *Local storage* is the storage media on an individual device, such as a hard drive in a laptop. Encrypting local storage is straightforward, regardless of the operating system you use. The steps, visualized in Figure 8.11, are as follows:

1. Create a password for encrypting the local storage.
2. Determine the operating system.
3. Use the encryption tool appropriate for the chosen operating system.

While encrypting local storage is straightforward and practical, remember that the encryption key is the only thing protecting the data. Make sure you store the encryption key in a secure location, for if the key is lost, you can no longer decrypt and access your data.

When using a shared drive, the security requirements are slightly more complex than with local storage. A *shared drive* is where groups of people can collaborate on shared documents.

FIGURE 8.11 Local encryption process flow

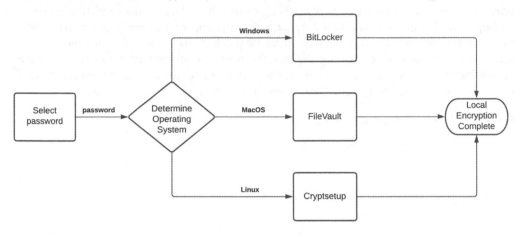

Apart from encrypting the physical media, you need to consider who needs access to the share and the type of access they need. When considering people, it's best to think in terms of groups. When considering access, you need to think about reading, creating, updating, and deleting content.

For example, suppose a hiring committee uses a shared drive to store candidates' cover letters and resumes. Only the search leader responsible for collecting and distributing the documents needs create access to the shared drive, whereas everyone on the hiring committee needs read access.

Shared drive permissions can get very complicated, since each file and folder has its own set of permissions. The safest way to manage shared drive permissions is by identifying groups of people and assigning them the appropriate roles. Every exception is the opportunity for a security compromise.

User-facing *cloud-based storage* is similar to a shared drive, except that the contents reside on computers run by the cloud provider instead of an internal IT team. By default, cloud storage offerings like Microsoft OneDrive, Google Drive, Box, and Dropbox all automatically encrypt files at rest using your login credentials. The same considerations about groups, roles, and permissions you use for shared drives apply to cloud storage.

Cloud storage offerings enable collaboration by design and offer advanced features like simultaneous editing in Google Docs. However, this collaboration by design philosophy means that the ability to share documents resides with the individual by default. When evaluating cloud storage offerings, an organization needs to assess the available administrative controls to minimize the risk of unintended data sharing.

Some organizations use cloud infrastructure to operate their enterprise computing environments. Amazon Web Services, Microsoft, and Google are three large providers of cloud infrastructure. When using infrastructure in the cloud, it is essential to ensure encryption at rest. Recall that if you have access to an encryption key, you can access the data it encrypts.

To ensure that only authorized people can access your data, consider using a customer-managed encryption key. With a customer-managed key, the cloud service provider can't decrypt and use your data.

Use Requirements

Use requirements specify how to collect, process, use, store, retain, and remove data. While understanding audience requirements is vital for creating impactful visualizations, understanding data use requirements is crucial to effective data governance. You need to consider requirements along each stage of the data life cycle, from the moment you create data until the point at which it gets removed or archived. Determining and documenting use requirements at each stage of the data life cycle facilitates effective data governance.

In terms of data processing, you want to identify where people can work with organizational data. You need to think through data sensitivity, encryption at rest, and encryption in transit. Not all data classifications have equivalent data processing requirements.

From a data retention perspective, you need policies that specify how long to keep data. There are legal data retention obligations to consider. For instance, you need to retain tax-related data for seven years. Suppose you terminate an employee. In that case, the U.S. Equal Employment Opportunity Commission (EEOC) specifies that you have to retain personnel and employment records for one year from the employee's termination date.

In addition to legal obligations, you should determine the organizational value of a given piece of data. For instance, if you work with a logistics operation, you may want to keep an archive of the transaction details for each package you deliver forever. While the value of these details diminishes with time, you can derive additional value as you apply statistical methods to identify patterns and trends.

In addition to retention considerations, think about data deletion requirements. Once you determine that the cost of keeping data exceeds its value to the organization, you need to govern its removal. For example, suppose you have a system that stores job applications for your organization. At some point, it no longer creates value for your organization to keep applications for filled positions. While the length of relevance differs per organization, you eventually want to delete old applicant data.

An *acceptable use policy (AUP)* defines an individual's responsibilities when accessing, using, sharing, and removing organizational data. While an AUP is a document with a broad scope, it has provisions for each type of data in an organization's data classification matrix. AUPs describe acceptable locations for storing proprietary information; what to do in the event of theft, loss, or unauthorized disclosure; and methods of disposal.

For example, suppose you are crafting an AUP using the classification matrix in Table 8.1. For the Public classification, you say that using any device to work with Public data is acceptable, and any loss or theft doesn't warrant escalation or reporting. However, for Highly Sensitive data, you limit access to organizationally owned encrypted devices. You also specify that it's necessary to report the event and escalate internally in the event of loss, theft, or disclosure.

Entity Relationship Requirements

Recall from Chapter 3, "Databases and Data Acquisition," that *Entity Relationship Diagrams (ERDs)* give database designers a way of visualizing the relationships between individual entities in a standardized format. Also, recall that during design, you model data as entities and that at implementation time, ERD entities become database tables. Also, recall from Chapter 3 that *cardinality* refers to the relationship between two entities.

Implementing foreign keys for the ERD relationships enforces data constraints. Looking at the customer system in Figure 8.12, an entry in the Address table must have a state that exists in the State table. Enforcing these data constraints is crucial as you consider the data governance implications of ERDs. Figure 8.12 illustrates how studying ERDs can surface data governance implications, as a comprehensive data warehouse design accounts for record link restrictions. *Record linkage* is when you duplicate data in multiple operational systems.

Figure 8.12 shows excerpts from a customer management and employee management transactional system. It also shows the record linkage table in an analytical system. Suppose Jack Johnson has been a customer of this company for 10 years. Due to this affiliation, Jack's information exists in the Customer system.

When a compelling employment opportunity presents itself, Jack takes it and joins the company. As part of Jack's new employee paperwork, he fills out his home address, which makes its way into the Employee system. Since the Customer and Employee systems fulfill different operational needs, the company is unaware that Customer 929349 is also Employee 347233. Having Jack's data in two separate places presents a record linkage problem. When data remains in distinct operational systems, it is difficult for the company to answer the following question: "Which of my employees are also my customers?"

To avoid data linkage problems, organizations invest in data professionals that design analytical systems. As part of the design process, data architects look for duplicate data across source systems and create linking tables, like the Customer_Employee_Link table in Figure 8.12, to provide a holistic view of data subjects.

Data Classification Requirements

Data classification is the process of analyzing data and organizing it into risk-based categories. Classifying data is appropriate for both structured and unstructured data. When classifying data, you put data elements into one of four classifications, similar to those in the data classification matrix found in Table 8.1. Note that the category names may differ. Instead of Public, Internal, Sensitive, and Highly Sensitive, you may come across Public, Internal-Only, Confidential, and Restricted. Regardless of the category names, it is vital to understand the attributes for each category so that you can make the appropriate category assignment.

Classifying data elements can feel like an overwhelming task. Fortunately, there are a variety of standards in place that simplify the classification process, enforce consistency, and protect privacy.

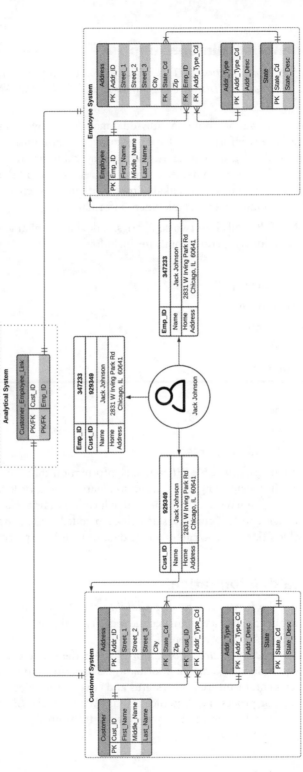

FIGURE 8.12 Record linkage example

Personally Identifiable Information

Personally Identifiable Information (PII) is any data that can uniquely identify a person. In the United States, the *National Institute of Standards and Technology (NIST)* defines PII as follows:

> PII is any information about an individual maintained by an agency, including (1) any information that can be used to distinguish or trace an individual's identity, such as name, social security number, date and place of birth, mother's maiden name, or biometric records; and (2) any other information that is linked or linkable to an individual, such as medical, educational, financial, and employment information.

According to NIST, PII falls into two categories: linked and linkable. *Linked PII* is data that you can use to uniquely identify someone, including:

- Full name
- Social Security number
- Date and place of birth
- Driver's license number
- Passport number
- Credit card numbers
- Addresses
- Telephone numbers
- Email addresses
- Login credentials and passwords

NIST goes on to identify *linkable PII*, which is information that you can use in combination with other identifying information to identify, trace, or locate an individual. For example, suppose you have access to medical, educational, financial, or employment information. Data elements like country, state, city, zip code, gender, and race are all examples of linkable PII, since you can join that data to identify a person, as shown in Figure 8.10 earlier.

Protected Health Information

In the United States, the *Health Insurance Portability and Accountability Act* (HIPAA) is a comprehensive healthcare law that regulates the security and privacy of health data. HIPAA applies to two categories of information.

Under HIPAA, *Protected Health Information* (PHI) is the broad category of data elements identifying an individual's health information. This information can be about the individual's past, current, or future health status and covers providing healthcare, processing healthcare payments, or processing insurance claims. Alternatively, *Electronic Protected Health Information*, or *e-PHI*, is any PHI you store or transmit digitally.

Exam Tip

The CompTIA exam objectives use the acronym PHI to mean "personal health information." However, HIPAA and common usage define it as "protected health information." This difference doesn't alter the meaning or intent of the rules governing this information, so you should treat them both as meaning the same thing if you see either one on the exam.

While HIPAA is a broad regulation, under the *Privacy Rule* provision, it identifies 18 data elements as PHI:

- Names
- All geographic identifiers smaller than a state, including street address, city, county, precinct, and zip code
- Dates other than year that relate to an individual, including birth date, admission date, date of treatment, etc.
- Telephone numbers
- Fax numbers
- Email addresses
- Social Security number
- Medical record numbers
- Health plan beneficiary numbers
- Account numbers
- Certificate or license numbers
- Vehicle identifiers and serial numbers, including license plate
- Device identifiers and serial numbers
- Web Uniform Resource Locators (URLs)
- Internet Protocol (IP) address numbers
- Biometric identifiers, including finger, retinal, voice, and facial prints
- Full-face photographs and any comparable images
- Any other unique identifying number, characteristic, or code, unless otherwise permitted by the Privacy Rule for reidentification

The rules around zip codes are slightly more complex. The first three digits of a zip code are not PHI. However, if all zip code combinations with the same first three digits contain fewer than 20,000 people according to the Bureau of Census, then the first three digits are PHI.

As you can tell by the list of data elements, PHI has a broad scope by design. However, there are two provisions in place if you need to share medical data without patient consent.

The first is *Expert Determination*, where you use statistical and scientific principles or methods to make the risk of identifying an individual very small. The second is *Safe Harbor*, where you deidentify a dataset by removing any PHI data elements.

Another aspect of HIPAA to be aware of is the *Security Rule*, which applies solely to e-PHI. While the Privacy Rule focuses on protecting patient privacy, the objective of the Security Rule is to ensure the confidentiality, integrity, and availability of e-PHI data. The Security Rule exists to ensure that digital records are in a secure location, that access is limited to authorized parties, and systems and processes are in place to prevent unauthorized access or accidental disclosure.

The PHI provisions of HIPAA apply only to covered entities. A *covered entity* is an organization legally obligated under HIPAA to protect the privacy and security of health information. There are three different types of covered entities under HIPAA:

- Healthcare providers (physicians, hospitals, clinics, etc.)
- Health insurance plans
- Healthcare information clearinghouses

Under HIPAA, several electronic transactions qualify as e-PHI. If a provider engages in any of these transactions in electronic form, they are a covered entity. These transactions include:

- Payment and remittance advice
- Claims status
- Eligibility
- Coordination of benefits
- Claims and encounter information
- Enrollment and disenrollment
- Referrals and authorizations
- Premium payment

Since this list has a broad scope, most medical facilities are considered covered entities.

HIPAA also extends beyond covered entities to business partners who handle PHI on the covered entity's behalf. HIPAA requires that covered entities enter into special agreements known as business associate agreements with their partners. A *business associate agreement (BAA)* requires that the business partner also complies with HIPAA provisions. For example, if you use cloud-based storage, the provider you use is a business partner under HIPAA.

It is vital to understand that information is about an individual's health does not automatically imply that the data is governed by HIPAA, as there are three important exceptions to HIPAA. These exceptions include:

- Employment records
- Student educations that are covered by the Family Educational Rights and Privacy Act (FERPA)
- Deidentified data

The laws surrounding PHI are complex. If you work in healthcare or with health-related data, you need to understand the Privacy Rule and Security Rule deeply. It is best to work with attorneys who specialize in the field if you have any doubts about PHI, processing, storing, and protecting e-PHI, or working with partners that require a BAA.

Payment Card Information

The *Payment Card Industry* (*PCI*) is a nongovernmental body that governs card-based financial payments. To protect the integrity of card-based financial transactions and prevent fraud, leading financial service companies, including MasterCard, Visa, Discover, American Express, and the Japan Credit Bureau, created the *PCI Security Standards Council* (*PCI SSC*). The PCI SSC develops policies to govern the processing, transmission, and storage of electronic payments.

The *PCI Data Security Standard* (*PCI DSS*) is the industry's core information security standard. The following six principles encompass the objectives set out by the PCI DSS:

- Building and maintaining a secure network
- Protecting cardholder data
- Maintaining a vulnerability management program
- Implementing strong access controls
- Regularly monitoring and testing networks
- Maintaining an information security policy

While all of the PCI DSS objectives ensure the security of financial transactions, understanding what it means to protect cardholder data is vital from a data governance point of view. In terms of data classification, there are two primary categories, according to PCI DSS. The first category is *Cardholder Data* (*CHD*). Cardholder Data includes data from the front of a card, including the cardholder's name, primary account number, and expiration date. The service code, a three- or four-digit number encoded on the magnetic stripe, is also Cardholder Data.

The second category is *Sensitive Authentication Data* (*SAD*). SAD includes complete track data from the magnetic stripe or embedded chip, Personal Identification Number (PIN), and the Card Verification Value (typically three digits on the back of a card).

The crucial thing to understand from a data governance perspective is that under PCI DSS, you can store Cardholder Data but cannot store Sensitive Authentication Data. Similar to PHI, complying with the PCI DSS is complex. If you need to process, transmit, or store electronic payment information, you must have a comprehensive understanding of PCI DSS. It is best to work with PCI DSS specialists if you have any doubts about complying with the PCI DSS objectives.

Jurisdiction Requirements

As you think through data governance, you must understand the impact of industry and governmental regulations on your organization. When thinking through regulatory and legal compliance obligations, there are four categories for you to consider. These categories include criminal law, civil law, administrative law, and private regulations.

The goal of *criminal law* is to discourage people from acting in a way that negatively impacts society. A legislative body creates criminal laws at the national, state, or local level. Legislative bodies include the U.S. Congress and state legislatures. There is a broad range of criminal offenses, including hacking, insider trading, espionage, robbery, and murder. One exclusive characteristic of criminal law is that punishment can include the deprivation of liberty, such as a jail sentence or probation.

The goal of *civil law* is to resolve disputes between individuals, organizations, and government agencies. Like criminal laws, a legislative body creates civil laws, which encompass almost anything not addressed by criminal law. For instance, civil law covers contractual disputes and liability claims. Instead of jail time, outcomes from civil lawsuits are typically monetary damages or orders by the court to perform or refrain from a specific action.

The goal of *administrative law* is to enable the effective operation of government by allowing government administrative agencies to propagate regulations. Administrative regulations frequently provide details missing from the criminal or civil law. For example, civil laws in the United States allow disabled individuals to receive government assistance. The Social Security Administration (SSA) is the administrative agency that implements social security and disability laws. Federally in the United States, the Code of Federal Regulations (CFR) defines administrative law.

The goal of *private industry regulations* is to govern activities of individuals and organizations without the force of law. However, it is common for contracts to specify compliance with non-governmental regulations. For example, if you process electronic payments, you will find language that ensures compliance with PCI DSS as part of the contract.

Especially for organizations that operate internationally, it is vital to understand the government with jurisdiction over your operations. Jurisdiction influences how and where to handle regulatory, administrative, civil, or criminal disputes. For example, the European Union has a law called the *General Data Protection Regulation* (*GDPR*). The goal of GDPR is to give individuals control over how their personal data is collected, stored, and used. GDPR is one of the strictest privacy and security laws in the world. If you have operations in Europe, GDPR applies. However, if you only operate within the United States, there is no legal obligation to comply with GDPR.

Breach Reporting Requirements

Despite people's best efforts, data breaches do occur. From a data governance standpoint, it is essential to understand how to react to a breach. You also need to understand the reporting obligations to which you are legally or contractually bound. While there are many frameworks to handle breaches, they generally include the following steps:

1. Verify the breach.
2. Stop the breach.
3. Assess the impact of the breach.
4. Notify the impacted parties.
5. Correct the cause of the breach.
6. Conduct a comprehensive review.

Breach reporting requirements vary by data classification. As you can imagine, if an unsecured laptop containing public data gets lost or stolen, there is no obligation to report the event. However, if the breach involves PII, PHI, or payment data, you must escalate to appropriate authority and notify impacted parties. Of particular note is the *Breach Notification Rule* for HIPAA, which provides a breach definition and notification requirements for individuals, the media, and the Secretary of Health and Human Services.

Within the United States, breach notifications are subject to state-level laws. Laws differ in the number of affected individuals that trigger a breach and the maximum number of days that can elapse before notifying people of the breach. On the other hand, there is greater consistency in the European Union, as the GDPR specifies a maximum 72-hour limit for violation notifications. Understanding the classification of your data, the laws and regulations you are bound to, and the jurisdiction for litigation is crucial to effective data governance.

Understanding Master Data Management

Master data management (MDM) is a data governance discipline that uses processes, tools, and technologies to ensure that data assets across an organization have a single source of truth. Successfully implementing MDM is a challenge regardless of industry or organizational size. As organizational complexity increases, identifying and maintaining an accurate, consistent, well-governed single source of truth becomes more challenging.

For example, consider the complexities of automobile manufacturers. Customers purchase vehicles from the manufacturer through a network of independently owned and operated dealerships. The manufacturer receives customer information from the dealership that lets it track ownership of its vehicles. Getting this data from dealerships is vital to the manufacturer's warranty and recall obligations over the vehicle's life.

At some point, customers sell their vehicles. Each vehicle may have many subsequent owners in the used market. Each time the vehicle is sold, the manufacturer's likelihood of receiving a sales transaction record diminishes. The lack of sales notification can cause the manufacturer to lose track of who owns its vehicles over time.

Automotive service shops also have a relationship with the manufacturer. For instance, repair shops need to acquire factory parts when performing a repair. If a manufacturer's warranty covers the repair, the shop may feed information about who the customer is back to the manufacturer.

To acquire new customers, manufacturers' marketing teams purchase mailing lists of potential customers. Marketing teams keep track of the people with whom they interact. Some of those people may be existing customers, past customers, employees, or entirely new customers.

By the time a car is 10 years old, the information about a vehicle, its previous owners, its service history, and its current owner exist in multiple operational systems. While the manufacturer owns some of these systems, others belong to dealers and repair shops. In addition, the quality of some data, like ownership status, degrades with time.

Each of these activities generates and collects data about customers. Since all of that data exists in separate systems, maintaining that data over time is challenging because different systems have different data, with no inherent mechanism for accuracy or consistency. A complex data lineage problem like this is the type of data challenge that MDM seeks to address.

Processes

The discipline of MDM is process-centric. For an organization with multiple separate operational systems, the consolidation of multiple data fields is part of a comprehensive duplicate resolution process. In Figure 8.13, you can see that person data comes from several different source systems, including an external vendor. Although the standardization of data field names is possible for internal systems, you need a translation process to map external data to your internal structure.

FIGURE 8.13   Duplicate resolution process

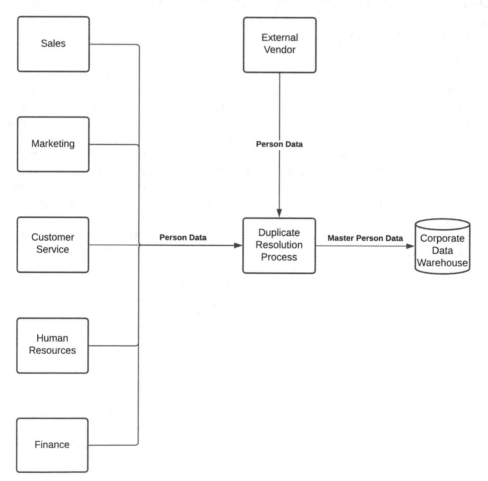

Maintaining a *data dictionary* is an essential component of effective MDM. A data dictionary is a document that contains metadata about your data structures. Consider Table 8.2, which is an example of a data dictionary entry.

TABLE 8.2   Breach notification requirements

Column name	Data type	Size	Description
ACNA_CODE	VARCHAR2	3	Access Customer Name Abbreviation Code, 3-digit ALPHA code assigned to identify carriers for billing/identification purposes
ACNA_NAME	VARCHAR2	30	Full-text I/CLEC carrier name corresponding to the ACNA code
CREATION_ DATETIME	DATE		Date on which a specific ACNA_CODE was inserted into this reference table
LAST_ UPDATE_ DATETIME	DATE		Date on which a given ACNA_CODE's information was last updated in this table

In addition to the details about each column in the table, a data dictionary includes other metadata, including:

- Purpose of the table
- Primary/foreign keys
- Column index definitions
- References by internal systems
- References by external systems

Maintaining a data dictionary takes a significant effort. Fortunately, tools exist that can extract most of the metadata about tables from a database. It is crucial to instill procedural discipline for maintaining column-level comments since they help orient new analysts to your systems.

When designing the processes that maintain a data dictionary, it is vital to define which system is authoritative for shared data elements over time. For example, a marketing system might be responsible for person data until someone becomes a customer, at which point a CRM system becomes authoritative for person data. The business rules for determining which systems are authoritative for which data elements are complex and unique to each organization.

Circumstances

Many circumstances lead an organization to pursue MDM. Typically, leadership identifies a difficulty that relates to having consistent information. To improve internal efficiency and reduce data quality issues, leadership recognizes the benefits of enhancing consistency across systems.

In addition, organizations want to streamline data access and realize that MDM can help them achieve this goal. For example, surrounding the master data source for person data with APIs improves consistency and streamlines access, as shown in Figure 8.14.

FIGURE 8.14 MDM for person data

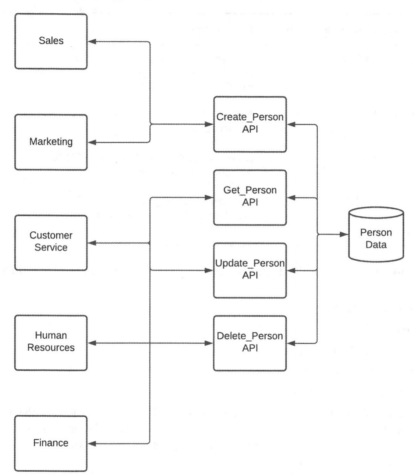

Another reason for adopting MDM is compliance with policies and regulations that require consistent handling of data. When the same data has different definitions in different systems, the cost of compliance increases. Using MDM to drive accurate and consistent data definitions leads to better data stewardship, which drives down the cost of compliance.

Mergers and acquisitions also drive MDM activity. For example, when two companies combine, the chances that their systems contain data about the same people is high. Additionally, mergers and acquisitions increase the scope and complexity of business operations. As the scope and complexity increase, organizations need to combine disparate data sources and reconcile any duplicates quickly. As organizational complexity increases, so does the value of achieving effective MDM through data governance.

Summary

Data is one of an organization's most important assets. Modern organizations have numerous systems that capture, process, transmit, and store data. Organizations also have a complex structure in terms of roles and responsibilities. Data governance is a discipline that takes an ordered, systematic approach to thinking about, organizing, managing, and using data. Data governance is vital to using data consistently and efficiently.

To govern data effectively, organizations appoint a data steward. A data steward is responsible for the overall success of the data governance effort, shepherding the development of policies, processes, and procedures. Data stewards work with data owners, their delegates, and data custodians to implement and enforce data governance.

One of the prime objectives of data governance is ensuring the right people have access to the right data at the right time. Data stewards use organizational structure and groupings within that structure to guide the creation of access controls. Access control policies describe the data subject area and access type, including reading, creating, updating, and deleting data. For example, while the leaders of Sales and Marketing both need access to financial systems for budgeting purposes, they shouldn't have access to each other's financial details. Additionally, people's roles change over time. Instead of granting data access to individuals, it's best to assign role-based access to groups of people.

Protecting an organization's data is vitally important to an organization. Creating policies that mandate data encryption at rest and in transit is a data governance principle that also accomplishes information security objectives. Using encryption technology appropriately helps ensure the safety of your data.

There are times when organizations need to share data, both internally and externally. For example, it is a common practice to use production data in test and training environments. However, people in the test and training environments don't need the actual production data. Instead, use simulated data in these environments. Data masking, or data obfuscation, is one way to accomplish removing sensitive data from non-production environments.

When sharing data externally, take care to deidentify data to avoid compromising individual privacy. When deidentifying data, you remove identifiers that can uniquely identify a person. Strong data governance is a boon to maintaining a list of identifiers to remove during the deidentification process.

In a modern organization, data exists on local devices, shared drives, and in the cloud. Each of these storage environments has its own unique set of considerations. Encrypting data at rest is foundational for all storage environments. If a physical device containing data is lost or stolen, encryption helps protect the data on that device. While this scenario is most likely with a local machine, encryption protects against that possibility regardless of the storage environment.

For shared drives and the cloud, it is crucial to implement group-based administrative controls. Just as data governance uses groups, departments, and divisions from an organizational chart to inform the creation of data access roles, the same process applies to defining role-based access to storage locations. When using user-facing cloud services, you want to pay close attention to what controls you can put in place to inhibit unintended external sharing.

Another aspect of data governance is to make it easy for people to accomplish their work while making it challenging to make mistakes. In addition to access controls, an acceptable use policy helps people understand how they can and cannot use the data they can access. Data use requirements define how to process data and how long to retain it. Use requirements also inform the decision to archive or delete data once it is no longer transactionally valuable.

When consolidating duplicate data from source systems into analytical systems, you need to consider record link restrictions. For example, suppose you have information about the same person in the human resources and CRM systems. In that case, you need to identify which system is authoritative for which person-specific data elements. You want to ensure consistency by reflecting changes from one system into the other. Ensuring consistency is particularly important when designing ETL processes to copy data into a data warehouse. You want to ensure you can uniquely identify an individual as the same person, regardless of their identity in the source system. Linking internal data with external data is also vital, as your organization may share person-related data with external partners.

The handling of certain data types has legal implications. Published standards define specific identifiers as PII and PHI, impacting how you handle the data internally, any necessary modifications before sharing, jurisdiction requirements, and data breach reporting timeframes. Other data types are subject to private regulations, like the PCI DSS. While private regulations don't have the force of law, it is common to see them as part of a contract between two organizations.

Data governance is a challenging discipline given the complexity of an organization, its external partners, and its systems. Master data management (MDM) describes the implementation arm of data governance. The goals of MDM are to establish the processes, tools, and technology to drive accuracy and consistency across an organization. Recall that MDM is a business discipline, not a technology. MDM uses technology to fulfill its goals, but purchasing a single piece of technology does not imply that MDM is successful.

Exam Essentials

Describe the role of a data steward.   A data steward leads an organization's data governance activities. A data steward is not a technical role. It puts a premium on creating policies and procedures, working across organizational divisions, and effectively looking after an organization's data.

Describe the four primary data classification categories.   Public is the most permissive category and applies to data intended for public consumption. Internal data applies to data for use within an organization. Sensitive data is for limited use within an organization, while Highly Sensitive data is the most restricted category. Certain PHI or PII identifiers fall within the Highly Sensitive category.

Describe the difference between person-based and role-based access.   With person-based access, you give individuals access to data. Person-based access is inefficient and prone to people having permissions linger after transitioning to a new area of responsibility. Role-based access assigns permissions to job roles. As people transition in and out of job roles, their access to data adjusts accordingly.

Describe the difference between storage environments.   Local storage is any storage media on an individual device, a shared drive is storage that allows for simultaneous connections from multiple computers, and cloud-based storage uses equipment external to your organization to hold data. Regardless of your storage environment, you should encrypt data at rest.

Describe master data management.   Master data management represents the processes, tools, and technologies that give an organization a single source of truth for shared data elements. MDM defines the processes through which an organization achieves data consistency. For example, when an organization stores data about people in multiple systems, an MDM process uses technology to ensure that the data is accurate and consistent across environments. In this manner, MDM is the application of data governance.

Review Questions

1. Which of these roles is directly responsible for an organization's data governance?

    A. Data owner

    B. Data custodian

    C. Data janitor

    D. Data steward

2. Which of these roles is assigned to a senior functional leader?

    A. Data owner

    B. Data custodian

    C. Data janitor

    D. Data steward

3. Which of these roles is assigned to an information technology professional who implements technical controls to further data governance objectives?

    A. Data owner

    B. Data custodian

    C. Data janitor

    D. Data steward

4. Eve is classifying data that is part of the interface between her organization and their health insurance provider. One of the fields in the data set is Social Security Number. What data classification is most appropriate?

    A. Public

    B. Internal

    C. Sensitive

    D. Highly Sensitive

5. Silas works in communications and has been asked to classify the assets on the organization's externally facing web site. What data classification is most appropriate?

    A. Public

    B. Internal

    C. Sensitive

    D. Highly Sensitive

6. Ian has a new job as a chemist at Guinness & Co. As part of his new job, he is given the chemical formula for Guinness Extra Stout. What is the most appropriate data classification for this chemical formula?

    A. Public

    B. Internal

    C. Sensitive

    D. Highly Sensitive

7. Deondre has a new job with the Coca-Cola Company. As part of his role, Deondre has access to a list of logistics suppliers and pricing information. What is the most appropriate classification for this data?

    A. Public

    B. Internal

    C. Sensitive

    D. Highly Sensitive

8. Clarence is developing a data access strategy for his organization which consists of 150 people across 5 groups, with 3 roles in each group. How many roles should Clarence expect to create to appropriately safeguard the data?

    A. 3

    B. 5

    C. 15

    D. 150

9. Zeke wants to protect his organization's data. What precautions should he take for cloud-based storage?

    A. Encryption at rest

    B. Encryption in transit

    C. Encryption at rest and in transit

    D. User-based encryption

10. Maxine is completing some new-hire paperwork using a form on the web. What should she do to ensure the connection is encrypted?

    A. Use HTTP

    B. Use the Chrome browser

    C. Check for the padlock icon is open

    D. Check that the padlock icon is closed

11. Zaid needs to share medical imagery data with a partner who is developing a machine learning model to identify cancer. What does Zaid need to do to ensure privacy? Choose the best answer.

   A. Deidentify the data

   B. Sort the data in random order

   C. Encrypt the data

   D. Aggregate the data

12. Zach is choosing an operating system for his organization that supports encrypted local storage. What option should he choose?

   A. Windows

   B. macOS

   C. Linux

   D. Any of the above

13. Jerry is looking at an ERD and sees a one-to-many relationship between the Person and Job Role tables. Which table should have a foreign key?

   A. Person

   B. Job Role

   C. Both Person and Job Role

   D. Neither Person nor Job Role

14. Cindy wants to use production data in a training environment for new human resources employees and wants to protect the privacy of the production data. What should she do?

   A. Use SFTP

   B. Use SCP

   C. Implement data masking

   D. Implement HTTPS

15. Fred has two deidentified datasets. The first contains medical treatment data, and the other contains biographic information. The zip code, sex, and birth date exist in both datasets. Is personal privacy at risk? Choose the best answer.

   A. No, the data is deidentified.

   B. No, the datasets are separate.

   C. Yes, reidentification is possible using zip code, sex, and birth date.

   D. Yes, reidentification is possible because one of the datasets has biographic information.

16. Which of the following is not considered PII?

   A. Passport number

   B. Favorite food

   C. Address

   D. Credit card number

17. Which of the following is not considered PHI?
    A. Account number
    B. Fingerprint
    C. Email address
    D. Color preference

18. Which of the following has the shortest maximum breach notification requirement?
    A. PCI
    B. PII
    C. GDPR
    D. PHI

19. Which of the following is considered Sensitive Authentication Data by the PCI DSS?
    A. PIN
    B. Name
    C. Account number
    D. Expiration date

20. Which of the following is not a situation that leads to pursuing master data management?
    A. Acquisition
    B. Arbitration
    C. Compliance
    D. Merger

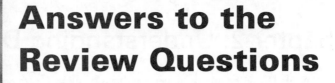

Appendix

Answers to the Review Questions

Chapter 2: Understanding Data

1. D. While UA 769 contains numeric and text components, selecting an alphanumeric data type is the best option if you store this information in a single field. Since there is no date information contained in UA 769, the date data type is not appropriate.

2. C. Voice transcripts are unstructured digital audio files. As such, the BLOB data type is the only viable choice. The alphanumeric, numeric, and date data types are all structured data types.

3. D. In order to facilitate precise mathematical operations on financial data, a numeric data type is the most appropriate choice. Smallmoney does not support values in excess of $1 million. Both smallmoney and money are subject to rounding errors. While alphanumeric could be used to store financial records, the data would have to be converted to numeric in order to facilitate mathematical operations.

4. B. At 45 minutes in length with an average of 102,400 KB per minute, each session would consume in excess of 4 GB of data ((45 * 102400) / 1024 / 1024). Only the BLOB data type in Oracle can accommodate binary data of that size. Microsoft SQL Server has a maximum size of 2 GB in the varbinary data type. The CLOB data type is limited to character data, and the numeric data type is limited to numeric data.

5. B. Alexander should select a CLOB. The text of 1,168 pages greatly exceeds 4,000 bytes, so varchar is not an option. The numeric data type holds only numeric data, whereas the BLOB data type is used for binary objects.

6. A. While defective or functional is categorical, the number of defects represents a count of an occurrence. As such, it is an example of discrete data. Since it is not possible to produce half a control arm, continuous is an inappropriate choice.

7. A. Since shoes are available only in half-size increments, shoe size is considered discrete.

8. B. As it is a measurement, Amdee's foot size is continuous. Shoe size is discrete, and categorical and alphanumeric are not appropriate in this case.

9. D. The range of values and degree of precision for measuring temperature are virtually infinite, making temperature a continuous variable. As such, a numeric data type is preferred when compared with integer.

10. B. Opinions are not numeric, so quantitative is not an option. Opinions vary widely, so they are not categorical. An opinion is an unstructured piece of text, so it is not dimensional. By definition, the text put into an open-ended response is qualitative.

11. C. Spreadsheets are designed to manage structured data. Each of the data elements (check number, date, recipient, and amount) fit easily into appropriately titled columns. As such, this scenario describes structured data.

12. A. A comma-separated values option supplies columnar structure with minimal overhead and is easy to ingest into Python. Plain-text or XML files would be harder to parse, and HTML is what is used to display the account export screen.

13. A. Based on the name-value pairing, the absence of tabs or commas as delimiters, and the lack of tags, the API is expecting data to be formatted as JSON.

14. A. Based on the name-value pairing, the absence of tabs or commas as delimiters, and the lack of tags, the API is expecting data to be formatted as JSON.

15. A. A comma-separated values file can be imported natively into a Microsoft Excel spreadsheet. While Excel is capable of reading the other listed file formats, the data would not be processed into neatly organized rows and columns.

16. C. In order for a person to interact with a web page, the web page needs to be packaged as HTML. While a web browser is capable of opening the other file types, Claire's JavaScript needs to be wrapped in HTML in order to function appropriately.

17. C. Examining the data, you can see the curly braces containing key-value pairs. This is JSON data that can be rearranged to be more pleasing to the eye as follows:

```
[
  {
    "eventType": "start",
    "sessionOffsetMs": 0,
    "mediaOffsetMs": 0
  },
  {
    "eventType": "playing",
    "sessionOffsetMs": 3153,
    "mediaOffsetMs": 0
  },
  {
    "eventType": "stopped",
    "sessionOffsetMs": 4818,
    "mediaOffsetMs": 559
  }
]
```

18. D. Google Sheets can import tab- and comma-separated files but cannot process a composite delimiter.

19. A. Since web server logs are generated automatically by a machine, this qualifies as machine data.

20. B. Since Dave's data has both structured (client name, date of commission) and unstructured (thumbnail image) elements, it is semi-structured. Since Dave is creating the website on his own, this is not an example of machine data.

Chapter 3: Databases and Data Acquisition

1. B. Key-value, column-family, and relational are not optimized for quickly identifying patterns in connected data, making a graph database the best choice.

2. B. Foreign keys enforce referential integrity. A primary key uniquely identifies a row in a table. A synthetic primary key is system-generated.

3. C. A data mart is too narrow, because Taylor needs data from across multiple divisions. OLAP is a broad term for analytical processing, and OLTP systems are transactional and not ideal for this task. Since Taylor is working with data across multiple different divisions, she will work with a data warehouse.

4. D. Initial and delta loads describe how much data is moving. Although ETL is a reasonable choice, ELT is optimal.

5. A. Both Start Date and End Date are necessary to understand when something happened. Middle Date is not a valid design criteria. Retrieving the current level of customer satisfaction is simple when you can match of the value of a flag variable in the where clause of a SQL statement.

6. D. Avalanche and Quasar are not common design patterns. A Snowflake schema is more normalized than a Star schema, which means that queries against a Snowflake schema will have more joins. The more joins a SQL statement has, the more complex the query. With a Star, dimensions are one join away from a fact table, reducing query complexity.

7. B. Static dimensions don't change over time. Counties are infrequently created, making C and D invalid choices. While the rate of change is low, counties do change over time, making county a slowly changing dimension.

8. C. A snowflake approach is more normalized, has more complicated queries, and requires less space than a star approach. The number of records in a fact table has no bearing on whether to use a snowflake or star approach.

9. A. While she may need to parse JSON to load the data into an OLAP environment, she is in danger of getting blocked if the terms of service prohibit programmatic data collection.

10. B. The extract and load phases typically use database-centric utilities. Purging data also uses database-centric tools. Since Python is a programming language external to a relational database, Maurice's team's existing skills are most relevant to the transform phase.

11. D. Surveys are completed by people, and public databases are unlikely to have information about a proprietary process. While Ellen may use sampling during her analysis, observation is the best approach for data collection.

12. C. Manually checking for updated data is error-prone and not sustainable. While an API would be nice, it is not necessary for data that is updated monthly. Since the data changes once per month, George should not be satisfied with the initial data load. Since George wants data to be refreshed on a regular basis, it is best to automate the data retrieval and upload process.

13. B. A complete purge and load removes historical data. ELT just changes the order in which data is loaded and transformed. While Martha may work with an ETL product, it is not necessary. Since Martha is prioritizing efficiency and wants to keep historical data in the data warehouse, copying over only the changed data with a delta load is the best approach.

14. C. A survey would include any bias the production staff has. Testing a sample of finished goods does not inform Bob of what is happening during quality control, and historical trends would not account for any changes in the production process. Observing the final quality check process will let Bob see whether or not defects are being accurately reported.

15. C. COUNT will return the number of rows. MAX will return the largest value, while AVG will return the average of a numeric column. The MIN function returns the smallest value.

16. A. Since Elena focuses on transactions in Italy, she does not need data from the entire European Union. Creating a province-specific subset may make sense after her initial analysis is complete. To allow Elena to focus efficiently on just the Italian transactions, she can reduce the data by filtering out all data not associated with Italy.

17. B. While ensuring an index on the county column is valid, it will not directly inform Jeff's analysis. Effective data logic may be necessary and would have to be to understand profitability over time—not just the profitability. Aggregating data at the county level does not inform analysis at the state or regional levels. Aggregating data at the region, state, and county levels lets Jeff perform the profitability trends at each organizational level.

18. D. SELECT identifies columns, FROM identifies tables, and WHERE filters the results. The ORDER BY clause lets Gretchen sort the result set in chronological order.

19. D. Removing the personalization features disservices customers. While talking with a DBA or verifying the existence of the index on Customer_ID is useful, parameterizing the query will reduce parsing and improve performance.

20. B. STDDEV retrieves the standard deviation on a numeric column. SUM adds numeric values together, and MAX returns the largest value in the column. The COUNT function returns the total number of rows in a table.

Chapter 4: Data Quality

1. A. While invalid, redundant, or missing data are all valid concerns, data about people exists in three of the four systems. As such, Jackie needs to be on the lookout for duplicate data issues.

2. C. Since the value −10 exists, this is not a case of missing data. With the data coming from a single source, it is not duplicate data. As the values exist over time, the data is not redundant. Since it's not possible to have negative rainfall, this is a case of invalid data.

3. C. Since the data is for a single movie and comes from a single dataset, it is neither redundant nor duplicate. Since the data exists, it is not missing. While star is a valid word, it isn't a valid movie genre; as such, this is an example of invalid data.

4. D. Since the data comes from multiple hospitals, the possibility of duplicate or redundant data exists. Although invalid data is certainly possible, the fact that an aggregation function in a programming language returned an error indicates that some values are missing.

5. D. There is no specification that dictates the price of concrete, so this is not a specification mismatch. The order of concrete pricing doesn't matter, which eliminates nonparametric data, and duplicate data doesn't make sense in this context. Since reported prices are significantly greater than in comparable countries, this is an example of a data outlier.

6. A. There may be duplicate or redundant data in the dataset, and an individual film might be an outlier. However, this scenario describes nonparametric data.

7. A. Since the data is coming from a single, well-designed system, redundant or duplicate data is unlikely. While outliers may exist, they do not cause database loads to fail. Since the data is coming from a well-designed transactional system, Raphael needs to validate the incoming data types to ensure they load into the data warehouse successfully.

8. C. The choice here is between redundant and duplicate data. In this case, Jorge is sourcing data from multiple systems, and redundant data comes from a single system, so duplicate is the correct answer.

9. B. Since Lars has numeric data and categorical definitions, there is no need to merge, impute, or parse the wind speed data. Since Lars is interested in Category 5 hurricanes, he needs to recode any windspeed value in excess of 157 miles per hour into Category 5.

10. D. Conversion and transposition are not necessary. While deriving an indicator may be beneficial, it is less valuable than merging the data from multiple sources.

11. B. As a data analyst, Ashley needs to work with IT to modify an ETL process. While she may be recoding or concatenating as part of this temporal work, Ashley is actively blending data.

12. B. It doesn't make sense to concatenate product IDs together, because you lose the ability to identify individual products. While some data may need recoding as numeric and price should be numeric, the ETL should append data from the four systems into a single, wide table.

13. A. Calculating an average is a single function call that produces unexpected results only when there is an underlying issue with the data. While looking online for the correct price may be useful to verify her hunch, checking for nulls herself is the best approach.

14. C. Since Sebastian wants to retain granular data, neither reducing the number of observations nor aggregating the data is the best approach. There is no need to normalize the income data. Since Sebastian is only interested in income data, he can remove the data that is superfluous.

15. D. While removing rows will nulls is appropriate, she needs to transpose by product category and summarize. Transposing by sales price or region will not help her current analytical goal.

16. B. Aggregation comes into play if there is a need to summarize the data by person. It is unlikely that a new column is needed for each Full Name. Dropping all missing values is a possibility, but not the best choice. Separating the Full Name into First, Middle, and Last Name columns allows Randall to easily sort and aggregate by each component of the name.

17. A. Aggregation is a good way to summarize data. Trusting his instincts does not help with model accuracy. Edgar may have normalized attributes during model creation. By cross-validating, Edgar can create a subset to train his model and another subset to test the accuracy of his model.

18. B. Accuracy is for measuring how an attribute and its intended use. Consistency measures an attribute's value across systems. Validity ensures an attribute's value falls within an expected range. While all of these dimensions are important, completeness is foundational to Jane's campaign.

19. C. Accuracy is for measuring how an attribute and its intended use. Completeness measures the minimum viable data necessary for a business objective. Validity ensures an attribute's value falls within an expected range. While all of these dimensions are important, ensuring the consistency of customer data across two different source systems is crucial to Ron's work.

20. A. Completeness measures the minimum viable data necessary for a business objective. Consistency measures an attribute's value across systems. Validity ensures an attribute's value falls within an expected range. While all of these dimensions are relevant, measuring a javelin in kilograms indicates a lack of accuracy.

Chapter 5: Data Analysis and Statistics

1. C. Sandy needs sample data. An observation is the weight of a single gorilla, and the population is all silverback gorillas, which Sandy will be unable to weigh. A specific weight, like 369 pounds, is an observation of the weight variable.

2. D. The interquartile range is a dispersion measure that includes the second and third quartiles, which contains 50 percent of the values in the dataset. The median represents the value in the middle of a sorted numeric list, the mode is the most frequently occurring value, and the mean is the average of all values. Median, mode, and mean are all measures of central tendency.

3. C. The mode is the most frequently occurring value, which is useful when working with categorical data like automotive color. The mean is the arithmetic average, the median represents the value in the middle of a sorted numeric list, and the range is the measure from minimum to maximum, which includes any outliers in the data.

4. C. The null hypothesis presumes the status quo, which in this case is that families are not willing to pay more for rooms near the swimming pool. Jenny is testing whether families are willing to pay more, so that rules out options B and D. Option A represents the alternative hypothesis.

5. D. Since the null hypothesis is that the proportion of green M&Ms is 24 percent, no more, no less, the alternative hypothesis must be that the proportion of green M&Ms is not 10 percent. While a proportion of greater than or less than 10 percent would point to the alternative hypothesis, the alternative hypothesis is that the proportion of green M&Ms is not 10 percent.

6.   D. Since you are trying to determine whether sales increased above the current average of $8,000, the population mean for the null hypothesis is 8,000, whereas the mean for the alternative hypothesis is greater than 8,000. Hypotheses are always stated in terms of the population you are working with, ruling out options A and B. The test is whether sales are higher than the average of $8,000 per day, which rules out option C.

7.   D. To get the mean, you add all the numbers of the dataset together and divide by the number of observations:

$$\frac{1+1+2+3+3+4+5+6+7+9}{10} = 4$$

1 is the minimum, 1 and 3 are the mode, and 3.5 is the median.

8.   C. To calculate range, subtract the minimum (1) from the maximum (8).

9.   C. Recall that the for a sample with even numbers, you calculate the median using the following formula:

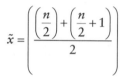

$$\tilde{x} = \left(\frac{\left(\frac{n}{2}\right) + \left(\frac{n}{2}+1\right)}{2} \right)$$

In this case, $\frac{n}{2} = 3$ and $\frac{n}{2}+1 = 4$. With those two numbers, you can proceed with calculating the median as follows: $\frac{3+4}{2} = 3.5$

10.   A. This statement describes a false positive (Type I error), when you reject the null hypothesis when you should accept it. A Type II error is a false negative, accepting the alternative hypothesis when you should accept the null hypothesis.

11.   C. Degrees of freedom is defined as 1 less than the total number of observations.

12.   D. Ari is assessing the relationship between categorical variables and should use a chi-square test. Both the Z-test and t-test compare numeric variables, whereas simple linear regression is used for determining whether you can infer the value of a dependent variable using the value of an independent variable.

13.   C. Simple linear regression explores the relationship between two variables, in this case the weight of an athlete and their time in a 400-meter run. Both the Z-test and t-test infer attributes of the population using sample data. A Chi-square test explores the relationship between categorical variables.

14.   C. A left skewed distribution typically has a mean less than the median, with the tail representing the lowest score.

15. B. Recall that the for a sample with even numbers, you calculate the median using the following formula:

$$\tilde{x} = \left(\frac{\left(\frac{n}{2}\right) + \left(\frac{n}{2} + 1\right)}{2} \right)$$

With an n of 16, $\frac{n}{2} = 8$ and $\frac{n}{2} + 1 = 9$. With those two numbers, you can proceed with calculating the median as follows: $\frac{8+9}{2} = 8.5$

16. D. Link analysis explores connections patterns between data points, making it ideal for social network analysis. Trend analysis compares data over time, performance analysis assesses measurements against defined goals, and exploratory data analysis uses descriptive statistics to summarize data and provide context for ongoing analysis.

17. A. Trend analysis compares data over time. Performance analysis assesses measurements against defined goals, exploratory data analysis uses descriptive statistics to summarize data and provide context for ongoing analysis, and link analysis explores connection patterns between data points.

18. B. Performance analysis assesses measurements against defined goals. Trend analysis compares data over time, exploratory data analysis uses descriptive statistics to summarize data and provide context for ongoing analysis, and link analysis explores connection patterns between data points.

19. C. According to the empirical rule, 95 percent are within two standard deviations. The rule also states that 68 percent of values are within one standard deviation, and 99.7 percent are within three standard deviations.

20. C. Exploratory data analysis can help orient Vidar to the data, including summary statistics and identification of outliers across datasets. Trend analysis compares data over time, performance analysis assesses measurements against defined goals, and link analysis explores connection patterns between data points. As Vidar is encountering this data for the first time, he should check for outliers as part of his orientation process.

Chapter 6: Data Analytics Tools

1. D. R is a programming language that is focused on solving analytics problems and is well known for its ease of learning. Python, Ruby, and C++ are all general-purpose programming languages that are not focused on analytics and would have a steeper learning curve.

2. C. The SELECT command is used to retrieve information from a database. It's the most commonly used command in SQL as it is used to pose queries to the database and retrieve the data that you're interested in working with. The INSERT command is used to add new records to a database table. The UPDATE command is used to modify rows in the database. The CREATE command is used to create a new table within your database or a new database on your server.

3. C. Spreadsheets are indeed widely used because they are easy to use and available on most modern business computers. The most commonly used spreadsheet is Microsoft Excel. Spreadsheets do not, however, provide powerful machine learning capabilities.

4. B. SPSS is a professional statistical analysis package and is the most likely choice of a professional statistician of the options presented. Excel is a spreadsheet that does not offer the powerful statistical tools offered by SPSS. Tableau is a data visualization package. Cognos is a fully functional analytics suite that would not be installed on a single user's computer.

5. A. RapidMiner is a machine learning tool that specializes in creating the visual designs that Vincent seeks. SAS is a statistical analysis package that is not used to create machine learning workflows. Vincent could create his own machine learning software in Python or R, but it would lack the visual workflow he desires.

6. A. It is likely that any of these tools could meet Carla's needs. However, the key requirement mentioned here is the tight integration with AWS services. AWS QuickSight is an AWS service itself, so it would be the best way to meet Carla's business requirements.

7. D. It is feasible that Simone might be able to create a scorecard using any of these tools. However, Metric Studio is the best tool for the job because it is designed to create scorecards for business leaders seeking to analyze key metrics from across their organizations.

8. C. Power BI Report Builder is a desktop tool that developers can use to create paginated reports. Report Server is a server-based tool where developers may publish those reports. Power BI Desktop is also a desktop tool, but it does not create paginated reports. The Power BI service is a SaaS offering of Power BI that would not be installed on an analyst's computer.

9. A. Tableau is arguably the most popular data visualization tool available in the market today. The focus of this tool is on the easy ingestion of data from a wide variety of sources and powerful visualization capabilities that allow analysts and business leaders to quickly identify trends in their data and drill down into specific details. Excel is a spreadsheet that offers only limited visualization capabilities. Stata is a statistical analysis package that also offers limited capabilities for visualization. QuickSight is a tool from AWS that is primarily focused on building dashboards.

10. C. The two primary tools available from Qlik are QlikView and Qlik Sense. QlikView is the original analytics platform offered by the company that focuses on providing rapid insights. Qlik Sense is a more sophisticated platform offering advanced analytics capabilities at a higher cost.

11. B. BusinessObjects is an enterprise reporting tool from SAP that is designed to provide a comprehensive reporting and analytics environment for organizations. RapidMiner is a machine learning package. Stata is a statistical analysis package. MicroStrategy is an analytics suite, but it is made by a company named MicroStrategy and not SAP.

12. D. The DROP command is used to remove an entire database or table from a database. The DELETE command is used to remove rows from a table but does not remove the table itself. The UPDATE command is used to modify rows within a table, while the ALTER command is used to modify the structure of a database or table.

13. D. Datorama is a marketing analytics tool made by SalesForce, so it is likely the best answer to Ty's needs. QlikSense and QuickSight may also be able to produce the results Ty needs, but they will likely have a longer integration time. SPSS Modeler is a machine learning tool and would not be able to produce the required report.

14. C. The Python Data Analysis Library (pandas) provides a set of tools for structuring and analyzing data. The Numpy package is used for numerical analysis. TensorFlow is used for high-performance numerical calculations. Keras is used for artificial intelligence applications.

15. C. Relational databases do not natively understand natural language queries. Any queries sent to a relational database must be written in SQL. This SQL may be written directly by an end user, created by an end user within a graphical interface, or written by software created in any other programming language. Natural language query applications seeking to retrieve data from a relational database must first translate that query into SQL before sending it to the database.

16. C. Minitab, SAS, and Stata are all statistical analysis packages that are unlikely to produce any reporting fit for consumption by a business leader. Power BI, on the other hand, is an analytics suite that produces highly visual reports that would be ideal for sharing with a business leader.

17. B. Event Studio provides real-time data monitoring and alerting, allowing business leaders to be immediately notified when certain events take place and/or providing automated responses to those events. Therefore, it would be the best choice for Amanda's needs.

18. D. The ALTER command is used to modify the structure of an existing database or database table. The UPDATE command is used to modify the data contained within a table, but not the table itself. The DROP command is used to delete an entire table or database. The MODIFY command does not exist.

19. C. SPSS Modeler is a machine learning tool that does not directly perform statistical analyses. Be careful not to confuse SPSS Modeler with the base SPSS software, which is a statistical analysis package. Stata, Minitab, and SAS are all statistical analysis packages that Kelly should consider.

20. D. The Data Manipulation Language (DML) contains the commands used to work with the data contained within a database. DML includes the SELECT, INSERT, UPDATE, and DELETE commands. The CREATE command is used to create a new database or table and is a component of the Data Definition Language (DDL).

Chapter 7: Data Visualization with Reports and Dashboards

1. C. Real-time reports reflect data at the moment the report runs. Hourly reports update every hour. Weekly reports update every week. Since the manager needs 3 days of lead time, a daily report is the best option.

2. A. While red/green, blue/orange, and yellow/purple are all complementary colors, the volume of printed reports means Jasmine should select a cost-effective color scheme that can be printed on any black-and-white printer.

3. B. The title page describes the title of the report and isn't appropriate for a paragraph. The appendix contains details that aren't necessarily relevant to the reader. While the report body could contains this kind of paragraph, it should be highlighted in the executive summary.

4. B. A scatter chart is an effective way to visualize the relationship between two numeric variables.

5. D. Since John's CEO wants to explore retail sales data, that rules out any type of static report.

6. A. As Ron is new to the organization, he needs to familiarize himself with corporate brand standards and any existing templates prior to working on distribution.

7. B. While Kelly needs feedback from the appropriate stakeholders, doing so without a watermark could lead them to believe the report they receive is the final product.

8. C. While all of the answers are relevant to determining requirements, Maggie should focus on key performance indicators for the organization as a whole.

9. B. Wireframes define the basic structure and content of a dashboard. A mockup provides details about the visual elements of a dashboard. Data marts and data warehouses are source systems.

10. D. A line chart shows the relationship of two variables, in this case sales data and time. A pie chart is best for categorical data, a tree map is for hierarchical data, and a histogram is for frequency data.

11. A. Since Celine is looking at South America, a geographic heat map is the best choice to contextualize precipitation.

12. C. Using a word cloud to signify the relative importance and commonality of words is the best approach.

13. D. A heat map uses color and location to illustrate significance, making highly correlated variables appear hot. A tree map is best for hierarchical data, a bar chart works well for categorical data, and an infographic is an effective tool for telling a story.

14. C. An infographic combines data with images and text to tell a compelling story. A tree map is best for hierarchical data, a bar chart works well for categorical data, and a heat map works well in a spatial context.

15. A. Tree maps are ideal for illustrating proportional relationships and are well-suited to interactive applications that facilitate data exploration by the user. A bar chart works well for categorical data, an infographic is an effective tool for telling a story, and a heat map works well in a spatial context.

16. A. A bubble chart illustrates the relationship between three variables. A bar chart works well for categorical data, an infographic is an effective tool for telling a story, and a heat map works well in a spatial context.

17. B. Since a stacked bar chart incorporates proportional segments for categories within each bar, it is effective at illustrating the percentage of brand profitability. A bubble chart works well for showing the relationship between three variables, an infographic is an effective tool for telling a story, and a heat map works well in a spatial context.

18. C. An infographic combines data with images and text to tell a compelling story. A bubble chart works well for showing the relationship between three variables, a stacked bar chart is useful for showing proportional segments for categorical data, and a heat map works well in a spatial context.

19. D. A bubble chart works well for showing the relationship between three variables, a stacked bar chart is useful for showing proportional segments for categorical data, and an infographic is for telling a story. Since the CFO wants to drill into data, that necessitates an interactive dashboard.

20. D. A scatter chart uses a dot for each observation, allowing the user to see the relationship between two variables for every data point. A bubble chart works well for showing the relationship between three variables, a stacked bar chart is useful for showing proportional segments for categorical data, and an infographic is for telling a story.

Chapter 8: Data Governance

1. D. A data owner is a senior leader over a functional unit, a data custodian is someone who implements technical controls, and a data janitor is not a valid role. By definition, a data steward is the role that is responsible for an organization's data governance initiatives.

2. A. A data steward is responsible for looking after an organization's data, a data custodian is someone who implements technical controls, and a data janitor is not a valid role. Senior functional leaders serve as data owners for their domains.

3. B. A data steward is responsible for looking after an organization's data, a data owner is a senior leader over a functional unit, and a data janitor is not a valid role. By definition, a data custodian implements technical controls to further data governance objectives.

4. D. Highly Sensitive data is reserved for restricted use. Public applies to data intended for public consumption, Internal applies to data for use within an organization, and Sensitive applies to data that is for limited use within an organization.

5. A. Public applies to data intended for public consumption. Internal applies to data for use within an organization, Sensitive applies to data that is for limited use within an organization, and Highly Sensitive data is reserved for restricted use.

6. C. Sensitive applies to data that is for limited use within an organization. Public applies to data intended for public consumption, Internal applies to data for use within an organization, and Highly Sensitive data is reserved for restricted use.

7. B. Internal applies to data for use within an organization. Public applies to data intended for public consumption, Sensitive applies to data that is for limited use within an organization, and Highly Sensitive data is reserved for restricted use.

8. C. With role-based access, Clarence should create a data access role that allows each person in a group to perform their job function. Five groups with three roles per group comes out at 15 roles.

9. C. To keep his organizational data secure, Zeke needs to encrypt his data at rest as well as during transmission.

10. D. Maxine wants to ensure she is using HTTPS, which browsers illustrate with a closed padlock.

11. A. While aggregation is an option, it's not viable for individual images. While the data need to be encrypted, especially in transit, it is more important to deidentify. The sort order does not matter.

12. D. Linux, macOS, and Windows all support local encryption.

13. B. Since a person can have multiple job roles, there needs to be a foreign key in the Job Role table referring to the identifier in the Person table.

14. C. SFTP and SCP are encrypted transfer protocols, whereas HTTPS is encrypted web traffic. Cindy can replace production sensitive data with synthetic data she generates, effectively masking the production data.

15. C. The point of this question is that using zip code, sex, and birth date, it is possible to reidentify individuals making personal privacy at risk.

16. B. Passport number, credit card number, and address are all considered PII. While favorite food is a preference, it cannot uniquely identify an individual.

17. D. Account number, fingerprint, and email address are all considered PHI. While color preference is a preference, it cannot uniquely identify an individual.

18. C. PCI has no notification requirement. PII is jurisdiction-dependent, PHI has a 60-day requirement, and GDPR has a 72-hour requirement.

19. A. Name, account number, and expiration date are all classified as Cardholder Data under PCI DSS. By definition, PIN is considered Sensitive Authentication Data.

20. B. Acquisitions, mergers, and compliance activities are all situations that can cause an organization to pursue MDM. Arbitration is a process what settles organizational disputes and is not likely to lead to MDM activities.

Index

E

Online Test Bank

Register to gain one year of FREE access after activation to the online interactive test bank to help you study for your CompTIA Data+ certification exam—included with your purchase of this book! All of the chapter review questions and the practice tests in this book are included in the online test bank so you can practice in a timed and graded setting.

Register and Access the Online Test Bank

To register your book and get access to the online test bank, follow these steps:

1. Go to www.wiley.com/go/sybextestprep (this address is case sensitive)!
2. Select your book from the list.
3. Complete the required registration information, including answering the security verification to prove book ownership. You will be emailed a PIN code.
4. Follow the directions in the email or go to www.wiley.com/go/sybextestprep.
5. Find your book on that page and click the Register or Login link with it. Then enter the PIN code you received and click the Activate PIN button.
6. On the Create an Account or Login page, enter your username and password, and click Login or, if you don't have an account already, create a new account.
7. At this point, you should be in the test bank site with your new test bank listed at the top of the page. If you do not see it there, please refresh the page or log out and log back in.

SYBEX®
A Wiley Brand